MODERN SPIRITUALISM
AND THE CHURCH OF ENGLAND,
1850–1939

GEORGINA BYRNE

THE BOYDELL PRESS

BF
1275
.C5
B79
2010

First published 2010
The Boydell Press, Woodbridge

ISBN 978–1–84383–589–9

The Boydell Press is an imprint of Boydell & Brewer Ltd
PO Box 9, Woodbridge, Suffolk IP12 3DF, UK
and of Boydell & Brewer Inc.
Mt Hope Avenue, Rochester, NY 14620–2731, USA
website: www.boydellandbrewer.com

The publisher has no responsibility for the continued existence or accuracy
of URLs for external or third-party internet websites referred to in this book,
and does not guarantee that any content on such websites is, or will remain,
accurate or appropriate.

A CIP catalogue record for this book is available
from the British Library

This publication is printed on acid-free paper

Printed in the United States of America by
Edwards Brothers, Inc, Lillington NC

STUDIES IN MODERN BRITISH RELIGIOUS HISTORY

Volume 25

MODERN SPIRITUALISM
AND THE CHURCH OF ENGLAND, 1850–1939

STUDIES IN MODERN BRITISH RELIGIOUS HISTORY

ISSN 1464–6625

General editors

Stephen Taylor
Arthur Burns
Kenneth Fincham

This series aims to differentiate 'religious history' from the narrow confines of church history, investigating not only the social and cultural history of religion, but also theological, political and institutional themes, while remaining sensitive to the wider historical context; it thus advances an understanding of the importance of religion for the history of modern Britain, covering all periods of British history since the Reformation.

Previously published volumes in this series are listed at the back of this volume.

For my father
Michael George Byrne

and in memory of my mother
Sheila Ann Byrne (1944–2000)

'… and perhaps when that wondrous hour comes, when the road leads down the last slope which all must follow, and I come near to the dark waters over which the evening mists lie thick, I shall find that true, faithful friend will be near at hand to give me a last word of cheer, and perhaps a first word of welcome when I set my foot upon the shore which is so far off and yet so near.'

William Boyd Carpenter, bishop of Ripon, *Further pages of my life* (1916)

CONTENTS

ACKNOWLEDGEMENTS

I owe thanks to the staff at Boydell & Brewer Ltd for their patience and support.

The Cleave Cockerill Trust generously assisted me in the initial funding of this project and grants from the dioceses of London and Worcester have also been very much appreciated.

I would like to thank Professor Arthur Burns for his wisdom, attention to detail, encouragement and good humour from the time that this project began – and for teaching a theology graduate the importance of dates. Thanks are also due to Professor Hugh McLeod, Dr Michael Snape and Dr Matthew Grimley for their encouraging words and occasional conversations about history over glasses of wine.

Dr David and Dr Maggie Crease, from the University of British Columbia, translated W. R. Inge's poem from Latin for me with great diligence and scholarship. Many thanks also to Sheila Mackenzie from the National Library of Scotland, who chased a particular item for me, and to Robert Beattie at Worcester Cathedral for his eagle eyes.

Over the last few years, as well as engaging with this project, I have been working as a priest in the dioceses of London and Worcester. I would like to thank the former bishop of Kensington, the Rt Revd Michael Colclough and the bishops of Worcester, the Rt Revd Drs Peter Selby and John Inge, for their support during this period. At the same time various colleagues have listened to me as I have shared the joys and woes of research, for which I am very grateful. In particular, Maureen Burton, John Everest, Rob Hall, Ant Petit, Ruth Heeley, Katryn Leclézio, Marilyn Hyland, Eva Field and, more recently, Robert Jones of the top corridor and Chapter colleagues at Worcester Cathedral have been those whose generosity and encouragement I have valued.

I would also like to pay tribute to the wonderful people of St Kenelm's Church, Romsley, who were, along the way, a real source of vitality and strength to me.

As I have spent time in libraries across the country Yvonne and Michael Pollitt, Simon Jones and Angus Ritchie have offered me hospitality and suitable refreshment. My family and friends have kept me grounded with their usual banter and, with good humour, have shown suitable interest and offered seemingly endless support.

My husband Tim has very patiently shared his wife with some strange characters from the nineteenth century and endured many stories, opinions and half-worked arguments over dinner. His love and encouragement have kept me going through the more stressful moments.

I would, finally, like to acknowledge my parents, who have been, since childhood, my greatest source of inspiration. My father Mick taught me the value of hard work and the importance of play. My mother Sheila, who died before this project began, was always my sharpest critic and my chief supporter. Had she lived to see its completion she would have been embarrassingly proud.

ABBREVIATIONS

IWM	Imperial War Museum
LPL	Lambeth Palace Library
n.d.	no publication date
n.p.	not published
ODNB	*Oxford Dictionary of National Biography*
SPR	Society for Psychical Research

1

The Church of England, spiritualism and the 'decline' of religious belief

The only correct answer to the question, 'Where are the dead?' consists, like the question, of four words: 'We do not know'.[1]

Such was the straightforward comment made by the eminent zoologist and philosopher J. S. Huxley, contributing to a collection of essays which sought to answer precisely that question. The publication, *Where are the dead?* (1928), drew together philosophers, clergy, atheists, scientists and spiritualists to answer an anonymous letter published in the *Daily News,* which wondered of the dead, 'Where *are* the mighty hosts of the dead ... what happens to the poor bewildered soul?'[2]

Similar questions have been addressed by all human beings at some point in their lives. An encounter with death, perhaps through personal bereavement, leads people to ponder what is, after all, one of life's greatest mysteries. Our natural human concern for family members or friends does not immediately cease with their death, and we speculate on the possibility of their continued well-being beyond the grave. The sense that a corpse does not resemble the living friend, and that 'something' is missing from the shell of the body, leads us to ask where that 'something' might have gone. Faced with the reality of death, even the most life-embracing person is forced to recognise his or her own mortality and the self-regarding question surfaces: what will happen to *me* when I die?

Nothing about this is new; the finality of death, the possibility of the survival of the human soul and the nature of the afterlife are matters that have been pondered for millennia. Huxley's stark, and all-too-obvious response to such questions ('we do not know') has not prevented speculation.

---

[1] Julian Sorell Huxley (1887–1975), in Sir Arthur Keith et al., *Where are the dead?* (London, 1928), 30.
[2] Ibid., viii.

This book offers an investigation into some of the lively speculation about life after death that took place between 1850 and 1939. More particularly it examines modern spiritualism, a phenomenon whose central tenet was that the living and the dead could converse with one another and that people could indeed 'know' what had happened to the departed. This study takes seriously the spiritualist visions of the afterlife and the theology that underpinned them, and offers the first thoroughgoing and systematic account of spiritualist beliefs. It then observes how the Church of England, already grappling with its own questions and speculations about the nature of the afterlife, engaged with modern spiritualism over the course of the period and refreshed the language and imagery employed in its own account of life beyond death.

Although claims to communicate with the dead are as old as questions concerning the afterlife, the particular phenomenon that was modern spiritualism began, quite precisely, in America in the early spring of 1848. By the end of 1852, the first spiritualist medium had crossed the Atlantic, landed in London and was offering séances – and spiritualism quickly became something of a national craze. What spiritualism offered was, primarily, an extravagant claim: that it was possible for the living to communicate with the departed. By various means, people across the country from all classes, religious traditions and educational backgrounds 'tried' the spirits, seeking to make contact with famous characters from history, or departed family members.

In addition, spiritualism offered, in some instances, spectacular signs and wonders: flying furniture, levitating mediums and ghostly presences, and for a time these attracted the attention of journalists. Fashions for such wonders came and went; the claim to communicate with the dead, however, remained at the heart of spiritualism.

Such a bold claim presented a peculiar challenge to the Church. If true, spiritualism might offer helpful 'proof' of the existence of life beyond death – an article of faith for Christianity. The nature of the afterlife revealed by the alleged spirits of the dead, however, bore scant resemblance to that proclaimed in traditional Church of England teaching in the mid nineteenth century, so if spiritualism were true then the Church needed to rethink what was taught about life after death. The Church was thus faced with a dilemma. Spiritualism became extremely popular: its language and ideas pervaded English society at all levels; it could not be ignored. Either the Church had to condemn it as untrue, misguided, fraudulent or even demonic, even though it appeared to offer proof of life beyond the grave, or else embrace it and discard some of its own traditional teaching about heaven and hell.

In all that follows we will see that what took place during the period

1850–1939 offers a case study of how religious belief is negotiated. Underlying the flamboyant external trappings of spiritualism was a system of belief that offered answers to questions about what the afterlife was like, who went there and what happened to them. This system of belief remained largely consistent over the course of this period. In contrast, the language that the Church used about the afterlife had, by the early twentieth century, changed considerably in its tone and, in some instances, as will be seen, sermons were preached and books were written containing phrases that closely resembled those regularly heard in spiritualist circles.

This is not to suggest in any way that the Church of England simply imported spiritualism lock, stock and barrel into its teaching. It did no such thing. Instead there are hints that spiritualist language and ideas that had already gained currency in all levels of English society were slowly incorporated into the Church's doctrine of the afterlife and presented as part of orthodox Christian teaching.

This process of 'negotiation' is significant, not least because it offers a fresh perspective on the ongoing debate among historians concerning the de-Christianisation or secularisation of Britain in the late nineteenth and early twentieth centuries. An examination of the Church's response to a phenomenon such as spiritualism allows us to appreciate religious belief as something *fundamentally* adaptable and changeable. Indeed, the Church of the late nineteenth century emerges as essentially syncretistic: it engaged with ideas and language beyond itself in order to refresh and re-present what it taught as Christian belief.

Classic accounts of secularisation have largely ignored or problematised the adaptable nature of belief, tending instead to connect belief too closely with the measurable outward signs of religious behaviour, such as church attendance. Thus, both E. R. Wickham, recording the non-attendance of the working classes in the churches of Sheffield, and K. S. Inglis, noting that non-churchgoing had become a 'social habit' of the poor, extrapolated from their studies a decline in religious *belief*.[3] The language employed by these studies suggested that the churches in the late nineteenth and early twentieth centuries saw severe decline and decay. Wickham wrote that, 'the weakness and collapse of the churches in urbanized and industrialized areas of the country should be transparently clear to any who are not wilfully blind'.[4]

---

[3] E. R. Wickham, *Church and people in an industrial city* (London, 1957); K. S. Inglis, *Churches and the working classes in Victorian England* (London, 1963).
[4] Wickham, *Church and people*, 11.

This narrative of a decline in religious belief was developed further by the work of sociologists of religion from the late 1960s, producing the secularisation thesis. Secularisation, the gradual removal of religious belief from its place of authority and influence within the life of a community, was seen as the inevitable consequence of social development and modern culture.[5] The secularisation thesis became compelling for historians, the challenge then being one of charting how and when the process began to take place in Christian Britain, by collecting church and chapel attendance figures and identifying trends of decline.[6]

More recently this thesis has been challenged. Peter Berger, one of the secularisation thesis' chief proponents in the 1960s, admitted in the 1990s that 'the assumption that we live in a secularized world is false'.[7] Certain religious institutions had lost power and influence but, he argued, both old and new beliefs had continued to play a part in the lives of individuals, in institutions, politics and society.[8] Bryan Wilson, having offered the classic account of secularisation, by contrast, remained convinced that it was a strong model.[9]

Some historians have questioned the assumption that church attendance provides the best and most reliable indicator of Christian belief. Much of this revision has come from detailed local studies. Thus Jeremy Morris, Jeffrey Cox and Simon Green have all noted vibrant church life in local community

---

[5] Thus Peter Berger states that, 'by secularization we mean the process by which sectors of society and culture are removed from the domination of religious institutions and symbols'. In other words, the Church is removed from areas previously under its control or influence, with the consequence that people look increasingly on the world without the benefit of religious interpretation or legitimisation. P. Berger, *The Sacred Canopy. Elements of a sociological theory of religion* (New York, 1969), 107. See also Bryan Wilson, *Religion in Secular Society* (London, 1966); Bryan Wilson, *Religion in a Sociological Perspective* (Oxford, 1982). For a brief and useful commentary on the secularisation thesis see Hugh McLeod, *Secularisation in Western Europe 1848–1914* (Basingstoke, 2000), 1.

[6] Alan Gilbert, for example, observed secularisation as 'latent' in the nineteenth century, its effects only being felt after the First World War. A. D. Gilbert, *Religion and society in industrial England. Church, chapel and social change 1740–1914* (London, 1976), viii. See also Robert Currie, Alan Gilbert and Lee Horsley, *Churches and Churchgoers. Patterns of Church growth in the British Isles since 1700* (Oxford, 1977).

[7] P. Berger (ed.), *The desecularization of the world. Resurgent religion and world politics* (Washington D.C., 1999), 2.

[8] Ibid., 3.

[9] Bryan Wilson, 'Reflections on a many-sided controversy', in Steve Bruce (ed.), *Religion and Modernization. Sociologists and Historians debate the Secularization Thesis* (Oxford, 1992), 195–210. Although, as the other essays of this book suggest, in maintaining this line Wilson is increasingly a lone voice.

contexts in the late nineteenth and early twentieth century.[10] Green, for example, argues that churches reached out to a wide range of people with rites of passage, Sunday schools and classes that were accessible and inclusive.[11] Jeffrey Cox contends that 'the Victorian churches were hardly a failure. They were arguably Victorian England's most important voluntary social institution'.[12] And Jose Harris, offering a broader sweep of social history, similarly notes large numbers of people attending clubs like the Boys' Brigade and Girls' Friendly Society, and sharing in Watch Night services, Harvest and Mothering Sunday in the 1870s.[13] Such accounts, although still acknowledging decline, have challenged the degree of its inevitability by modifying previous assumptions about the usefulness of church attendance figures, and pointing us rather to the Church's role in wider society.

Others have challenged notions of decline by examining boundaries between belief and unbelief within personal accounts of faith. Frank Turner has urged caution in assuming that the 'crisis of faith' device in some Victorian literature is a reliable indicator of a wider decline in belief.[14] James Moore has identified in the late-Victorian period a struggle for meaning, and the negotiation of new doctrines in the light of technological changes, rather than a straightforward loss of faith.[15] More recently, Timothy Larsen, from his study of Victorian secularists, has demonstrated that there was a fluid movement between faith and doubt in the period, and gives an account of unacknowledged 'reconversions' to Christianity that do not fit the 'crisis of faith' thesis.[16]

Sarah Williams has similarly argued that studies of religious belief should not be determined by questions of decline.[17] From her study of Lambeth between 1880 and 1939, she describes patterns of religious belief and practice

---

[10] J. N. Morris, *Religion and urban change: Croydon 1840–1914* (Woodbridge, 1992); J. Cox, *The English Churches in a Secular Society. Lambeth, 1870–1930* (Oxford, 1982); S. J. D. Green, *Religion in the age of decline. Organisation and experience in industrial Yorkshire, 1870–1920* (Cambridge, 1996).

[11] Green, *Religion in the age of decline*, 22–3.

[12] Cox, *The English Churches in a Secular Society*, 7.

[13] Jose Harris, *Private Lives, Public Spirit. A Social History of Britain 1870–1914* (Oxford, 1993), 154–9.

[14] F. Turner, 'The Victorian crisis of faith and the faith that was lost', in R. J. Helmstadter and B. Lightman (eds.), *Victorian Faith in Crisis. Essays on Continuity and Change in Nineteenth-Century Religious Belief* (London, 1990), 9–38.

[15] J. Moore, 'Theodicy and society: the crisis of the intelligentsia', in ibid., 153–86.

[16] Timothy Larsen, *Crisis of Doubt. Honest Faith in Nineteenth-Century England* (Oxford, 2006).

[17] S. C. Williams, *Religious belief and popular culture in Southwark c.1880–1939* (Oxford, 1999), 4–5.

that lay beyond the boundaries of the churches, arguing that, although not conventionally 'orthodox', these practices should be taken as legitimate indicators of religious belief in their own right. Drawing on oral history and working-class autobiographies, she claims that middle-class definitions of religiosity are inadequate when dealing with working-class belief. Within the parameters of 'popular religion' she notes belief in luck, magic and folk remedies for healing sitting alongside occasional church attendance and locally negotiated systems of morality. Together these formed their own 'narrative of meaning'.[18]

In addition, she argues that although some of the religious practices were claimed to be 'traditional' by working-class inhabitants of Southwark, often they were recently acquired. Referring to them as 'traditional' gave them a superior status and helped to foster the idea of a popular religious heritage and a degree of continuity with the past.[19] At the same time older rural traditions were reinterpreted in a new urban context. Rather than representing a problematic survival of older folk belief in the context of secularisation, the religious life of working-class Southwark was developing and accommodating new ideas, while retaining connection with the past.

Sarah Williams offered a welcome fresh perspective on religious belief. Importantly, she moved away from the trend for quantifying belief, suggesting instead that belief was something much more complex and elusive. However, her work does not go quite far enough. In the first place her examination of 'popular belief' is concerned with the working classes alone and this is too narrow a perspective. Surely there might also be a permeable boundary between 'orthodox' belief and middle-class 'narratives of meaning' to be examined? Also, although rightly identifying the ways in which popular (i.e. working-class) beliefs were shaped by a variety of factors, she still assumes a degree of stasis in the teaching of the Church. Thus the impression is formed of a vivid, sincere and thriving working-class belief, formed out of traditional and contemporary concerns, connecting with a rather monolithic, middle-class institutional Church for rites of passage and Sunday school classes. The static, orthodox, Church belief was absorbed into the more dynamic popular belief.

By contrast, this study demonstrates that what took place in the nineteenth and early twentieth century was a lively negotiation of belief: an ongoing conversation between the Church and what is here identified as 'common culture', which led to the Church reshaping and re-presenting its own

[18] Ibid., 56.
[19] Ibid., 57.

teaching. In her comments about political thought in the early twentieth century, Jose Harris identified a 'space', which she named as 'popular culture', shared by academic and non-academic worlds, where people of all classes and backgrounds absorbed and discussed issues of the day.[20] It was a space that 'produced a great deal of sometimes amiable, sometimes nauseating rubbish; but it produced also many serious and systematic attempts to analyse the role of the state and other political institutions, in a context of advanced capitalism, urban conglomeration and modern mass democracy'. It was inhabited by a rich variety of people, for whom 'political theorising' was 'virtually a national sport': professors of philosophy, statesmen, economists, historians, scientists, doctors, clergymen, social workers, soldiers, business men, labour leaders, fellow-travellers and 'a host of others'.[21]

Harris sees this cultural 'space' as beginning to flower in the 1870s. This does not mean that such a 'space' is unidentifiable before then. Juliet John, writing about Charles Dickens, notes that although historians tend to connect 'mass culture' with the technological advances enabling mass communication in the late nineteenth century, a dramatic widening of political and cultural participation took place much earlier. Dickens, she argues, used terms such as 'masses' and 'the mass' in his writings on America as early as 1842, in order to make sense of 'emerging cultural and social formations'. His attempts to understand, address and engage with the 'masses' suggests, she says, that these terms had 'imaginative and political potency'.[22] It also suggests that Dickens, at least, believed that large numbers of people shared some common opinions – not least about him and his work.

Jose Harris is comfortable using the phrase 'popular' to describe the shared cultural space. However, given that 'popular culture' can too readily mean 'working-class culture' in histories of the late-modern period (as can 'mass culture'), I am choosing to refer to this shared space as 'common culture', allowing it to be inhabited by people from a variety of educational backgrounds and classes: by Dickens' 'masses' as well as by intellectuals and aristocrats. This was a space where new scientific discoveries could be discussed by eminent scientists like Michael Faraday as well as by the audiences who flocked to see him at his Friday lectures, or who read about him in the newspapers. This was a space where the performances of magicians or the latest

---

20 J. Harris, 'Political thought and the state', in S. J. D. Green and R. C. Whiting, *The boundaries of the state in modern Britain* (Cambridge, 1996), 15–28.
21 Ibid., 17.
22 Juliet John, ' "A body without a head": The Idea of Mass Culture in Dickens's American Notes (1842)', *Journal of Victorian Culture*, 12, 2 (Autumn 2007), 173–202, at 175.

remedies for good health could be analysed both by the well-to-do and by servants, alongside local and national politics, and matters of religion.

Church teaching was itself shaped, influenced and redefined by the beliefs and practices circulating within this common culture. This meant that religious belief in the nineteenth century, *within* the Church as well as beyond it, was fluid, dynamic and subject to accretion. Far from being monolithic or impervious to cultural and religious change, Church teaching emerges in this study as susceptible to change, and religious belief – which is not the sole preserve of the Church, but rather lies within and without it – is seen to be constantly in a process of negotiation.

If religious belief, rather than being a measurable commodity, is caught up in a process of negotiation, and susceptible both to Church teaching and to common culture, then both signs of belief and crisis of belief can be expected. In the predominant narrative of decline, the secularisation thesis, all signs of religious belief are problematic, or else interpreted as the last gasps of a dying institution. The secularisation thesis assumes a *telos* of complete non-belief which, as Jeffrey Cox has put it, 'strips away the legitimacy of a religious point of view in individuals'.[23] Yet if belief is understood as a process of negotiation, naturally syncretistic, dynamic and fluid, then occasional signs of religiosity are typical. As the sociologist Grace Davie has claimed, 'the sacred does not disappear'.[24] Callum Brown noted recently how religiosity is capable of increasing as well as declining. In 2001 he charted 'the death of Christian Britain', concluding that 'Britain is showing the world how religion as we have known it can die'.[25] He was forced to admit five years later that 'religion is back on the agenda', even if in a slightly different guise.[26] Conversely, we may also treat with seriousness the sense of 'crisis' felt by some churchmen in the nineteenth and twentieth centuries as a perception of their situation, even in places where the church attendance figures would indicate growth.[27] The

---

[23] J. Cox, 'Master narratives of long-term religious change', in Hugh McLeod and Werner Ustorf (eds), *The decline of Christendom in Western Europe, 1750–2000* (Cambridge, 2003), 204.
[24] Although she rightly points out that the measurable links between society and the institutional Church have weakened over time. This has not stopped religiosity from finding other outlets. G. Davie, *Religion in Britain since 1945: believing without belonging* (Oxford, 1994), 43.
[25] Callum Brown, *The Death of Christian Britain* (London, 2001), 198.
[26] Callum Brown, *Religion and Society in Twentieth-century Britain* (Harlow, 2006), xv. Brown identifies the resurgence of religious militancy and the refashioning of religion as 'spiritual experience devoid of central authority' alongside de-Christianisation as the three trends of late-twentieth-century religion.
[27] Perceptions and reality are not always the same. Jeremy Morris has noted that for all the evidence of local church growth in mid Victorian Britain, a sense of crisis persisted among

feeling that some long-cherished or 'traditional' beliefs were being sacrificed or lost in the process of negotiation might well have led to a sense of 'crisis'.

Rather than attempting to understand religious belief by measuring indicators of commitment to a religious institution, this study takes instead one aspect of Christian teaching and places it alongside a new and appealing set of ideas. By doing this it becomes possible to observe something of the process of negotiation in religious belief. The teaching in question concerns the ideas about the afterlife: what happens to people when they die, and the nature of heaven and hell. Spiritualism, with its claim to converse with the departed, offered a particular set of answers, and it is the contention here that the Church of England shaped what it presented as a Christian belief in the afterlife *in part* by engaging with the claims, the language and ideas of modern spiritualism that had become embedded in the common culture by the late nineteenth century. Over the course of the period 1850–1939 religious beliefs regarding the afterlife changed substantially, meaning that ideas dismissed as unorthodox in the 1850s had become part of mainstream Church of England teaching by the 1930s. Religious belief in this analysis did not 'decline'; it adapted and changed.

Parameters

The period under consideration begins in 1850 and ends in 1939. This has the advantage of allowing a *longue durée* approach, but the parameters were set primarily in order to take into account three key texts. The first of these is F. D. Maurice's *Theological Essays* (1853).[28] In this work Maurice countered the belief, widely accepted at the time, that after judgement God punished the wicked for an endless period. For this Maurice was accused of 'universalism' – teaching that God would ultimately save all people – and he lost his position at King's College London. The *Theological Essays* are important here in part because they were written just a year after spiritualism arrived in London, but also because they highlight the fact that the idea of universal salvation was regarded as controversial in the mid nineteenth century.

The second text is the 1938 report *Doctrine in the Church of England.* The document was the work of a committee set up in 1922 and chaired by Hubert

---

some clergy. J. N. Morris, *F. D. Maurice and the crisis of Christian authority* (Oxford, 2005), 27. Robin Gill has helped to disconnect perceptions of church attendance from the reality of overbuilding. [Robin] Gill, *The myth of the empty church* (London, 1993).

[28] (John) Frederick Denison Maurice (1805–72). F. D. Maurice, *Theological Essays* (London, 1957. 1st pubd 1853).

Murray Burge (1862–1925), the bishop of Oxford, and, after his death, by William Temple, who by 1938 was archbishop of York.[29] The committee was invited 'to consider the nature and grounds of Christian doctrine with a view to demonstrating the extent of existing agreement within the Church of England and with a view to investigating how far it is possible to remove or diminish existing differences'.[30]

Regarding the afterlife, the committee argued that beyond death there was possibility for spiritual growth and even universal salvation. 'It would not be easy to find in the New Testament a basis for definitely and rigorously excluding all hope of further opportunity; indeed there are passages which taken by themselves are universalist in tendency.'[31] The Church of England admitted, albeit long after his death, that F. D. Maurice might have had a point.

The third work is the 1939 Report of the Archbishop of Canterbury's Committee on Spiritualism. Although between 1852 and 1939 a number of pamphlets, books and sermons were written about spiritualism, the Church of England took a long time to offer an institutional response to its presence. A committee was set up in 1935 after the dean of Rochester, Francis Underhill, put a motion to the National Assembly. The motion stated: 'that, in view of the growth of Spiritualism among the clergy and communicant laity of the Church, this Assembly respectfully requests their Graces the Archbishops to consult with the Convocations as to the appointment of a Commission to investigate the matter and report to the Assembly'.[32] In the report, which was not released into the public domain until the 1980s, the conclusions of the majority tentatively suggested that, in some cases, 'the hypothesis that they [the alleged communications] proceed from discarnate spirits is a true one'.[33]

There are two further boundaries to this work. The first concerns denomination and the second geography. Although from time to time brief mention may be made of non-Anglican responses to spiritualism, it is the development

---

[29] William Temple (1881–1944) was bishop of Manchester from 1920, archbishop of York from 1929 and archbishop of Canterbury from 1942. *Oxford Dictionary of National Biography* (hereafter *ODNB*).

[30] *Doctrine in the Church of England. The report of the commission on Christian doctrine appointed by the archbishops of Canterbury and York in 1922* (London, 1938), 19.

[31] Ibid., 217.

[32] Motion to National Assembly, 10 July 1935. Lambeth Palace Library (hereafter *LPL*): *Lang Papers*, Vol. 70, fol. 4.

[33] Archbishop's committee on spiritualism, *Report of the committee to the Archbishop of Canterbury* (n.p., 1939), 22.

of belief within the Church of England that is of chief concern here. The reason for this is mostly to do with manageability; in order to effect a proper analysis of how religious belief works as a process of negotiation it is much easier to keep to one area of doctrine within one denomination. A multiplicity of Christian traditions might muddy the waters. The same argument can be made to justify the focus on England rather than Britain as a whole. Spiritualism was prevalent in Scotland, Wales and Ireland, as in England but, in order to keep this study manageable, the area of primary concern is England.

In addition, this study deliberately examines spiritualism as separate from other 'alternative' forms of religious belief and practice in evidence in this period, which might fall under the broad category of occultism, such as, for example, Theosophy or the Hermetic Order of the Golden Dawn. Alex Owen, in her assessment of the 'mystical revival' of the 1890s, remarks that 'spiritualism prided itself on its democratic appeal and practice'. It was crude, sometimes materialist and 'extremely catholic' in its attitude to conventional religious belief. It held huge appeal for 'men and women of all classes and shades of belief'.[34] By contrast, the fin-de-siècle occult revival she describes was inhabited by small, self-consciously esoteric, intellectual and exclusive societies, whose members viewed spiritualism as vulgar, naive and overly concerned with spirit phenomena. Fin-de-siècle occultism was, Owen suggests, more serious in its pursuit of a hidden spiritual reality.[35] Although it might be argued that spiritualism can be placed within the spectrum of the occult, it is precisely spiritualism's democratic appeal that is crucial here. Whether those who dabbled in spiritualism did so in the sincere belief that the spirits could communicate with them, or because they wanted to see tables spinning and flowers falling from the ceiling, they dabbled in great numbers, unencumbered by the narrower intellectualism of a more serious and exclusive occultism. The popularity of spiritualism and its appeal to a broad section of the general public is a key feature of this study.

A new history of spiritualism

There are already a number of histories of modern spiritualism in existence, written from a variety of perspectives, yet none has addressed the teachings of spiritualism with the same attention as this study. The earliest account is given

---

34 Alex Owen, *The Place of Enchantment. British Occultism and the Culture of the Modern* (Chicago, 2004), 18.
35 Ibid., 19.

by a medium, Emma Hardinge Britten in 1883. Her work, *Nineteenth Century Miracles, or spirits and their work in every country of the earth. A complete historical compendium of the great movement known as 'Modern Spiritualism'* (1883) was born out of her tours around Britain and the world. She was well known as a medium and spiritualist writer who, for many years, contributed accounts of spiritualism in English towns to spiritualist newspapers.[36] Her work glossed over the fraudulence prevalent among mediums and concentrated instead on proffering vivid accounts of spirit manifestations and séances that took place across the country and the world, claiming that the activity was a vigorous attempt on the part of the spirit world to communicate with the living.

By contrast, two accounts of spiritualism published in the early twentieth century were more critical. Frank Podmore, president of the Society for Psychical Research (SPR),[37] saw spiritualism as the natural result of a combination of mesmerism and witchcraft.[38] It appealed, he thought, to a variety of people: the curious, the scientific and the 'utopians', who sought either consolation in grief or the answers to the mysteries of the universe. Although Podmore was keen to investigate spiritualism further, he was generally sceptical of its claims, persuaded that much of what took place in séance was the result of telepathy. He recognised, though, that many people were drawn to spiritualism as they had been drawn to similar movements in the past:

> We learn from the whole history of witchcraft and kindred superstitions, and from the extraordinary persistence down to our own day, and amongst persons of some scientific attainments, of the belief in fluidic emanations from magnets, crystals, drugs and other substances, that belief in such agencies is apt in such material to breed its own justification.[39]

Joseph McCabe, writing in 1920, took a different, slightly less serious approach than Podmore, detailing the careers of the 'star' mediums, and the chaos and rivalry among them. He described the spectacular phenomena at séances, and the equally spectacular unveiling of fraudulent mediums in the 1870s and 1880s. Despite the frauds, spiritualism appealed to people, he thought, because it offered 'proof' of heaven at a time when science was

---

[36] Emma Hardinge Britten, *Nineteenth Century Miracles, or, spirits and their work in every country of the earth. A complete historical compendium of the great movement known as 'Modern Spiritualism'* (Manchester, 1883).
[37] See chapter three, pp. 51–53.
[38] Frank Podmore, *Modern Spiritualism. A history and a criticism*. 2 Vols. (London, 1902), 2: 348.
[39] Ibid., 2: 360.

unsettling belief; it suggested that beyond death all were saved and, importantly, it offered a vision of heaven that was vivid and attractive.[40]

In the late 1960s the social scientist Geoffrey Nelson moved away from describing the personalities involved in spiritualism and instead examined it as a social movement. After offering a narrative of the development of spiritualism in America and Britain, he attempted to analyse it in the light of social theory, concluding, however, that spiritualism ultimately defied analysis. Choosing to operate H. Richard Niebuhr's 'Church–Cult–Sect' continuum, spiritualism should have moved from being on the 'cultural periphery' to a place in the 'cultural centre'.[41] This, he argued, never happened; despite the popularity of spiritualism, it never became part of the 'cultural centre'.

Part of the problem with Nelson's analysis lies in his need to fit spiritualism into a ready-made sociological model, and part in his readiness to accept the conclusions of Wickham and Inglis, that the urban working classes were alienated from religion. Spiritualism, he claims, was largely urban and working class, and therefore, like the working classes, lay on the 'cultural periphery'. It gave to people who were deprived of traditional religion an alternative ethical and spiritual pattern for their lives.[42] It was, therefore, a 'by-product' of secularisation and urban industrialisation.[43] The assessments of religious belief made by Wickham and Inglis have, as has been noted, been challenged. In fact, as we shall see, far from being the preserve of the urban working classes, spiritualism was vibrant among all classes in rural as well as urban areas of the country.

More recently a small number of social and cultural historians, in particular Ruth Brandon, Janet Oppenheim, Logie Barrow, Alex Owen and Jenny Hazelgrove, have explored spiritualism.[44] With the exception of Jenny Hazelgrove, these historians have employed aspects of the secularisation thesis in their work, assuming that spiritualism represents a response to a crisis of faith

---

[40] Joseph McCabe, *Spiritualism. A popular history from 1847* (London, 1920), 23–5.
[41] Niebuhr's work, *Social Sources of Denominationalism* (New York, 1929) was itself a reworking of the thinking of Ernst Troelsch, but suggested a dynamic movement along the different stages of the continuum. G. K. Nelson, *Spiritualism and Society* (London, 1969), 222.
[42] Ibid., 260–66.
[43] Ibid., 269.
[44] Ruth Brandon, *The Spiritualists. The Passion for the Occult in the Nineteenth and Twentieth Centuries* (London, 1983); Janet Oppenheim, *The Other World. Spiritualism and Psychic Research in England, 1850–1914* (Cambridge, 1985); Logie Barrow, *Independent Spirits. Spiritualism and English plebeians, 1850–1910* (London, 1986); Alex Owen, *The Darkened Room. Women, Power and Spiritualism in Late Victorian England* (London, 1989); Jenny Hazelgrove, *Spiritualism and British Society between the Wars* (Manchester, 2000).

in mid Victorian Britain. Thus Oppenheim argues that Victorians, anxious that their 'social fabric was slipping', sought to 'counter that insecurity, to calm their fears' with spiritualism.[45] In the face of modernity and science, spiritualism offered a 'vigorous response'. Owen notes that spiritualism appeared as Christianity and the Bible lost their authority in society.[46] Hazelgrove has attempted to counter this crisis of faith thesis, by examining spiritualism beyond the time of the First World War. From this vantage point she notes that, well into the twentieth century, there was evidence of a widespread, if fragmented, belief in the supernatural that was impervious to modernism and science, and that belied any sense of crisis.[47]

Some historians have argued that spiritualism was particularly attractive to those who lacked power in mid Victorian society. Both Logie Barrow and Janet Oppenheim thus claim spiritualism as a movement among the working classes. Barrow's work redresses the earlier narratives of spiritualism which concentrated on its rise among the middle classes in London, revealing the significance of spiritualism for previously existing radical working-class organisations in the north of England.[48] Jay Winter, similarly, writing about spiritualism and the First World War, agreed that Victorian spiritualism was mostly the preserve of political radicals – although no evidence is offered for this beyond Barrow's work.[49]

Oppenheim goes further, suggesting that spiritualism caused consternation among 'the great' precisely because it was a working-class movement.[50] Alex Owen has drawn attention to the 'disproportionate' numbers of women involved in spiritualism as mediums, suggesting that women who were excluded from power in traditional Churches found in spiritualism a sphere for the exercise of spiritual authority.[51] By contrast, this study shows that spiritualism embraced people from a wide variety of backgrounds and interests.

In the narrative of crisis and declining religious belief, spiritualism is identified as either problematic – the 'pathological outcome of science's triumphant but traumatic shedding of religion'[52] – or else as the preserve of people alienated from traditional religion. In this identification the Church of

---

[45] Oppenheim, *The Other World*, 1.
[46] Owen, *The Darkened Room*, introduction.
[47] Hazelgrove, *Spiritualism and British Society*, 23.
[48] Barrow, *Independent Spirits*, 10.
[49] J. M. Winter, 'Spiritualism and the First World War', in R. W. Davis and R. J. Helmstadter (eds), *Religion and Irreligion in Victorian Society* (London, 1992), 186.
[50] Oppenheim, *The Other World*, 86.
[51] Owen, *The Darkened Room*, introduction.
[52] Hazelgrove, *Spiritualism and British Society*, 5.

England has no real place. Oppenheim notes five clergymen who were spiritualists, and concedes that Christian spiritualists claimed that spiritualism had renewed the Christian faith for some.[53] However, alongside this the 'official' line of the Church of England was 'negative' and 'cautious'.[54] Hazelgrove claims that spiritualism offered a sensual and romantic experience of religion more akin to Roman Catholicism than Anglicanism,[55] which had in any case seen its traditions 'eroded' by the time of the First World War.[56] Once again, the impression emerges of the Church of England static in its teaching, the preserve of the upper and middle classes, generally unable to understand the popularity of spiritualism.

On closer analysis, though, we find that spiritualism was not a 'fringe' or working-class movement, and neither did the Church of England's own teaching remain unaffected by it. Instead, spiritualism was widespread among all classes, and clergy as well as laity engaged with it, tried the spirits and, more importantly, employed the language and ideas of spiritualism in their own presentations of Christian belief.

Historians of spiritualism thus far have failed to take seriously the theological language and ideas inherent in modern spiritualism. This is a surprising oversight. The chief claim of modern spiritualism was that it was possible to communicate with the dead. The dead did, indeed, according to convinced spiritualists, arrive at séances and 'speak' through mediums and through other means. Given this belief among spiritualists, it might be assumed that historians would be interested in the revelations from the afterlife. This has not been the case, and although much has been written about spiritualism as a movement, a haven for disaffected social groups, a branch of psychic science or a gathering point for flamboyant personalities, little has been written about the communications made by the spirits themselves. Neither has any attempt been made to analyse the language and ideas about the afterlife presented by convinced spiritualists in journals, pamphlets and books. In order to remedy this oversight, this study offers the first thorough analysis of the theology of spiritualism.[57] Such an analysis is central to the argument that the ideas and language of spiritualism, circulating in the common culture, helped to shape beliefs about the afterlife.

The importance of language and linguistic analysis in historical study has

---

[53] She notes William Williamson Newbould, Thomas Colley, Hugh Haweis, William Stainton Moses and Charles Maurice Davies. Oppenheim, *The Other World*, 69–79.
[54] Ibid., 68.
[55] Hazelgrove, *Spiritualism and British Society*, 53–8.
[56] Ibid., 271.
[57] See chapter four, 83–103.

been frequently observed in the past quarter century, famously in the modern British context by Gareth Stedman Jones, in relation to issues of class.[58] In the context of questions about de-Christianisation, both Sarah Williams and Callum Brown have similarly highlighted language. Williams, affirming her contention that studying belief by reference to 'formal indices' is inadequate, has argued that instead

> There is a need to recover the many and various ways in which individuals developed their own distinctive religious idioms, to look at how different fields or narratives of experience intermeshed with one another and to consider the language in which these ideas were structured. What role does religion play, for example, in the creation of meaning in the complex network of associations and constructions of reality which characterise Victorian popular culture not merely as operated within working class society but throughout all social levels and contexts?[59]

Callum Brown similarly argues for the importance of understanding Christianity as essentially 'discursive'. By examining fiction, musical lyrics, personal testimony and religious tracts he thus offers an account of a Christian discourse that he claims spread far beyond the boundary of institutional religion. This discourse remained significant in Britain until the mid 1960s.[60]

As Jeremy Morris has argued, Brown's analysis presents a useful alternative approach to the de-Christianisation discussion, although essentially flawed.[61] Morris points out that Brown is apt to make sweeping generalisations, neglecting small but important changes in Christian doctrine as well as social and political change that took place before the 1960s. More importantly, Morris argues that 'discursive Christianity', as Brown describes it, 'floats' between popular belief and the theology of the Churches, relating properly to neither. Once again, the teaching of the Churches emerges as detached from working-class culture, and monolithic. 'Reading Brown one could get the impression that there was no change to Christianity in the period. This is implausible.'[62]

---

[58] G. S. Jones, *Languages of Class. Studies in English Working Class History 1832–1982* (Cambridge, 1983).
[59] Sarah Williams, 'The language of belief: an alternative agenda for the study of Victorian working-class religion', *Journal of Victorian Culture*, 1, 2 (Autumn, 1996), 313–14.
[60] Brown, *The Death of Christian Britain*, 176.
[61] J. Morris, 'The strange death of Christian Britain: another look at the secularization debate', *Historical Journal*, 46, 4 (2003), 963–76.
[62] Ibid., 970.

For all of the flaws in the overall analysis, however, Brown's insistence on the role of discourse in historical study is valid. Christianity must be discursive, engaging with different discourses, he argues, or else it is inconceivable.[63] Christian discourse may be identified in protocols of behaviour, such as saying grace before meals or going to church, but will also be manifest in the 'voices' of the people, in testimony or autobiography.

Close attention, therefore, needs to be paid to the language of belief. As will be seen in this study, in the interface between spiritualism and Church teaching a rich variety of tropes and discourses emerge which were not straightforwardly contained by particular societies and social groups, but which rather pervaded a common intellectual and social space. By studying one aspect of Christian doctrine – the nature of the afterlife – and placing it alongside the alternative theological system of modern spiritualism, it becomes possible to observe both the importance of language in the development of belief, and also the way in which religious belief, rather than being a fixed entity that is eroded over time, is in fact a thoroughly dynamic process of negotiation, susceptible to the common culture in which it also plays a part.

---

[63] Brown, *The Death of Christian Britain*, 13.

17

2

Spiritualism in context

The story of modern spiritualism begins in America, and, more precisely, in a house in Hydesville, New York State, in 1848.[1] The village of Hydesville was made up of wooden houses and the people were farmers. The nearest significant town was Rochester, which was thirty miles away, and New York itself was two hundred and fifty miles away – at least two days' journey. One of the wooden houses was inhabited by John Fox, who lived with his wife and two of their children, Margaretta (or Maggie), aged fifteen, and Catherine (Katie), aged twelve. Their married daughter, Leah Fish, lived in Rochester and their son, David, lived two miles away. From February 1848 strange rapping sounds were heard whenever the two younger girls entered a room. The family decided that the rapping sounds were the communications of a departed spirit; they spoke to the unseen spirit and the spirit duly responded to their yes–no questions by means of the raps – when the girls were present. Neighbours came to witness the phenomenon and 'heard' the spirit claim to be a murdered man. The girls were separated and sent to stay with relatives, but the rapping continued around them. After a time other spirits presented themselves, and made it clear through raps that they wished Maggie and Katie to give public displays of their talents in spirit communication, and that the sisters should charge people to watch. Thus began the Fox sisters' careers as mediums.

---

[1] The story is told in detail in McCabe, *Spiritualism*, 27–102. For an early account, albeit written in mocking tone, see *Blackwood's Edinburgh Magazine*, LXXIII (May 1853), 629–46. *Blackwood's* dates the story from *March* 1848. The story of the Fox sisters is accepted as the beginning of modern spiritualism. However, there were instances of people being overtaken by spirits and incidents of disturbances among Shakers in the 1830s. Also of significance was Andrew Jackson Davis, an American shoemaker who became a mesmeric healer and clairvoyant. He began to receive spirit messages in 1847. See Emma Hardinge Britten, *Modern American Spiritualism*, 3rd edn (New York, 1870).

The sisters were investigated by the press, legal representatives and politicians, and were initially rewarded with favourable reports. Horace Greeley, the editor of the *New York Tribune*, declared himself impressed with the sisters. In 1851, Judge Edmonds of the New York Supreme Court not only accepted the veracity of the phenomena, but he then discovered his own mediumistic powers. The daughter of Governor Tallmadge of New York found a hitherto hidden gift for mediumship which included the ability to play music and speak several languages. The Fox sisters, guided by their sharp-minded elder sister Leah, began to move in the higher social circles of New York and Washington, even performing for the wife of the President. As early as 1851, however, as their careers were in ascendancy, the sisters' integrity was questioned. The *Tribune* published a sworn affidavit from a Mrs Culver, a friend of the Fox family, saying that Katie had confessed that the raps were made by the cracking of her joints and that questions were answered by the 'spirits' as the sisters carefully watched the faces of those attending the meetings.[2] Mrs Culver's claims were denied, but the sisters were dogged by rumours of fraud thereafter. These rumours were exacerbated as both Maggie and Katie took to drink and, at one point or another in the course of the next thirty years, confessed fraud and then recanted their confessions. They remained, however, in the public eye and their popularity continued.

Spiritualism flourished despite the Fox sisters' personal successes and failures. In 1852 the *Olive Branch*, an American Methodist newspaper, noted that 'scarcely a village can be found which is not infected with it … in most small towns several families are possessed'.[3] In 1853, Henry Spicer, an Englishman investigating the phenomena of spiritualism, stated that 'there were not less than *thirty thousand* recognised media practising in various parts of the United States'.[4] At the American Roman Catholic Congress in 1854, one speaker estimated that in a total national population of twenty-five million, some eleven million had embraced spiritualism. This was clearly an exaggeration; even the spiritualists themselves guessed that the number was only somewhere between one and two million.[5] Nevertheless, such exaggeration suggests that the rapid spread of spiritualism had caused a degree of alarm in at least one Christian denomination.

Spiritualism came to England in the autumn of 1852 when the medium

---

2 McCabe, *Spiritualism*, 39.
3 *The Olive Branch*, 19 June 1852.
4 Henry Spicer, *Sights and Sounds: The Mystery of the Day: comprising an entire history of the American 'spirit' manifestations* (London, 1853), 4.
5 McCabe, *Spiritualism*, 64.

Maria Hayden, the wife of the editor of the *Star-spangled Banner*, was invited to London by a mesmeric lecturer, Mr Stone, who had met her when visiting America. She became fashionable in London among the wealthy who 'flocked to communicate with their dead ... for a ½ Guinea'.[6] Despite Mrs Hayden being 'treated disgracefully by the leaders of the press, pulpit and college ... and subjected to a storm of ribaldry, persecution and insult',[7] spiritualism quickly became popular in London and beyond.

The Times noted with disdain in 1857 that spiritualism was 'all about and around',[8] and it was caricatured by the *Daily News* in the 1860s as being a 'fashionable excitement' for 'ladies of the Mrs Leo Hunter type'.[9]

Away from the fashionable drawing rooms of London, spiritualism flourished in a different way in the towns of Yorkshire, and in Keighley in particular. It was taken to Yorkshire by David Richmond, a man who, although originally from the area, had spent eleven years in America, where he had encountered the Fox family and discovered his own talent as a medium. He brought spiritualism with him on his return in 1853, where it found particular favour among secularist groups. The *Westminster Review* commented in 1862 that 'in Bradford, Bingley and other Yorkshire towns there are [secularists] once notorious for believing nothing, now equally notorious for believing everything'.[10]

The *Yorkshire Spiritual Telegraph*, the first spiritualist newspaper in England, noted as early as 1855, however, that spiritualism was not confined to one class or opinion:

> Besides, it is not to any particular sect or party that those manifestations are confined. We find there are Clergymen of the Church of England – Ministers belonging to almost all that various dissenting denominations, not excepting either Swedenborgians, Quakers, Shakers, Unitarians or even our popular advocates of Sceptical opinions. Then again, such manifestations are not confined to the preachers, or teachers of those various creeds but are equally common among the members of those various bodies. Even in the town of

---

6 Ibid., 103.
7 Britten, *Nineteenth Century Miracles*, 129.
8 *The Times*, 5 May 1857, pg. 6, col. C.
9 *Daily News*, noted in *Spiritualist*, 3 Dec. 1869. 'Mrs Leo Hunter' was a character in Charles Dickens' *The Pickwick Papers*, who held parties for people of beauty, fashion and literature, who 'talked considerable nonsense ... no doubt with the benign intention of rendering themselves intelligible to the common people about them'. Charles Dickens, *The Pickwick Papers*, Oxford World Classics edn. (Oxford and New York, 1998), 182.
10 *Westminster Review* (1862), 89. See Barrow, *Independent Spirits*, 11.

Keighley we find members belonging to a variety of those classes, who are susceptible of spirit influence.[11]

Spiritualism's chief claim was that living human beings could communicate with the spirits of the dead. Yet this claim was embellished by a variety of phenomena that became irrevocably attached to the whole spectacle that was modern spiritualism. In its beginnings the phenomena were crude: people seated around a table at a séance found that when the alleged spirits were present the table span or tilted to answer yes–no questions.[12] Rapping sounds were sometimes made to answer a question, or else were heard as a pencil or marker was moved up and down letters of the alphabet: thus, slowly, the 'spirit' tapped out a word.

Over time, mediums became more proficient at enabling the alleged spirits to communicate quickly and clearly. 'Automatic writing' was popular in domestic settings, where an individual would allow his or her hand, holding a pen, to be directed by the spirits into writing text or drawing pictures. Spirits communicated through 'direct voice', as a medium would allow his or her larynx to be used for communication, resulting in strange voices emanating from the medium. Sometimes a medium would go into a 'trance', where his or her own spirit would temporarily leave the body, to be replaced by the spirit of a dead person who then 'controlled' the medium. In many cases this discarnate spirit would become a familiar and habitual 'control', acting as a go-between and passing on messages from others in the spirit world to living friends or relatives. Sometimes the 'control' would summarise the messages, rather than give them directly, which, according to spiritualists, accounted for mistakes in the message. Controls were often child spirits; Native Americans were also popular.

Mediums, as well as enabling communication from the spirits, displayed other talents, such as clairvoyance and clairaudience: the ability to see things and hear sounds and voices beyond the limits of the natural realm. Some were able to contact a spirit by touching an object once owned by the dead person: this was known as psychometry. Others claimed to heal, or to be able to move objects without touching them.

More spectacularly, a number of mediums began to offer 'materialisations'. These were sometimes 'apports', flowers falling from ceilings, music being heard when there were no musicians present, objects floating as if in

11 *Yorkshire Spiritual Telegraph*, May 1855.
12 See, for example, Charles Maurice Davies' account of his first encounter with spiritualism, 'A Church of England clergyman', *The Great Secret and its unfoldment in Occultism* (London, 1895), 33–5.

mid air and the production of strange fragrance. Even more impressive were 'full body manifestations', where the medium would be bound and locked into a cabinet, from which a ghostly apparition would then appear. These manifestations were developed in the 1870s, but proved the undoing of many fraudulent mediums.[13] 'Partial manifestations', of hands, for example, were also part of the repertoire. With the advent of photography came 'spirit photographs', which showed images of the living surrounded by ghostly presences.

Spiritualism was a strange and fascinating American import; it became tremendously popular in England and appealed, as we will see, to a wide variety of people. Perhaps one reason for the appeal was its distinctiveness, particularly the claim that it was possible to converse with the dead. This foreignness and distinctiveness, however, may lead us to overlook quite how quickly and easily it became embedded into a receptive common culture. Put simply, despite its originality, spiritualism nevertheless contained many features that were already familiar to countless English men and women, and it connected with some long-established cultural tropes. Tilting tables, ghostly forms, mediums displaying knowledge of events that could not be explained, bouquets of flowers falling from ceilings: none of these was particularly novel or unheard of before Mrs Hayden's arrival.

Such phenomena, as well as the claims made by mediums that they could communicate with the dead, could have been described, communicated and explained by means of three significant discourses already in evidence by 1850. These are identified here as the 'preternatural' discourse, the 'scientific' discourse and the 'Christian' discourse. This chapter considers the first two of these – the relationship between spiritualism and the Christian discourse forming the substance of later chapters. Importantly, neither of the discourses now described represented a reflection of only minority interests. Indeed, what emerges from the following observations is a vibrant tapestry of ideas, customs and language, already present in 1852, and into which spiritualism became woven. Significantly, as we will see, members of the Church of England, even clergy, were not unfamiliar with these discourses.

The preternatural discourse

The term 'preternatural' here refers to phenomena understood to be irregular, yet still within the natural order, as distinct from 'supernatural', meaning phenomena judged to be above and beyond the natural way of things. The

---

[13] McCabe, *Spiritualism*, 138–47.

eighteenth century, as Sasha Handley has observed, had witnessed long debates about the correct classification of natural and spiritual phenomena. She suggests that 'preternatural wonders should be located somewhere in between the natural and supernatural worlds, as something out of the ordinary, yet potentially explicable by a combination of natural law and divine agency'.[14] Handley's own definition of 'preternatural' as 'out of the ordinary, yet potentially explicable' serves us well, covering as it does a wide variety of phenomena, ranging from alleged sightings of ghosts or apparitions to the supposed magical properties of amulets and the theatrical performances of magicians.

For a number of years, the prevailing narrative of the preternatural, as expounded by Keith Thomas in *Religion and the Decline of Magic* (1971) and expanded by Eamon Duffy in *The Stripping of the Altars* (1992), supposed a post-Reformation enlightened world gradually pushing a once cherished belief in the preternatural into the realm of superstition.[15] The English Reformation was seen to have done much to 'obliterate' the 'imaginative world' of the late Middle Ages,[16] and England in the sixteenth and seventeenth centuries became increasingly rational and less magical.

In recent years some historians have worked to revise this narrative, describing instead how communities retained and even developed a sense of the mysterious and the preternatural. Phyllis Mack has described a lively seventeenth-century world where women in particular saw spectacular visions and offered prophetic utterances, a far cry from Duffy's dull Protestantism.[17] Jane Shaw, Peter Lake and Alexandra Walsham have similarly revealed how strands of Protestantism in England developed their own pattern of wonders and miracles.[18] Sasha Handley has observed that the eighteenth century was alive with ghost sightings and ghost stories and that these were not simply retold for entertainment but played a real part in shaping the cultural landscape of their time.[19]

---

[14] Sasha Handley, *Visions of an unseen world: ghost beliefs and ghost stories in eighteenth-century England* (London, 2007), 9.
[15] Keith Thomas, *Religion and the Decline of Magic* (London, 1991. 1st pubd 1971), 799.
[16] Eamon Duffy, *The Stripping of the Altars* (New Haven and London, 1992), 593.
[17] Phyllis Mack, *Visionary Women. Ecstatic prophecy in seventeenth-century England* (Berkeley, 1992).
[18] Jane Shaw, *Miracles in Enlightenment England* (New Haven and London, 2006); P. Lake with M. Questier, *The Antichrist's Lewd Hat. Protestants, Papists and Players in Post-Reformation England* (New Haven and London, 2002); A. Walsham, *Providence in Early Modern England* (Oxford, 1999).
[19] Handley, *Visions of an unseen world*.

This vivid preternatural discourse was certainly still in operation in the mid nineteenth century. The plethora of ghost stories, the widely articulated fascination for the uncanny and the unexplained, as well as thrilled responses to performing magicians and mesmeric practitioners, suggest a buoyant interest in out of the ordinary yet potentially explicable phenomena. There were several strands to this discourse. It was possible, for example, to maintain an aesthetic appreciation of ghost fiction and a 'scientific' curiosity concerning unexplained phenomena alongside a vehement scepticism towards 'superstitious' beliefs in ghosts and the alleged magical properties of rabbits feet. *Aesthetic* appreciation of fictional ghost stories and magical tricks was something distinct from a lived *experience* of the ordinary world as being daily shot through with irregular phenomena. Yet these two strands at times became entwined as alleged experiences of unusual occurrences were related as narrative, even printed and published, taking on a life of their own as fiction.

Aesthetic tastes for the preternatural were further encouraged by late-eighteenth- and early-nineteenth-century Romanticism. The heightened emphasis on emotion, imagination and the mysterious in literature, art and music associated with Romanticism, along with a burgeoning interest in folk culture and the occult, encouraged a fresh examination of the preternatural. This was especially the case with the gothic novel. Although literature scholars tend to date the period of the gothic novel in its purest form from 1764 to 1820, beginning with *The Castle of Otranto* by Horace Walpole and ending with Mary Shelley's *Frankenstein*, ghost stories and tales designed to alarm continued to appeal long after this period.[20] By the mid nineteenth century short dramatic tales, such as 'The Haunted and the Haunters: or the House and the Brain' by Sir Edward Bulwer-Lytton and 'Madam Crowl's Ghost' by Joseph Sheridan Le Fanu, were enjoyed in collected works and periodicals.[21] Charles Dickens included ghost stories in his journals *Household Words* and *All the Year Round*, and his 1843 novel, *A Christmas Carol*, was extremely popular.

---

[20] See Julian Wolfreys, *Victorian Hauntings. Spectrality, Gothic, the Uncanny and Literature* (Basingstoke, 2002), 8–9. Also Michael Charlesworth (ed.), *The Gothic Revival 1720–1870. Literary Sources and Documents*. 3 Vols. (Mountfield nr. Robertsbridge, 2002).

[21] For Bulwer-Lytton's story, see V. H. Collins, *Ghosts and Marvels. A Selection of Uncanny Tales from Daniel Defoe to Algernon Blackwood* (London, 1924), 71–126. It was described by the *Guardian* as 'that greatest of all ghost stories', in the preface to M. R. James, *More Ghost Stories of an Antiquary* (London, 1911), 11. 'Madam Crowl's Ghost' was first published anonymously in *All the Year Round* (1870–71), but may also be found in M. R. James (ed.), *Madam Crowl's Ghost and other tales of mystery by Joseph Sheridan Le Fanu* (London, 1923).

Ronald Finucane has claimed that people knew the difference between fictional ghost stories and accounts of 'real' incidents, and enjoyed both, and that an aesthetic appreciation of ghost stories could coexist alongside either personal belief or disbelief in preternatural experiences.[22] This was true for the president of the English Church Union, Lord Halifax, who, despite his great antipathy towards spiritualism and its claim to communicate with the dead, was nevertheless a serious collector of ghost stories and accounts of ghost encounters.[23]

Yet at the same time, the boundary between ghost stories and accounts of ghostly encounters was decidedly porous. Experiences alleged to be 'true accounts' of hauntings found their way into collections of ghost stories. Thus the 'true' account of the ghost of Cottenhall Court in Worcestershire, whose nocturnal habits led to the living inhabitants moving out of the house, became part of a collection of *Ghost stories and presentiments* (1888).[24] Some accounts were handed on through generations and across families, a number of which appeared in *Lord Halifax's Ghost Book* (1936) or the collections of M. R. James.[25] Some of these 'stories' originated as reported accounts of uncanny or ghostly experiences and, vice versa, fictions were often told in the first person, giving them the aura of an authentic account.[26]

Some early advocates of modern spiritualism, although keen to show that it was superior to and distinctive from ghost experiences, nevertheless set spiritualism within a preternatural discourse which included ghosts. William Howitt, in *The History of the Supernatural. In all ages and nations, and in all Churches, Christian and Pagan: demonstrating a universal faith* (1863); Alfred Russel Wallace, in the new edition of *Chambers' Encyclopædia* (1888–92); and Emma Hardinge Britten, the American medium working and writing in Britain in *Nineteenth Century Miracles* (1883), all set spiritualism at the end of a long line of popular examples of preternatural wonders and ghost activity that had already caught the imagination of the public.[27]

[22] R. C. Finucane, *Appearances of the Dead. A Cultural History of Ghosts* (New York, 1984); see especially 177–205.

[23] Halifax, *Lord Halifax's Ghost Book. A collection of stories made by Charles Lindley, Viscount Halifax* (London, 1936).

[24] B. Dunston, *Ghost stories and presentiments* (London, 1888).

[25] For example, James, *More Ghost Stories.*

[26] Halifax, *Lord Halifax's Ghost Book.* See especially the story of 'The death of Lord Tyrone', originally from the eighteenth century, passed down through family members, 56. Also 'Colonel P.'s ghost story', a story in the first person but written by Halifax himself, 6–7.

[27] William Howitt, *The History of the Supernatural. In all ages and nations, and in all Churches, Christian and Pagan: demonstrating a universal faith*, 2 Vols (London, 1863);

Such examples included rappings at Rushton Hall, near Kettering, which in 1584 had disturbed Sir Thomas Tresham as he sat down to read a treatise entitled 'Proof that there is a God'. There were disturbances at the Palace at Woodstock in 1649 and at Mr Mompesson's at Tedworth in 1661, where drumming and knocking sounds imitated music or claps made by family members.[28] The famous Cock Lane ghost, investigated by Dr Johnson and Bishop Percy, was described,[29] as was the disturbance in 1716 at Epworth parsonage, home to John Wesley's family.[30]

In the nineteenth century, a house was haunted by rappings and poltergeist activity in Sandford, near Tiverton, Devon, in 1812. In 1834 Major Moor of Great Bealing, near Woodbridge, Suffolk, heard a sudden ringing of bells in his house. The bells stopped ringing after fifty-three days as suddenly as they had started. Major Moor published an account of the disturbances in a pamphlet called 'Bealing Bells', and inspired correspondence between people who had had similar experiences. One of these was the clergyman John Stewart of Sydensterne, near Fakenham, Norfolk. He gave details of how he had lived in a house which had, 'rappings, groans, cries, sobs, heavy trampings and thundering knocks.' This happened, according to his account, during the nine years of his occupancy.[31]

Both Britten and Howitt cited the case of Mary Jobson of Bishop Wearmouth, who was suddenly struck deaf, dumb and blind in 1839, at the age of about thirteen. Several doctors tried medical treatments, to no avail, and during the illness strange sounds were heard and a mysterious painting of the sun, moon and stars appeared on the girl's bedroom ceiling. The painting returned after being whitewashed by her father. In June 1840 she recovered as suddenly as she had become ill and the attendant phenomena ceased. The report of her illness was written up by Dr Reid Clanny, physician in ordinary to the duke of Sussex, based on the testimony of doctors who attended her.[32]

The account of a Mr Lenox Horne's ghostly vision was embellished by the appearance of modern spiritualism. In 1829, at his home in Hatton Garden,

Chambers' Encyclopædia, new edn (London, 1888–92), IX; Britten, *Nineteenth Century Miracles*.

[28] Howitt, *History of the Supernatural*, 2: 172.

[29] The fact that this 'ghost' proved to be fraudulent didn't appear to put off the spiritualist chroniclers.

[30] *Chambers' Encyclopædia*, IX: 646.

[31] Britten, *Nineteenth Century Miracles*, 93–6. Her account is flawed – John Stewart, originally from Belfast, was in Sydensterne for only one year before being made rector of Twaite in 1832.

[32] Unfortunately there is no reference for this report, but it appears in Britten, *Nineteenth Century Miracles*, 99–102; Howitt, *History of the Supernatural*, 2: 174.

Horne had witnessed – with friends – a vision of a masked ball from the period of Charles II, where the guests wore animal masks. The vision gradually faded and disappeared from view to the astonishment of Horne and his guests. He remained apparently untroubled by this vision until 1853, when he attended a party at which a séance was proposed (modern spiritualism having recently arrived in Britain). In attendance was Mademoiselle Josephine, the eleven-year-old daughter of a French medium, Madame Albert. Josephine used automatic writing to convey a message from the spirit of 'one who was known in the day and time of Charles Stuart as the finest woman of her age – Lady Castlemaine'. She reminded Horne of his vision and offered it as a warning against licentious living. Her 'base passions' in life, and the passions of her companions, had become so engraved upon their spirits that after death they had taken on animal form. 'Our hell,' she wrote through Josephine, 'is not to pass into other states, but to live in our own.' There was still hope, however, and it was possible, 'by the knowledge of what we have made ourselves, to grow into higher conditions.'[33] Spiritualism, the spiritualists argued, made sense of the previously unexplained, and out of the ordinary, phenomena.

If the relationship between ghost stories and 'factual' accounts of ghost encounters was ambiguous, the relationship between magic tricks and belief in the magical was less so. Enjoyment of magic was not exclusive of belief in the magical, but it was distinct from it. Tricks performed by magicians, whether in large halls or privately at home, were undertaken with the audience tacitly accepting that a human agent would entertain them with actions that they themselves would not be able to explain. They knew, in other words, that the magician was 'tricking' them. A person who believed that a charm would bring luck, or a potion a desired love, on the other hand, occupied a world where out of the ordinary or unusual events might be explained as the actions of either human or divine agency. A belief in the magical meant belief that an external agent could alter a person's life or destiny. To people who appreciated magical tricks, spiritualism offered seemingly impossible feats to be enjoyed and possibly investigated: mediums levitating, flowers falling from ceilings, music being played by invisible musicians. For those who believed in the magical properties of amulets, or who hoped to know their future, spiritualism produced healing magnets and voices from beyond the grave to advise them.

Magic performance, which by the nineteenth century had been largely divested of any suggestion of witchcraft or satanic agency, appealed to those seeking to be entertained. The most famous magician of the period, John

---

[33] Britten, *Nineteenth Century Miracles*, 98.

Nevil Maskelyne (1839–1917) began his career as a performing magician when he was still a boy, before joining with George Alfred Cook (1825–1905) and entertaining crowds to popular acclaim. In 1873 the pair took out a lease on the small hall at the Egyptian Hall in Piccadilly, aiming their entertainment at the middle and upper classes, and becoming so successful with their art of 'entertainment as pure trickery' that they had to move into the large hall.[34] Maskelyne and Cooke developed a number of 'signature' magical tricks, which included a fake séance and the appearance of ghosts, thus making use of the popularity of stories of the uncanny and poking fun at spiritualists and séances.[35] Into the twentieth century the American escapologist Harry Houdini (1874–1926) continued the tradition of drawing crowds with magic and spectacle, travelling around the north of England between 1902 and 1920, apparently defying the laws of nature with his performances.[36]

The enjoyment of magic tricks on a smaller, domestic, scale was also evident, as the publication of *Magic at Home* (1890), a 'how-to' collection for young people, reveals.[37] The book was styled as 'scientific', and the tricks presented were designed to illustrate and instruct the operations of natural law, employing optical illusions, buoyancy and gravity. The illustrations of the book implied that an air of theatricality could be employed even in the home. Newspaper advertisements suggest that domestic magic tricks were popular; *The Times*, for example, carried advertisements for conjuring sets, as well as small-time magic performers and ventriloquists for hire.[38]

When mediums began to include seemingly impossible feats and unusual phenomena – levitation, apports and manifestations – in their séances, a few critics initially accused them of relying on satanic agency.[39] Over time this accusation was replaced by the more common charge of fraud or trickery. Magicians such as Maskelyne, and later Houdini, sat alongside convinced spiritualists at séances in order to detect and then to explain to a credulous public how the 'tricks' were performed.[40] Conversely, spiritualists like Alfred Russel Wallace and Arthur Conan Doyle were convinced that Maskelyne and

---

[34] See Anna Davenport and John Salisse, *St George's Hall. Behind the scenes at England's home of mystery* (Pasadena, 2001), 23.
[35] Ibid., 26.
[36] Ruth Brandon, *The life and many deaths of Harry Houdini* (London, 2001); Brian Lead and Roger Woods, *Harry Houdini. Legend and Legacy* (Accrington, 1993).
[37] 'Professor' Hoffman, *Magic at Home. A book of amusing science* (London, 1890).
[38] *The Times*, 1 Jan. 1861, pg. 1, Col. 1.
[39] See chapter six, pp. 150–51.
[40] See McCabe, *Spiritualism*, esp. the exposure of the Davenport Brothers, 122, and further exposures of fraud, 154–67.

Houdini possessed mediumistic powers, which they chose not to acknowledge.[41]

Popular appreciation of magic 'tricks' sat apart from but alongside an ingrained belief in the magical: that certain items had power to change the course of events, for example, or that the future could be foretold. The folklorist Edward Lovett (1852–1933) claimed to have been interested in collecting 'superstitions' since his boyhood in the mid nineteenth century, particularly in London. In *Magic in Modern London* (1925) he catalogued beliefs in, for example, the lucky properties of horseshoes, the ability of tortoiseshell cat fur to cure chest troubles, and the use of love potions and mandrakes to bring romance and fertility.[42] The Folk-lore Society, founded in 1877 by anthropologist Sir Edward Tylor (1832–1917) and folklorist Sir Laurence Gomme (1853–1916), collected evidence of belief in the magical across the country. They noted the potentially unlucky properties of flowers in Inkberrow, omens of death and the hidden meanings of natural phenomena (in Cumberland, for example, sun shining on the woods foretold that the pigs would fatten well).[43]

The Folk-lore Society's pejorative designation of such beliefs as 'superstition' suggested that the observers viewed themselves as rational objective collectors of oddities. Yet the sheer prevalence and variety of such articulated beliefs in their journal reveals something of the strength and depth of the preternatural discourse. Seemingly out of the ordinary events did occur, and sometimes were explained as being the result of human agency. But clearly there were people across the country who identified a world located between the natural and supernatural, where unusual phenomena could not be explained simply, and where spiritual or divine agency was therefore a legitimate interpretation of events. These people did not necessarily believe in the magical all of the time, but it meant that when they encountered spiritualism they were susceptible to its claims to communicate with the dead. Spiritualism offered the possibility of hidden knowledge and advice for the living dispensed by those lurking in the afterlife.

The scientific discourse

Occasionally the preternatural discourse overlapped with the scientific discourse; although it was not simply the case that science was used to cast

---

[41] Brandon, *Life and many deaths of Harry Houdini*, 230.

[42] Edward Lovett, *Magic in Modern London* (Croydon, 1925).

[43] *Folk-lore Journal*, Mar. 1917, 52; Sept. 1917, 311–12.

doubt on the existence of ghosts. Indeed, scientific language was sometimes used to embellish accounts of unusual experiences: the presence of doctors attending Mary Jobson, for example, gave the story a degree of scientific credibility. Science also appeared in ghost fiction. Joseph Taylor used knowledge of phosphorous in the story of a 'ghost' who attempted to seduce a girl in France,[44] and Bulwer-Lytton's story, 'The Haunted and the Haunters', included scientific investigators.[45] Scientific method was employed by the Folk-lore Society in order to catalogue and categorise beliefs in the magical.[46]

In the nineteenth century a diverse audience followed contemporary scientific developments with great interest. The natural philosopher and scientist, Michael Faraday (1791–1867), for example, credited with the discovery of electro-magnetic induction and the development of the practical applications of electricity, cultivated such interest. Crowds of people gathered at his public Friday evening lectures at the Royal Institution (founded in 1826) and many more came to read about the latest scientific progress through the newspaper reports of these events.[47] The Great Exhibition of 1851 attracted six million visitors, marvelling at the technological and industrial developments of the day.[48] Yet the public fascination with science included what would now be described as 'heterodox' or 'alternative' science as well as that propounded by Faraday and his colleagues at the Royal Institution, a fascination which embraced mesmerism, phrenology and the power of herbs – much to Faraday's disgust.[49]

There were few 'professional' scientists at this time, and it was possible for people who did not make their living in science laboratories to engage enthusiastically and seriously in 'scientific' experiment. In one significant instance the scientific and preternatural discourses were brought together when, in the 1850s, a group of men in Cambridge, intrigued by the possibilities of ghost

[44] In this instance the 'ghost' turned out to be a lecherous Dominican friar, unmasked by science. J. Taylor, *Apparitions; or, the mystery of ghosts, hobgoblins and haunted houses, developed* (London, 1814), 29–38.

[45] The investigators were unable to explain the uncanny experience. Collins, *Ghosts and Marvels*, 71–126.

[46] As it was by William James in 1902. *Varieties of Religious Experience* (London, 1985. 1st pubd 1902).

[47] James Hamilton, *Faraday. The Life* (London, 2002), 194.

[48] Jeffrey Auerbach, *The Great Exhibition of 1851. A nation on display* (New Haven and London, 1999), 137.

[49] Despite his best efforts to disprove the claims of mesmerism, he was largely ignored. See Alison Winter, *Mesmerized. Powers of the Mind in Victorian Britain* (Chicago and London, 1998), 26.

experiences, decided to investigate them scientifically and formed a society, called the Cambridge Ghost Club, to do so.

Another society, the London Ghost Club, was formed in 1862, and from these two the Society for Psychical Research eventually emerged in 1882. The Cambridge and London Ghost Clubs, as well as the SPR, included, as will be seen, many clerical members. Indeed, founder members of the Cambridge Ghost Club included a future bishop and future archbishop.[50]

The vocabulary of experiment, energy, health, investigation, telegraphy and electricity was enthusiastically embraced by some spiritualists. It was already a common and popular discourse, and it helped to present spiritualism as modern, new and exciting. In 1858 the first edition of the spiritualist newspaper, the *Two Worlds*, embracing the possibilities of science, announced that its mission was to deal with various aspects of 'spiritualism, social science, mental philosophy and physiology'. In addition, it included in its pages debates concerning homeopathy, vegetarianism and teetotalism, judging that these matters were of importance to its readers.[51] Another title, the *Medium and Daybreak*, included advertisements for lectures about phrenology and claims for the spiritual power of crystals.[52] From a cursory reading of spiritualist newspapers two observations can be made. In the first place, at least some spiritualists saw spiritualism as important to physical and spiritual health. Secondly, the pages of spiritualist newspapers reflect the vivid kaleidoscope of cures, treatments and medical theories available in mid-nineteenth-century Britain.

As Roger Cooter, Logie Barrow and Ian Burney have all observed, it would be a mistake to imagine an easy distinction between 'orthodox' and 'heterodox' medical theory and practice in this period. Indeed, much of what would now be termed 'orthodoxy' in medicine was in the process of being fiercely negotiated when spiritualism entered English life. These historians have noted that qualified, regular medical practitioners worked alongside bonesetters, chemists and herbalists in the early nineteenth century.[53] Yet a new,

---

[50] The SPR itself included professional scientists as well as interested clergymen, novelists, politicians and women. The ghost clubs and the SPR are examined more fully in chapter three, pp. 50–53.

[51] *Two Worlds*, 2 Oct. 1858.

[52] *Medium and Daybreak*: for phrenology see 14 June 1872; for crystals for sale to aid clairvoyance, 29 Apr. 1870.

[53] R. Cooter (ed.), *Studies in the History of Alternative Medicine* (Basingstoke, 1988); L. Barrow, ' "An imponderable liberator": J. J. Garth Wilkinson', ibid.; I. Burney, 'Medicine in the Age of Reform', in Arthur Burns and Joanna Innes (eds), *Rethinking the Age of Reform. Britain 1780–1850* (Cambridge and New York, 2003).

'pure' medical profession was slowly being fashioned by men like surgeon and medical journalist Thomas Wakley (1795–1862) and his fellow contributors to the journal he founded, the *Lancet*. Roy Porter goes so far as to suggest that the early nineteenth century saw these radical medical campaigners consciously constructing a world of 'quacks' and irregulars in order to further their ambition to purify and regulate the medical profession.[54] This 'irregular' world included 'prescribing clergymen', who offered their services to the sick.[55]

The pages of spiritualist newspapers suggest that spiritualism was less comfortably accommodated into the world of Wakley and the professionals, and more easily at home in an unregulated environment alongside the 'quacks'. The therapeutic properties of magnetised portraits,[56] herbs and crystals were extolled, and their potential for healing was treated with great seriousness.

Studies made by historians into the world of what would now be termed 'alternative' medicine in the early nineteenth century have revealed more of this kaleidoscope of theories, practices and remedies into which spiritualism was accommodated. The 'big four' medical 'alternatives' were hydropathy, herbalism (medical botany), homeopathy and mesmerism.[57] In addition to these four, Kathryn Gleadle has added vegetarianism and hygeism, the practice of purging the blood by using James Morrison's vegetable pills.[58] Each of these 'alternatives' had its supporters and enthusiasts. Importantly they were not confined to a particular geographical location or class and, as Roy Porter noted of the eighteenth century, when it came to the possibility of cures, 'the sick, given the opportunity, would shop around'.[59]

Hydropathy became part of the British medical landscape from the 1840s, being introduced and practised by men inspired by the techniques of the Austrian Vincent Preissnitz. It included complicated systems of bathing underpinned by a theory of how the body was divided into two parts comprising lower and higher orders. By 1891 Britain had sixty-three substantial and reputed 'hydros', enjoyed mostly by middle-class patrons and a few

---

[54] R. Porter, 'Before the Fringe: "Quackery" and the eighteenth-century medical market', in Cooter (ed.), *Studies*, 1–10, at 2.
[55] Cooter (ed.), *Studies*, xv.
[56] *Medium and Daybreak*, 20 May 1870.
[57] Cooter (ed.), *Studies*, xiv.
[58] Kathryn Gleadle, 'The age of physiological reformers: rethinking gender and domesticity in the age of reform', in Burns and Innes (eds), *Rethinking*, 200–219.
[59] Porter, 'Before the Fringe', 3.

aristocrats.[60] Hydropathy had 'celebrity' enthusiasts, such as Darwin and Tennyson, and flourished in places like Malvern and Matlock, where water was plentiful and access by train was possible. Although enjoyed by the respectable middle classes, it claimed to be egalitarian, and was associated with radical Quakers and Unitarians and a zealous Methodism espoused by Joseph Smedley, the proprietor of the Matlock hydro.[61]

Homeopathy offered a holistic approach to the treatment of bodily ailments in conjunction with the laws of nature. Introduced to England in the 1820s, it enjoyed a boost to its reputation by the reported relief it gave to the marquis of Anglesey, who tried it on a visit to Naples in 1834.[62] The British Homeopathic Society was established in 1844 by Frederick Hervy Quin, who had practised in Naples before returning to London, and who was connected with Whig nobility. The English Homeopathic Association was founded the following year by John Epps, and sought, by contrast, to encourage homeopathy in domestic settings.

Herbalism, sometimes called 'medical botany' or 'Coffinism', was more commonly associated with lower classes and northern industrial towns. John Wesley had actively encouraged the use of herbs and plants to heal, but it was under the influence of an American, Samuel Thompson, that interest in herbalism grew. His ideas were shared by an Englishman, Albert Isaiah Coffin. He promoted medical botany in Manchester from the 1840s and began a fortnightly journal in 1847. As Kathryn Gleadle has noted, the journal boasted of its connections with 'ordinary' people.[63] Societies were formed in the industrial towns of the north, where, as Ursula Miley and John Pickstone have suggested, the distance from fields and rural landscape imbued herbs with a special and mysterious character.[64]

Spiritualism connected with a world of healing, herbs, water cures and crystals, and spiritualist newspapers reveal that some proponents actively sought to use the language of healing and health to describe the benefits as well as the claims of modern spiritualism.[65] Yet, purely for the combination of

---

[60] See Kelvin Rees, 'Water as commodity: hydropathy in Matlock', in Cooter (ed.), *Studies*, 28.

[61] Gleadle, 'Age of physiological reformers', 205; Rees, 'Water as commodity', 32.

[62] Glynis Rankin, 'Professional organisation and the development of medical knowledge: two interpretations of homeopathy', in Cooter (ed.), *Studies*, 47.

[63] Gleadle, 'Age of physiological reformers', 206.

[64] Ursula Miley and John Pickstone, 'Medical botany around 1850: American medicine in industrial Britain', in Cooter (ed.), *Studies*, 141.

[65] It was believed, for example, that clairvoyance, or trances, brought health to the 'brain-system'. Spiritualists connected this with the benefits of mesmerism. *Spiritual Magazine*, Nov.

an explicit concern for health coupled with flamboyant theatricality, out of all of the medical theories and practices around in the mid nineteenth century, the one that spiritualism most resembled was mesmerism.

Mesmerism developed in the eighteenth century, although the ideas that underpinned it were, even then, long established. In the seventeenth century the idea began to develop that the universe was knit together by forces of rhythm and flux. The individual person was a microcosm of the universe, responding and reciprocating the same universal forces. These ideas, usually attributed to Robert Fludd (1574–1637), were taken up in the eighteenth century by Franz Anton Mesmer (1734–1815). Mesmer studied as a doctor in Vienna, entitling his thesis *de l'influence des Planettes sur le corps humain*. In it he argued that the universe was surrounded by an invisible, universally distributed fluid that flowed everywhere and served as a vehicle for influence between heavenly and earthly bodies. This fluid, sometimes described as a 'force', was, Mesmer thought, the cause of universal gravitation.[66]

After qualifying as a physician Mesmer applied his theory of fluids to the treatment of hysteria, moving to Paris in 1788 where his ideas found favour. The medical establishment shunned him, but his claims to heal patients by a combination of stroking, touching, hypnotic staring and magnets continued to arouse interest among the people whom he treated.

According to Frank Podmore, early-twentieth-century chronicler of spiritualism and psychic science, mesmerism was introduced to England by a Dr Bell – who had witnessed its effects in Paris.[67] The spiritualist Emma Hardinge Britten claimed it was introduced through an Irishman called Mr Chevenix in 1828, he likewise having witnessed it in Paris.[68] These were only minor events; mesmerism, or 'animal magnetism' as it was sometimes called, arrived more seriously in 1837, when Charles Dupotet de Sennenevoy reached London. 'Baron' Dupotet, along with two others, had, in 1826, persuaded the Academie de Medicine in Paris to convene a committee investigating mesmeric phenomena by means of a series of experiments. The most

1860. A correspondent to the *Yorkshire Spiritual Telegraph* claimed to have been healed of cancer by spirits via a 'healing medium'. *Yorkshire Spiritual Telegraph*, Oct. 1856.

[66] Podmore, *Modern Spiritualism*, 51–66.

[67] Ibid., 111.

[68] Britten, *Nineteenth Century Miracles*, 124. This account was confirmed by the *Zoist*, the mesmerist journal. Richard Chevenix witnessed it in France and Germany in 1803 and tried it himself in Ireland in 1828, mesmerising and curing a peasant woman with epilepsy. Between May 1828 and January 1829 he claimed to have mesmerised 164 people, of whom 98 manifested 'undeniable effects'. *Zoist*, Vol. 1 (Mar. 1843–Jan. 1844), 58.

astonishing of these experiments was a surgical operation carried out on a woman who, when in a mesmeric state, apparently felt no pain.[69]

With such medical credentials Dupotet appealed to the newly emerging medical elite of London, as well as to fashionable society. Initially his experiments in London attracted interested parties to his private rooms, but it was his collaboration with John Elliotson (1791–1868), professor of medicine at University College London, that had the greater impact on mesmerism in England.[70] Elliotson became interested in mesmerism and conducted a series of experiments. Thomas Wakley, editor of the *Lancet*, was at first sympathetic, but he became increasingly sceptical and published reports that were critical of both Elliotson and his claims for mesmerism.[71] By the end of 1838 the *Lancet* had concluded that mesmerism was a fraud and Elliotson resigned from his position.[72] He continued to practise, establishing a mesmeric hospital in Wimpole Street by 1845.[73]

Mesmerism, although discredited by the *Lancet*, went on to become something of a national craze. Alison Winter has charted how mesmerism gained both popular appeal and, once more, the support of some in the medical community. Elliotson and a few others continued their work in private, but away from London experiments took place on public stages up and down the country, conducted by travelling lecturers. During the 1840s lecturers (who had a variety of backgrounds and credentials) demonstrated the phenomena of mesmerism to audiences in temperance halls, mechanics' institutes, public houses and rented rooms. In showy experiments – which often involved subjecting mesmerised individuals to forms of torture to prove that they had lost their sense of feeling – lecturers entertained and instructed large numbers

---

[69] Winter, *Mesmerized*, 41–2.

[70] Elliotson was a pioneer of stethoscope use. He was also interested in acupuncture and phrenology. See Cooter (ed.), *Studies*, xiv. For some of Elliotson's phrenological experiments see *Zoist*, 1, 41.

[71] For example, 'Dr Elliotson's experiments in "Mesmerism" at the house of Mr Wakley with two girls deceiving', *Lancet*, 1 Sept. 1838. It was thought that many of the patients were deceiving: *Lancet*, 28 July 1838.

[72] The *Lancet* also derided Elliotson's other concern, phrenology; *Lancet*, 2 July 1842. Elliotson's fury at his treatment by Wakley was still tangible in 1846. He bit back, for example, in his own journal, in April 1846; *Zoist*, 4, 20–21. Ironically, it transpired that Dupotet was using mesmerism for financial gain. When it became clear that he was making money out of the poor, as well as the rich, Elliotson fell out with him. *Zoist*, 1, 89.

[73] He attracted influential supporters, such as Richard Whately (1787–1863), the archbishop of Dublin, professor of mathematics at the newly formed University of London, Augustus de Morgan (1806–71) and Thomas Makdougall Brisbane (1773–1860), astronomer and president of the Royal Society in Edinburgh.

of people. It was in this context, Winter argues, that mesmerists triumphed in the 1840s, spreading enthusiasm and interest and offering people a language to describe the powers of the mind, performing before audiences that could number anything between a dozen and a thousand people.[74] In this respect, mesmerism paved the way for the large 'performance' séances in the next decades.

There were two periodicals associated with mesmerism: the *Zoist*, founded in 1843 by Elliotson, and the *Phreno-magnet*, founded in the same year by Spencer Hall, a former stocking maker, printer and travelling mesmerist. The *Zoist*, which continued until 1856, offered a forum for discussions about mesmeric experiments, trances and the possibilities for their use in medicine. It also offered space to other subjects, such as phrenology, clairvoyance and the theories of sleep. After 1852 the claims of spiritualism and the phenomena displayed by mediums were also hotly debated in its pages.[75] The *Zoist* presented itself as a serious journal for medical minds. The *Phreno-magnet*, by contrast, was directed at factory workers, artisans and tradesmen, and the sort of people that Spencer Hall encountered on his lecture tours. It wasn't as successful as the *Zoist*, and lasted for only eleven months.

The *Zoist* gave details of clergymen who not only supported the claims of mesmerism, but even engaged in mesmeric healing themselves. Thomas Pyne, the incumbent of Hook, Surrey, for example, engaged enthusiastically in a ministry of healing. He claimed he cured a child of deafness, a woman 'in pain' and a seven-week-old child who was not sleeping. He received many letters of thanks from grateful parishioners.[76] The vicar of Flixton, Suffolk, George Sandby, wrote a book in 1844 defending mesmerism against charges that it was satanic. Called *Mesmerism the gift of God*, it was, according to the *Zoist*, well received in the London and provincial press.[77]

Mesmerism offered a discourse of trance states, hypnotic stares and the relation between the unseen universe and the individual. The fact that a handful of scientists were also prepared to give it credence meant that when spiritualism arrived in England spiritualists could claim that it was, similarly, 'scientific'.[78] Mesmeric and 'scientific' vocabulary, already present in the

---

[74] Winter, *Mesmerized*, 110–36.
[75] See, for example, an edition of 1854, *Zoist*, 12, 5–17. Elliotson and one of his supporters, Dr Ashburner, fell out over spiritualism. Ashburner became an adherent; Elliotson remained sceptical of its claims until near to death.
[76] *Zoist*, 2, 538.
[77] *Zoist*, 2, 217. The sermon that had prompted Sanby's response, given by Hugh M'Neile and called 'Satanic agency and mesmerism', had apparently sold three thousand copies.
[78] *Medium and Daybreak*, 3 June 1870.

common culture, was used by spiritualists to bolster their own claims. Thus spiritualism was 'phenomenal and philosophical, corresponding with inductive and deductive methods of reasoning'.[79] It was claimed as part of a noble history of science; its philosophy was in line with the thinking of, among others, Copernicus, Kepler, Galileo and Newton.[80]

Scientists themselves, on the other hand, were divided in their opinions of spiritualism. The mathematician Augustus de Morgan and the biologist Alfred Russel Wallace became convinced by its claims, but Michael Faraday wrote to *The Times* in 1853 arguing that table-tilting could be effected by involuntary muscle movement rather than unseen spirits.[81]

In 1852 the cultural climate was nevertheless generally receptive to spiritualism. Spiritualists understood this, often explaining their practices and the belief that the dead could communicate with the living in terms that people could already grasp. They employed popular scientific language, using words like 'telegraph', 'energy', 'electricity' and 'fluid' to express how the world of the dead and the world of the living connected.[82] They directed their written material towards people interested in health and healing. At the same time, bolstering their claim that the dead walked among the living, they employed the language of ghosts, wonders, unusual occurrences and unexplained events.[83] They presented spiritualism as simultaneously modern and scientific, and yet also ancient and mysterious, and were able to do so because these discourses were already part of the common culture – and not mutually exclusive.

In addition, as we have seen, these discourses were not unfamiliar to Anglicans. There were clergy and other serious-minded churchmen who 'collected' ghost stories, wrote of their ghost experiences or formed societies to investigate 'scientifically' accounts of ghost activity. There were clerical healers and even clergy mesmerists. But although spiritualism slipped easily into these available discourses it also offered something that made it distinctive: the claim that it was possible to make contact with the dead and that the dead

---

[79] Ibid., 27 May 1870.

[80] Ibid., 30 Dec. 1870. The list also included Descartes, Plato and Jesus.

[81] *The Times*, 30 June 1853, pg. 8, col. D. Spiritualists had the last laugh. After Faraday had died his 'spirit' returned to a séance to admit that he was wrong in life and that the claims of spiritualism were valid. Winter, *Mesmerized*, 26.

[82] So much so that Cromwell Varley, Atlantic cable electrician and spiritualist, cautioned against the overuse of the words 'electricity' and 'magnetism': *Spiritualist*, 15 Feb. 1871. For reference to 'spiritual telegraphy' see *Spiritualist*, 15 July 1872.

[83] A lecture was delivered, for example, explicitly connecting ancient magic and witchcraft with spiritualism. *Medium and Daybreak*, 18 Aug. 1871.

spoke to the living about the nature of the afterlife. It was this claim that brought spiritualism into the orbit of Church of England teaching. Had spiritualism offered only unusual phenomena at séances and some extravagant claims for healing, then the Church could have ignored it; instead spiritualism taught people about the departed state in vivid terms that were quickly and readily absorbed, along with the phenomena, into the common culture. In so doing it presented a challenge to the Christian Church's unique authority to teach on such matters. Similarly, had it been the preserve of a few eccentrics or enthusiasts, the Church could have dismissed it. The following chapter demonstrates, however, that spiritualism became so popular with such large numbers of people of all types and backgrounds that it could not be overlooked.

3

Spiritualism and English common culture

Spiritualism quickly became embedded within English life. It gained committed followers and offered flamboyant mediums and the hint of scandal, as well as strange, even indescribable phenomena. At the same time, and importantly, the language and ideas of spiritualism became familiar in the homes, meeting halls, newspapers and workplaces of many more people than would have acknowledged themselves as 'spiritualists'. The central claim to communicate with the dead became widely known to men and women, adults and children alike, who came into contact with the language and ideas of spiritualism regardless of whether or not they believed its claims or witnessed the phenomena.

Experimentation at home

It is difficult to establish how many people experimented privately with spiritualism, as home séances tended to remain private affairs unless they were reported by either a convinced participant or a committed spiritualist. Throughout the period spiritualist writers were quick to boast about what they saw as widespread experimentation across the country. Thus the more impressive evidence comes from reports in non-spiritualist newspapers, and the comments of critical observers, who suggested that extensive experimentation with séances did indeed occur throughout the whole of the period. The American spiritualist Maria Hayden introduced modern spiritualism to London in 1852 and it soon became something of a 'craze'. Another American, Mrs Roberts, soon followed, but then English mediums quickly began to discover their own talents and, within a couple of years, these home-grown talents became well known. Mediums of note were Mrs Thomas Everitt, the wife of a Pentonville tailor who began her mediumship in 1855,[1] followed in

---

[1] McCabe, *Spiritualism*, 115.

1858 by Mrs Mary Marshall and her niece Mary Brodie, who offered séances that included tricks with handkerchiefs.[2] Two male mediums, David Richmond, mentioned earlier, and Daniel Dunglas Home, also appeared on the scene. Home was a flamboyant medium, originally from Scotland, who had conducted séances in the fashionable salons of Europe before travelling to London in 1859.

The sceptical *Blackwood's Edinburgh Magazine*, in an 1853 article, was horrified to note that 'many men' seemed to have 'taken leave of their senses. We have gone back to the old trash of King James's witchcraft.'[3] Spiritualism was fashionable very quickly, and so some assumed that it would disappear as speedily as it had arrived. Thus the *Scottish Review* described spiritualism in July 1854 as 'the epidemic which has recently prevailed in our country and which has now, we trust, so nearly run its course that we may treat it as a matter of history. We refer to the various "spiritual manifestations" made through "mediums" of various kinds, intelligent and unintelligent; and especially to that phase of it, which is commonly known under the designations of "table-turning" and "table-tapping", or "table-talking." '[4] In 1857, however, *The Times* found that spiritualism was not a passing fashion. Five years after Mrs Hayden had first conducted her séances in London, spiritualism had been 'digested into a science with its forms, its nomenclature, its inductions and its rules'.[5] It had become something recognisable, something to be commented upon. Five years later *The Times* complained that English civilisation was still beset by a prevalent passion for tampering with the supernatural and feared that rather than dwindling as a fashion, spiritualism was, in fact, on the increase, and in evidence in all classes of society:

> So far from superstition being dormant we have clear proofs of its existence, and some reason to fear that it is on the increase both in the

---

[2] Mrs Marshall was noted for her lack of education, and often finished a séance with the words: 'The sperrits is gone. I heard their feet a-patterin' away jest now', according to 'A Church of England clergyman' (Charles Maurice Davies), *The Great Secret*, 136. She was described by the London Dialectical Society as the 'high priest' of the movement. See the account of the chairman, Dr James Edmunds: London Dialectical Society, *Report on Spiritualism, of the Committee of the London Dialectical Society* (London, 1871), 79. Despite her lowly education, she performed for people like William Cowper-Temple (1811–88) and his wife Georgina. See Van Akin Burd, *Christmas Story. John Ruskin's Venetian Letters of 1876–1877* (Newark, 1990).

[3] *Blackwood's Edinburgh Magazine*, Vol. LXXIII (May 1853), 629–46, at 634. The article concluded that spiritualism was 'humbug and deliberate imposture'.

[4] *Scottish Review*, Vol. VII (July 1854), 193–208, at 199.

[5] *The Times*, 5 May 1857, pg. 6, col. C.

highest and the lowest classes of society. While Mr Home and Mr Forester hold their fashionable séances at the West-end of London, gipsies and fortune-tellers are pandering to a like morbid craving for communion with the kingdom of darkness among peasants and servant girls.[6]

The fascination certainly continued in London, as the *Daily News* observed in 1869, writing that society ladies were 'made acquainted with the methods of conversing with departed friends' over tea.[7]

Polite experimentation in spiritualism came to the notice of critics and commentators in the twentieth century. Writing in 1908, a Roman Catholic priest working in Bayswater noted that it was still commonplace to find people experimenting with séances at home: 'It is not an uncommon amusement, as some people call it, in drawing rooms to evoke the spirits, and to obtain answers to rappings.' He was keen to point out that although spiritualism was becoming prevalent among members of Roman Catholic congregations, outside Catholicism spiritualism was 'rampant'.[8]

Séances reportedly took place among soldiers during the First World War, according to the recollections of some of the army chaplains. One commented that, 'a very dangerous belief in spiritualism is gaining ground, and a tendency towards dabbling in it'.[9] Incidents of séances within the army, however, were as nothing compared with the abundance of séances among those bereaved by the war. Yet the very word 'dabbling' is suggestive of the amateurish experimentation that took place in private homes through the whole of the period, as people 'had a go' at contacting the dead. In 1921 one spiritualist convert, McLaren Post Macfie, wrote of how, although he had not previously believed in spiritualism, he experimented with a ouija board one day with a friend and became convinced.[10] In the late 1930s friends and family members still gathered around tables to test the spirits of the dead with ouija boards and glass tumblers, and Noel Coward's 1941 play, *Blithe Spirit*, could assume that

---

6   Ibid., 15 Mar. 1862.
7   *Daily News*, 3 Dec. 1869.
8   A. V. Miller OSC, *Sermons on Modern Spiritualism* (London, 1908), 47.
9   *The Army and Religion. An enquiry and its bearing upon the religious life of the nation* (London, 1919), 19–20. Michael Snape has challenged the idea that spiritualism was as prevalent in the trenches as the chaplain's words suggest. Instead, he argues, what soldiers believed was a diffuse Christianity that included ghosts and the supernatural. M. Snape, *God and the British Soldier. Religion and the British Army in the First and Second World Wars* (London, 2005), 39–40. He suggests that it was much more common at home than in the trenches.
10 McLaren Post Macfie, *From Heaven to Earth. Messages Automatically Written* (London, 1921), 4.

audiences would be familiar with the notion of a light-hearted spiritualist séance held at a private dinner party.[11]

Experimentation did not imply that those who took part either believed or disbelieved the claims made by spiritualists to communicate with the dead. In the privacy of the home a spiritualist séance might just as much be performed as a parlour game, or a way of showing off skilful magical trickery, as be a seriously intended conversation with those beyond the grave. Nevertheless, from the observations of the unconvinced and even hostile critics of spiritualism, it must be concluded that many private experiments in communicating with the dead certainly did take place.

Those looking to experiment were not short of advice and encouragement as to how to proceed when they turned to spiritualist publications. Thomas Shorter, a Christian spiritualist writing in 1859, advised those trying a séance at home to begin with prayer to God, asking permission for spirit friends to attend. He also thought that a collect or the Lord's Prayer might be said, and a hymn might be sung if people were in good voice.[12] The *Spiritual Magazine*, in February 1862, advised enquirers to set up their own séances: 'Let the members of the family sit around a good-sized table, in a calm but cheerful spirit and in a child-like manner as the privilege of witnessing the phenomena.'[13] The *Spiritualist* offered advice as to how to set up a spirit circle at home. The advice included the optimum number around a table and how to create the right atmosphere.[14] In the summer of 1874, at a spiritualist conference, an Anglican priest and convinced spiritualist, Charles Maurice Davies, advised people to try spiritualism at home.[15]

Several well-known people experimented with spiritualism. It became common knowledge that Queen Victoria had tried it,[16] as had such figures as Gladstone, Thackeray and Trollope.[17] Holman Hunt attended a séance.[18] John

[11] Noel Coward, *Blithe Spirit. An Improbable Farce in Three Acts* (London, 1976. 1st pubd 1941).

[12] Thomas Shorter, *Confessions of a Truth Seeker. A Narrative of Personal Investigations into the Facts and Philosophy of Spirit-Intercourse* (London, 1859), xvi.

[13] *Spiritual Magazine*, Feb. 1862.

[14] *Spiritualist*, 19 Nov. 1869. The newspaper issued the same advice in subsequent publications.

[15] Ibid., 21 Aug. 1874.

[16] *Medium and Daybreak*, 10 Nov. 1871 noted that she had been to séances.

[17] Thackeray included a positive description of spiritualism in the July 1860 edition of the *Cornhill Magazine*, which he edited; *Cornhill Magazine*, Vol. 2 (1860), 219–24.

[18] Georgiana Houghton, *Evenings at Home in Spiritual Séance. Prefaced and welded together by species of autobiography* (London, 1881), 167.

Ruskin tried it in 1875 after the death of Rose de la Touche.[19] Elizabeth Barrett-Browning was convinced by spiritualism, having been at séances with D. D. Home, although her husband Robert Browning was not. Aristocrats met for séances: the earl of Dunraven noted a séance held in September 1868 at the home of Mrs Hamilton, with the baron de Veh and his wife, the Princess Karoli, Mrs Watkins, Mrs Gregory, the count de Mons, General Brevern, the medium and himself present.[20]

Emma Hardinge Britten noted that large numbers of society ladies and gentlemen, discovering their talents, offered their mediumistic gifts to friends and acquaintances.[21] At the same time, in the 'large and thickly-populated districts of Yorkshire, Lancashire and Northumberland' miners, pit-men, weavers and factory hands found their mediumistic voices, and were known to 'pour forth moving trains of exalted eloquence' inspired by the spirits.[22] Among their own class, she noted, uneducated people found powers of spirit healing, trance speaking, automatic writing and spirit drawing, so much so that it was 'impossible' to visit any town or hamlet without discovering the 'way-marks' of spiritual power.

Thus there are grounds for taking seriously the observations of the spiritualist William Howitt, who noted in 1863 the 'thousands and tens of thousands daily sitting down in families and circles of intimate friends and quietly and as people of common sense, successfully testing those angels under their own mode of advent and finding them real'.[23] Spiritualism was practised in the home more widely, he thought, than in public meetings, and far more people had experience of private séances than of the public displays of mediums. 'Not one man in a hundred has ever seen a public medium. Public mediums have, in reality, only inaugurated the movement: it has been, of necessity, carried on by private and family practice.'[24]

Although advice was given as to how to begin a séance, private experiments in spiritualism were not controlled, and therefore differed in how they originated. This can be clearly observed in three accounts given by convinced spiritualists that reveal how they each began to 'try' the spirits. The first, by the medium Georgiana Houghton, writing in 1881, tells of private experiments that had begun some years before:

---

19 Burd, *Christmas Story*, 34.
20 Earl of Dunraven, *Experiences in Spiritualism with D. D. Home* (Glasgow, 1924), 104.
21 Britten, *Nineteenth Century Miracles*, 165.
22 Ibid.
23 Howitt, *History of the Supernatural*, 2: 219.
24 Ibid., 2: 220.

It seems curious to look back upon my first experiences in Spiritualism, in days when it was not spoken about at all, whether believingly
or unbelievingly, so that I had never even heard the subject mooted
when, in the summer of 1859, my cousin, Mrs Pearson, told me there
were some persons living near her by whose means the spirits of those
we had lost could communicate with us who were still remaining
upon earth.

It appears that Miss Houghton was intrigued and she decided to accompany
her cousin in order to judge the communication for herself.

I accordingly did so, and made my first visit to Mrs. Marshall, who
with her niece (introduced as Mary Brodie, although clandestinely
married to her cousin Emanuel Marshall), sat with us at a round table.
In a short time the raps came, and the various manifestations, now so
well known, filled me with astonishment.[25]

Miss Houghton received a communication from her dead sister Zilla, on a
subject unknown to others in the room, which gave her reason to believe the
validity of the séance. She continued to attend séances with friends who were
mediums and received much from them by way of both comfort and information. Having attended séances for a while she decided to try mediumship for
herself:

Mamma and I had at once set fairly to work to gain the happiness for
ourselves, and every evening at dusk sat for about half an hour with
our hands on a small table, in quiet talk on spiritual matters, of which
we had learned something, having read Mr. Shorter's 'Confessions of
a Truth Seeker' with much interest; but our constancy was severely
tried for nearly three months had elapsed, when, on December 31,
1859, the table was gently tipped, and thus the communication was
opened by what might now seem the slow process of the alphabet, but
then each word was gladly spelt out, nor did we feel any impatience
for a quicker method; and we gradually received short messages from
the very many dear ones who were as anxious as ourselves that they
might make their presence known to us who had mourned them.[26]

The spirits advised them not to communicate too often; once a week was
enough. Sunday was suggested as the best day because the sitters would be
less likely to be disturbed by earthly callers, and the communication would
not interfere with earthly duties.

---

[25] Houghton, *Evenings at Home*, 1.
[26] Ibid., 4.

Georgiana Houghton's dedication to spiritualism, attempting to communicate with the spirits for three months without response, if true, suggests either great patience or else a strong desire to acquire the same mediumistic gifts as her friends. Her tone regarding her experimentation, however, is sincere and reverent; she takes the words of Thomas Shorter to heart and approaches her séances in an attitude of quiet prayer. She writes of how she held a séance at Pentecost and gave it much prayerful thought beforehand. Reflecting on the séance afterwards she wrote: 'May it indeed be given to us in these days to be gathered into that Kingdom, for the New Wine of the outpouring of the Spirit has been bestowed upon us in full measure.'[27]

Her reverential tone contrasted with another, later, advocate of spiritualism, Mrs Mabel St Clair Stobart, who viewed her early experiments as something of an amusing game. St Clair Stobart was an outspoken and enterprising woman, the founder of the Women's Convoy Corps who, after a time living in South Africa with her husband, gathered groups of women to nurse soldiers in the front line in Turkey, Bulgaria and the Balkans.[28] She claimed to have always been interested in spiritualism. 'When did I become a spiritualist? As a matter of fact I don't remember the time when I was not a spiritualist.'[29] Writing about her childhood in the early part of the twentieth century she described the visits of a local friend and medium, Kate Wingfield:

> She would come to our house in the evening, and without lowering the lights or any need for gramophones or the painful singing of 'Onward Christian Soldiers', etc, we would sit informally around the fire, whilst we listened to an old French doctor, who had lived in the eighteenth century, speaking through K. W.'s lips in a fluent French of which K. W. was incapable.[30]

Kate Wingfield was also able to write in languages of which she had no knowledge. 'It all came so spontaneously, we could not fail to realize the genuineness of the phenomena.'

Mabel wrote of how she then decided to develop some of her own talents; she began experimenting with her sister in thought-reading. The family was visited by Frederic Myers, a friend of Wingfield and founder of the Society of Psychical Research.[31] Mabel's mother became alarmed at her daughter's

---

[27] Ibid., 135, 141.
[28] M. St Clair Stobart, *Miracles and Adventures. An Autobiography* (London, 1935).
[29] Ibid., 20.
[30] Ibid., 20.
[31] See below, p. 51.

activities, believing that it was a sign that 'the devil was getting a foothold'.[32] The spiritualist and psychic activities were curtailed. Mabel got married soon afterwards and the spiritualism stopped.

Although she viewed her childhood experiments, with hindsight, as frivolous, her attraction to spiritualism remained. After the Great War in 1918 she began to study it again, this time with a greater seriousness. As she worked to promote spiritualism she saw more evidence of it in society, claiming that it 'was spreading like a prairie fire, and my work grew with the increasing interest in the subject shown by the world at large'.[33]

Georgiana Houghton had approached spiritualism with earnestness; Mabel Stobart, initially, with amusement. F. J. Theobald, writer of many pamphlets and articles in defence of spiritualism, came to it through conversations with a friend. He was introduced to it first as a theory by the doctor, J. J. Garth Wilkinson. Wilkinson was a homeopathic doctor, a fellow of the College of Surgeons and interested in mesmerism. He was also a member of the Swedenborgian Church.[34] Theobald, hearing about spiritualism as an idea, was initially repelled by the thought of spirits conversing through table-raps but discussed it with Wilkinson in an 'objective' manner. Spiritualism was for him at this point still a theory to be discussed, rather than an activity to be experienced. He then became friendly with neighbours in Highgate, William and Mary Howitt – 'a charming family'. With them Theobald and his wife set up a 'home circle' and the group soon found that they possessed mediumistic powers.[35] After this, Theobald's whole family, children and even servants, discovered mediumistic talents, which were catalogued at length.[36]

Although most séances took place privately in people's homes, the spiritualist press reported some of them, and noted the presence of observers as well as 'sitters'. The *Spiritualist*, for example, in 1869, told of a séance held at a private house in Clerkenwell where non-participants were present. The house must have been of a good size as there were seven people around the table and thirty visitors.[37] In East London it was known that regular meetings took place on Sunday evenings at 7pm and on Tuesdays at 9pm at the home of a Mrs

---

32 Stobart, *Miracles and Adventures*, 21.
33 Ibid., 371.
34 Barrow, 'Imponderable liberator', 94. Swedenborgianism bore some resemblance to spiritualism.
35 F. J. Theobald, *Homes and Work in the Future Life*, 3 Vols (London, 1885, 1886, 1887), 2: 45–6.
36 See, for instance, Theobald, *Homes and Work*, 1: 16–17 and 3: 109–13.
37 *Spiritualist*, 17 Dec. 1869.

Main in Bethnal Green,[38] which suggests that guests were welcome. Increasing numbers of visitors meant that, occasionally, spiritualists were forced to move out of private homes. In 1881 *Light* reported that a group of spiritualists in Bingley had recently purchased a hall, having grown significantly in number from the twelve that had first met privately in the home of a Mr Illingworth only twelve months before.[39]

It is possible only to speculate on how many unreported private experiments in spiritualism took place. It is equally difficult to ascertain what happened when people undertook their experiments and whether, having achieved positive results, they became committed believers in the claims of spiritualism and held regular séances. However, both the excited accounts of committed spiritualists and the more scornful comments of critics suggest that people did experiment with séances in their homes and with friends. If they did experiment, then they also understood what to do and what to expect at a séance, which meant either that they had experienced them in other people's homes, or at open séances, or else had taken advice from acquaintances or the spiritualist press. From wherever they procured their advice, this unquantifiable number of people was familiar with the expected phenomena of spiritualism. More importantly, they knew the language of the séance, the claims of spiritualism to communicate with the dead, and the ideas of the afterlife articulated by convinced spiritualists.

Public séances, meetings and lectures

Public séances presented by professional or well-known mediums, as well as open meetings and lectures, gave people an opportunity to hear the claims of spiritualism and observe the attendant phenomena without participating in a table séance. They are also easier for the historian to assess, as both spiritualist and non-spiritualist writers and journalists reported them as public events, thus affording more reliable evidence of participation than vaguer claims of widespread private experimentation. Such reports offer an insight into where and how spiritualism grew; often they include the numbers of people attending, the questions asked by audiences and the places where the meetings and séances took place. On the whole, and as might be expected, the spiritualist writers reported séances and spiritualist meetings in a positive light, emphasising the breadth and variety of class and opinion among enquirers and

---

[38] Ibid., 31 Dec. 1869.
[39] *Light*, 19 Feb. 1881.

the large numbers that attended. The reports from the non-spiritualist press were more sceptical of spiritualism in tone, but did not disagree with the claims of large numbers.

Opportunities to hear the claims of spiritualism were plentiful. Meetings and public séances were held during the course of the period across the country and in many different venues. In April 1870, for example, a young American medium called Jesse B. Sheppard gave a demonstration in London of his talents. He played the pianoforte, allegedly under the influence of the spirits, to great acclaim.[40] In Bradford another visiting American medium, James Peebles, usually noted in the spiritualist press for being the United States Counsel in Trebizond as well as a leading spiritualist, gave a series of four lectures at the Mechanics' Hall in May 1870. The first was, according to the *Spiritualist*, given to a 'small but attentive audience'. The final lecture, however, was given to 'upwards of 1000 people'.[41] Local mediums shared the platform with Mr Peebles and displayed their talents. The *Spiritualist* noted:

> Among the more remarkable mediums in Bradford is Mr Thomas Tate, a working man, who appears to be under the influence of Indian spirits principally. He is a healing medium and cures by the laying on of hands. Elizabeth Sagar, a physical medium, has many striking manifestations ... Mary Ann Illingworth Bowling is a remarkable medium as a speaker, considering her uneducated mind; she can neither read nor write.

The report of the meeting concluded by noting that 'the room was crowded to excess'.

In 1872 a public meeting took place in Chelsea that was 'well attended' with a 'lively debate'.[42] In April the same year a lecture was given in Norwich to a 'large and intelligent audience'.[43] In 1879 a meeting in London on the religion of spiritualism was forced to close its doors to the public before the appointed starting time, there being no room left for those who had come to hear the lecture.[44] The Leicester Liberal Club provided a 'good audience' to a trance medium in 1895.[45]

Spiritualists shared their views on matters other than the claims of spiritualism, and people were quite ready to hear their perspectives. Thus in Walsall

[40] *Medium and Daybreak*, 8 Apr. 1870.
[41] *Spiritualist*, 15 May 1870.
[42] Ibid., 15 Feb. 1872.
[43] Ibid., 15 Apr. 1872.
[44] The Cavendish Rooms, Mortimer Street, held 250 people. Ibid., 10 Jan. 1879.
[45] *Medium and Daybreak*, 3 May 1895.

in 1881, a 'very large' audience listened to lectures on a variety of subjects including 'Conscience', 'Saints, Sinners and Saviours' and 'Somnambulism'.[46] In Newcastle upon Tyne two thousand people were allegedly present to hear a lecture about what spiritualism had to say regarding capital punishment.[47] In Leicester the audience that gathered to observe Mr Walter Howell, a trance medium, chose the subjects for his two addresses, indicating where their interests lay: 'the Second Coming of Christ' and 'What the Spirits can tell us of the state in which they live'.[48]

In 1900 a newly secured hall in Wolverhampton was filled with people wanting to hear about spiritualism. *Light* reported that, 'At the evening service the crush was very great and the stewards, after filling every available spot, including the ante room, yard and lobby, were compelled very reluctantly to turn scores away.'[49] The following month, in the same hall, a lecture on the subject of 'The Judgement Day – what and when?' was given to an audience of around one hundred.[50] A local newspaper reported the opening of the hall in a reasonably sympathetic manner and was impressed by the clairvoyance of Mrs J. M. Smith of Blackpool, who was described as 'a rather striking personality, especially on the platform'.[51]

In 1916 Edmund McClure, an honorary canon of Bristol, despaired that spiritualism was widespread and that professional mediums offered their services 'in all our large towns'.[52] In 1919 *The Times* reported severe overcrowding at a séance in Aberavon. A council sanitary inspector had found that spiritualist services were being conducted for one hundred and seventy people in a room that would have held only eighteen people comfortably, with no means of ventilation.[53] In the same year Arthur Conan Doyle, the writer and committed spiritualist, claimed that he had given fifty lectures around the country to something like a hundred thousand interested people.[54] And in 1925 the *Christian Spiritualist* reported a debate held in the Temperance Hall, Bolton, on the subject, 'Is spiritualism true?' The debate took place over two nights, with 'deep interest' taken by the 'large audiences'.[55]

---

[46] *Light*, 26 Feb. 1881.
[47] Ibid., 3 May 1890.
[48] Ibid., 26 Mar. 1881.
[49] Ibid., 28 Apr. 1900.
[50] Ibid., 19 May 1900.
[51] *Express and Star* (Wolverhampton), 25 Apr. 1900.
[52] Edmund McClure, *Spiritualism. A Historical and Critical Sketch* (London, 1916), iv.
[53] *The Times*, 20 Mar. 1919, pg. 8, col. C.
[54] Arthur Conan Doyle, *Our Reply to the Cleric: Sir Arthur Conan Doyle's Lecture in Leicester, October 19th, 1919, following the Church Congress* (Halifax, 1920), 4.
[55] *Christian Spiritualist*, 20 Oct. 1925.

Across the country, and throughout the period under consideration, in halls and meeting rooms people gathered to listen to the claims of spiritualism and to witness the practices of mediums for themselves. It is reasonable to suppose that people went to public meetings and séances for a variety of reasons: to witness bizarre phenomena, to contact the dead and to listen to the ideas of the afterlife offered by spiritualism. However, for whatever reason they went, once they were there they came into contact with the language and the imagery of spiritualism. Regardless of whether they left the meeting believing the claims of spiritualism or not, at the meetings they met other interested people, they conversed, they listened, they saw and they encountered the spiritualist discourse.

Scientific experimentation

Although a significant number of people were comfortable attending séances and public meetings in order to find out about and experiment with spiritualism, others preferred to observe from the sidelines. For the interested sceptic and the cautious experimenter alike, spiritualist phenomena could be observed, and séances could be attended, as part of a pursuit of truth and science.

As we noted briefly in chapter two, in 1851 a group of men connected with the University of Cambridge founded a society committed to investigating unusual phenomena. They called the society 'The Ghost Club' and advertised for members of the public to offer them examples of dreams, apparitions, visions, spectral appearances (more commonly known as 'fetches' or 'doubles'), coincidences, and instances of people appearing in visions to others at the moment of their death or after death. These examples were requested for 'a serious and earnest enquiry into the nature of the phenomena which are vaguely called supernatural'.[56] The communications were to be addressed to the Reverend Brooke Foss Westcott at Harrow. Westcott, a renowned biblical scholar and future bishop of Durham, founded the society along with Edward White Benson, later archbishop of Canterbury, Arthur Balfour, who became prime minister, the moral philosopher Henry Sidgwick, and psychical researchers Frederic Myers and Edmund Gurney.[57] The origins

---

[56] The printed circular from the Ghost Club can be found in the appendix of Robert Dale Owen, *Footfalls on the boundary of another world* (London, 1860), 377–80.

[57] Having been a fellow at Trinity College, Cambridge, Brooke Foss Westcott (1825–1901) was assistant master at Harrow School in 1852. After returning to the academic life for a time, he became bishop of Durham in 1890. Edward White Benson (1829–96) knew Westcott from

of the Cambridge Ghost Club are somewhat obscured by the founding of the London Ghost Club in 1862, which included the same men, along with some others.[58] The London Ghost Club dwindled in numbers, but was revived in 1882 and became something of an exclusive dining club with, at various points in its history, the physicist Sir Oliver Lodge, the ghost enthusiast Harry Price, the newspaper editor William Stead and Sir Arthur Conan Doyle as members.

In the same year, 1882, the SPR was formed, following a proposal by Professor William Barrett[59] during a meeting of the British National Association of Spiritualists.[60] The SPR had its roots, however, in the Cambridge Ghost Club, and the first president of the SPR was former Ghost Club member Henry Sidgwick. Frederic Myers, Edmund Gurney and Arthur Balfour were also members of both societies, suggesting that in their minds, at least, there was a connection between ghost appearances and spiritualism.[61]

The SPR grew rapidly, from a membership of a hundred and fifty in 1883 to three hundred in 1884.[62] In the following year the number was over five hundred. The membership at this point included scientists, literary figures and academics. There were a number of clergy members, many of whom, like the bishop of Carlisle, Harvey Goodwin, and the hymn writer Clement Cotterill Scholefield, conduct of Eton College, had connections with Cambridge colleges.[63] William Boyd Carpenter (the bishop of Ripon and another Cambridge graduate) was a member, along with archdeacons, canons and other clergy. Academics, MPs and some aristocrats joined: among them Arthur Conan Doyle and W. E. Gladstone. In 1920 *The Times* noted the mixture of people who were members of the SPR: 'All sorts of scholarly men

King Edward's School in Birmingham. He was also at Trinity College, Cambridge. He became archbishop of Canterbury in 1883. Benson was married to Mary, sister of Henry Sidgwick (1838–1900). Sidgwick was a fellow of Trinity. He became professor of moral philosophy at Cambridge in 1883. He was married to Eleanor Balfour, sister of Arthur Balfour (1848–1930), Conservative politician and later prime minister (1902–5). Other leading figures in the early SPR were psychical researchers Edmund Gurney (1847–88) and Frederic W. H. Myers (1843–1901), both of whom had been members of the Ghost Club along with Balfour. *ODNB*.
[58] Peter Underwood, *A short history of the Ghost Club Society* (Haslemere, 2000), 1.
[59] Sir William Barrett (1844–1925) was professor of physics at the Royal College of Science, Dublin from 1873–1910. He was knighted in 1912. *ODNB*.
[60] See later in this chapter, 61.
[61] Benson's wife, Mary, became a member. For an account of the SPR's history, see Alan Gauld, *The Founders of Psychical Research* (London, 1968).
[62] *Journal for the SPR*, No. I (February 1884), 2.
[63] Ibid., No. VI (July 1884), 91; No. VII (Aug. 1884), 110.

– some philosophers, some clergymen, some politicians, and men of science – in recent years have resolved to inquire into the assertions of spiritualists that they are able to converse with the souls of the dead.'[64]

The SPR offered the opportunity for the sceptic and the believer alike to foster an interest in spiritualism without needing to make a judgement concerning the veracity of its central claim to communicate with the dead. Instead, members of the SPR investigated the external phenomena of the séance. The society proposed that by utilising modern scientific method any fantasy and exaggeration on the part of mediums could be controlled; science could also help to verify the nature of séance phenomena.[65] The society held lectures, encouraged papers, began a journal and set up committees to investigate all claims of unusual, or psychical, activity. Thus one member, Henry Carvill Lewis, interviewed a medium, William Eglington, who had received numerous positive testimonials in *Light*.[66] Lewis tested the medium's ability to effect automatic writing on a slate, and found that Eglington cheated, looking up the answers to questions in a dictionary.[67] There were committees dedicated to investigating such matters as telepathy and haunted houses.[68] Edmund Gurney, Frederic Myers and fellow SPR member Frank Podmore published a two-volume account, *Phantasms of the Living* (1887) containing some of the SPR's investigations.[69]

Myers realised that investigating spiritualism under the auspices of scientific enquiry was problematic. In his introduction to *Phantasms of the Living* he admitted that it was difficult to examine matters of religion using scientific experiment. Some people had, he knew, hoped that scientific enquiry would confirm religious belief in life beyond death:

> We could not take for granted that our inquiries would make for the spiritual view of things, that they would tend to establish even the independent existence, still less the immortality of the soul. We shrank from taking advantage of men's hopes and fears, from representing ourselves as bent on rescuing them from the materialism

---

64 *The Times*, 20 Nov. 1920, pg. 4, col. E.
65 Edmund Gurney, Frederic Myers and Frank Podmore, *Phantasms of the Living*. 2 Vols (London, 1886), 1: xxxvi.
66 *Light*, 16 Oct. 1886.
67 H. Carvill Lewis, *The alleged psychical phenomena of spiritualism. An account of two séances* (From the Proceedings of the SPR) (London, 1887).
68 *Journal for the SPR*, No. II (Mar. 1884), 31. A clergyman, Rev. William Done Bushell, assistant master at Harrow School, sat on this committee.
69 Gurney, Myers and Podmore, *Phantasms of the Living*.

which forms so large a factor in modern thought, or from the pessimism which dogs its steps with unceasing persistency.[70]

Indeed, he found that studying unusual or 'supernormal' occurrences in the present necessarily led to questions concerning the miracles of the past, challenging religious faith. Yet at the same time he identified what he saw as 'materialism', present not only in science but in wider society. He thought this materialism too narrow; there was a need for scientists to try to understand the importance of emotion in human beings.[71]

In 1917 the spiritualist newspaper, the *Two Worlds*, recognised the same tension. Some people investigated spiritualism from the perspective of psychic science and were interested in the phenomena alone; others, the newspaper suggested, were more interested in the religious aspect and the question of survival and life beyond death. Of these two strands, the *Two Worlds* thought that more people fell into the latter category, and suggested that psychic science had become 'spiritualism without the spirits'.[72] Nevertheless, the tension was ever present in spiritualism, and among the membership of the SPR, some of whom remained intrigued by the possibilities of the afterlife, others of whom became increasingly interested in telepathy and the power of the human mind.

Debates about spiritualism

As soon as modern spiritualism entered English life in 1852 it became a popular subject for discussion as well as a new fashion to be experienced. Many of the meetings and debates concerning the veracity of spiritualist phenomena – as well as the chief claim of spiritualists to converse with the dead – took place beyond the control of convinced spiritualists. The very fact that debates took place indicates not simply that spiritualism was a matter of interest to non-spiritualists, but also that it was a significant enough feature of public life to be recognised as worthy of discussion. Thus the Oxford Union, for example, registered the presence of spiritualism and debated in 1873 whether it deserved scientific investigation – and voted by a large majority that it did.[73]

A similar conclusion had been reached by a sub-committee of the London

---

[70] Ibid., 1: xlviii.
[71] Ibid., 1: liv.
[72] *Two Worlds*, 19 Jan. 1917.
[73] *Spiritualist*, 15 July 1873.

Dialectical Society two years earlier. The committee had been formed in 1869 to 'investigate the phenomena alleged to be spiritual manifestations and to report thereon'.[74] The report was made in 1871, with the chairman of the committee, Dr James Edmunds, stating that:

> In presenting their report, your committee, taking into consideration the high character and great intelligence of many of the witnesses to the more extraordinary facts, the extent to which their testimony is supported by the reports of the sub-committees and the absence of any proof of imposture or delusion as regards a large portion of the phenomena; and further, having regard to the exceptional character of the phenomena, the large number of persons in every grade of society and over the civilised world who are more or less influenced by a belief in their supernatural origin, and to the fact that no philosophical explanation of them has yet been arrived at, deem it incumbent upon them to state their conviction that the subject *is worthy of more serious attention* and careful investigation than it has hitherto received.[75] [my italics]

In making the report the committee invited the opinions of spiritualists, mediums, 'scientific men' and sceptics.[76] Edmunds acknowledged that they had found that those who were convinced by spiritualism were much more willing to speak than were those who thought it fraudulent. Further sub-committees were formed to examine various types of séance phenomena, spiritual manifestations and the involuntary movement of furniture. Séances were visited and interviews undertaken.

Not all invited members of the committee were happy with the investigations. Professor Thomas Huxley wrote that he had no intention of assisting with it on the grounds that he had no interest in the subject.[77] He believed spiritualism to be fraudulent, but even if it proved genuine, he said:

> If any body would endow me with the faculty of listening to the chatter of old women and curates in the nearest cathedral town, I should decline the privilege, having better things to do. And if the folk in the spiritual world do not talk more wisely and sensibly than their friends report them to do, I put them in the same category. The only good that I can see in a demonstration of the truth of 'spiritualism' is to furnish an additional argument against suicide. Better live a

---

[74] London Dialectical Society. *Report on Spiritualism*, vi.
[75] Ibid., 5.
[76] Ibid., 1.
[77] Ibid., 229.

crossing-sweeper than die and be made to talk twaddle by a 'medium' hired at a guinea a séance.[78]

The writer George Henry Lewes (1817–78) also declined to take part in the committee, arguing that, 'When any man says that phenomena are produced by no known physical laws, he declares that he knows the laws by which they are produced.'[79]

The favourable report given by the London Dialectical Society was hailed as a triumph by spiritualists.[80] The fact that distinguished sceptics, such as Huxley and Lewes, refused to join the committee, however, meant that for some the triumph was not as credible as it could have been.[81]

The Church Congress discussed spiritualism in 1881, 1919 and again in 1920.[82] The speeches in the Congresses, encouraging of and critical of spiritualism, will be discussed in greater detail later, but it is sufficient to say here that the Church of England engaged with the subject because spiritualism was so widespread in the parishes. In 1881 the Congress noted that it was 'undoubtedly exercising a potent influence upon the religious beliefs of thousands'.[83] The same concern was voiced almost forty years later. At the 1919 Congress, according to John Arthur Victor Magee, the vicar of St Mark's, in the fashionable area of St John's Wood, London:

> Spiritualism, like the spirits, is in the air. It is more than a craze. It is a passion. There is a wave of psychic feeling, I will not call it altogether power, which is passing through England today … Sir Arthur Conan Doyle is moving from city to city, casting out common sense and ministering to popular crazes. Every third or every fifth young lady whom you meet imagines herself, because she is a little bit psychic, to be a modern St. Theresa or a St. Catherine.[84]

Magee's words suggest that he encountered spiritualism at least often enough to believe it to be pervading society around him. Even without the

---

[78] Ibid., 230.
[79] Ibid., 230.
[80] See, for example, *Medium and Daybreak*, which reported on the Society's findings on 10 Nov., 17 Nov., 24 Nov. and into Dec. 1871.
[81] McCabe, *Spiritualism*, 136.
[82] The Church Congress, begun in 1861, was an annual meeting of members of the Church of England. The Congress was made up of lay and clerical members who discussed religious, moral and social matters. The location of the Congress changed each year, and was presided over by the bishop in whose diocese it was held.
[83] *The official report of the Church Congress held at Newcastle-on-Tyne* (London, 1882), 60–61.
[84] *Authorized report of the Church Congress held in Leicester* (15 Oct. 1919), 113.

hyperbole, he conveyed to his hearers that spiritualism was not simply around, it was flourishing. 'Every third or fifth young lady' was more than just a handful of people. 'A wave of psychic feeling' suggested a growing rather than a diminishing tide, even forty years after the first Church Congress debate about spiritualism. Moreover, even if his words exaggerated the extent of spiritualism in St John's Wood, they revealed much about his response to it, and his belief that it *was* widespread.

Indeed, the Church Congress in 1881 and those that followed in 1919 and 1920, discussed spiritualism *as though it were* prevalent. It was not an alternative or a comparable religion to Christianity, but it excited the popular imagination enough for the Church to discuss it with seriousness and, indeed, for some to view it as a force that might be embraced or appropriated for Church teaching.

At the end of the debate at the Congress of 1919, the archbishop of Canterbury, Randall Davidson, announced that the bishops were to discuss spiritualism at the Lambeth Conference in the following year. By that point they would have before them the results of enquiry by 'our best men and our best women who have knowledge, experience and thought on this great subject'.[85] Davidson thought the subject 'great' enough to commit the best people to investigate it. His words led, eventually, to the formation of a committee in 1936, which, after investigations and interviews, gave a considered opinion on the matter in its report of 1939.[86]

Debates about spiritualism raged in the columns and letters pages of newspapers, as well as in private societies and public meetings. These debates further enhanced the public's familiarity with spiritualism, although historians have tended to overlook the extent and importance of this public debate. In 1873 there was, for example, a brief correspondence concerning spiritualism and science in *The Times*, for which the editor felt the need to apologise: 'Many sensible readers, we fear, will think we owe them some apology for opening our columns to a controversy on such a subject as spiritualism, and thus treating as an open or debatable question what should be dismissed at once as either an imposture or a delusion. But even an imposture may call for an unmasking.'[87] The correspondence nevertheless continued. There was another brief flurry concerning spiritualism and anthropology in *The Times* from 16 to 22 September 1876.

[85] Ibid., 116.
[86] See chapter six, pp. 177–81.
[87] *The Times*, 6 Jan. 1873, pg. 7, col. E. The correspondence began on 27 Dec. 1872.

In November 1926 the *Daily News* invited readers to contribute stories of their experiences of ghosts and 'uncanny' events, rather interestingly making a connection between ghost appearances and spiritualism.[88] This call for contributions was presented as a serious enquiry, rather than a search for stories to excite or frighten. The subject of ghosts had, the paper claimed, aroused fear and ridicule, but (and here the link was made with spiritualism) 'in recent years the names of so many prominent and influential people have been associated with it *and used in support of the existence of spiritual intercourse* that it has become worthy of careful examination'.[89] The newspaper received three thousand stories from readers and the diversity of authorship was thought worthy of comment:

> Most of the stories prove honesty of purpose on the part of the narrators, and the fact that the writers of some of the most striking occurrences represent every class, from the poor and unlettered, to those well placed in the world is an indication that the subject of ghosts or spirits has an amazing interest for the public.[90]

Following this call for stories and experiences, in the beginning of December 1926 the *Daily News* published an article written by Robert Blatchford, self-proclaimed soldier, socialist, sceptic and spiritualist. The article, favourable to the claims of spiritualism, inspired the newspaper to enquire further. On 6 December it published an article by Sir Oliver Lodge, eminent scientist and spiritualist, and began a public debate between various interested writers. On 10 December the Right Hon. John Mackinnon Robertson, secularist writer and Liberal MP for the Tyneside division, argued against spiritualism; on 11 December E. P. Hewitt KC, a bencher in Lincoln's Inn, wrote in favour.

The *Daily News* called its debate 'Spiritualism on trial', and although the trial ended in the middle of January without drawing any conclusion, during the course of almost six weeks various people, from all walks of life and religious opinion, offered their thoughts. They included Estelle W. Stead, who claimed to have been in touch with her father William Stead, the publisher and advocate of spiritualism who had died on the Titanic.[91] The list of debaters

---

[88] As has already been noted, some spiritualists also made this connection. *Light*, 15 Oct. 1881.
[89] S. Louis Giraud, *Ghosts in the Great War and True Tales of Haunted Houses. Thrilling Experiences of 'Daily News' Readers* (London, 1926), iii.
[90] Ibid., iv.
[91] W. T. Stead was the 'amanuensis' for a woman named Julia, who dictated her experiences in the afterlife through automatic writing to him. See W. T. Stead, *After death. A personal narrative. 'Letters from Julia'*. 9th edn. (London, 1914, 1st pubd 1897).

also included the Rev. D. E. S. Waterhouse, a Wesleyan minister, who argued that spiritualism had failed in its claims; the countess of Westmorland, who had received a message from beyond the grave; and H. G. Wood, a Quaker, who was cautious and believed that messages from the dead only came unsought, if they ever came at all.[92]

Just over two years later, in early January 1929, the *Daily News* began examining spiritualism again. On this occasion the newspaper invited the comments and experiences of its readers and was met with an overwhelming response. Lilian Baylis, who produced Shakespeare plays at the Old Vic, was conciliatory towards spiritualism. She stated that, as a Christian, she believed in the Communion of Saints and, although never having experienced the feeling of departed friends near her, 'should not dream of denying the affirmations of serious people'. A Mr R. Humphrey from Grimsby told of how his son was missing in the war and one night had appeared to him and told him how he died. A few days later, news came that his body had been found. Mr A. J. Howard Hume from Brighton described how he and his wife had established a pact with a lady friend that, if she died, she would get over to them a 'rather amusing phrase'. She had died and had communicated the phrase to them twice. Mrs M. Clifford from Rhyll had lived abroad for many years and, returning to London, received a message at a séance full of strangers that was for her from a long dead family member. E. M. Patchett from Grantham had received good news about an ill son, who got better. A. Kenway from Fleet believed spiritualism all to be lies and sin. Mrs A. M. Barton from SW17 had heard her son's voice at a séance. Maud Barton from Bridgport had received spirit photographs. A. H. Darby from Wood Green had been converted from atheism to spiritualism by a séance and thereafter attended a spiritualist church.

What this correspondence did, in effect, was once again raise the public profile of spiritualism and encourage discussion of its claims. As a result, the spiritualist discourse was as common to readers of the *Daily News* as it was to its committed advocates.

Proselytising

Innumerable people experimented with spiritualism at home; large numbers attended public lectures, or read about debates and discussions concerning the claims of spiritualism and its phenomena in newspapers. The spiritualist

[92] *Daily News*, from 6 Dec. 1926 to 17 Jan. 1927.

discourse was pervasive. However, through the course of the period, some of those who counted themselves as convinced and committed spiritualists endeavoured further to encourage the numbers of people encountering spiritualism by spreading their beliefs in a more active way. This they did by a variety of methods. Some spiritualists organised themselves into societies and gatherings and invited members of the public to attend. Some committed themselves to the education of children. Others spread their claims through a variety of spiritualist newspapers, and some supported and encouraged the culture of 'celebrity' or star mediums as a means of engaging the attention of the public. Also of significance was the role played by famous converts, such as Arthur Conan Doyle and Oliver Lodge, whose eminence lent weight to the claims of spiritualism.

Attempts made to organise spiritualists into a coherent body were uneven in their results. This was in part due to the nature of spiritualism. It was, after all, often very domestic; a practice that could be 'dabbled' in at home around a table or over tea. In addition, not all of those who believed themselves to possess mediumistic talents wanted to be organised or registered, and chose to offer their gift in private, and only to family and friends. As we have seen, people curious about spiritualism were not always prepared to be acknowledged as members of a spiritualist organisation, or 'believers' in its claims to converse with the dead. Some were happier observing from time to time from the sidelines, or examining it as members of the Society for Psychical Research.

There were some spiritualists, however, who did want to organise spiritualism into a structured movement, who thought that the message of spiritualism would be proclaimed more widely and effectively if spiritualists organised themselves and campaigned more vigorously across the country.[93] Some of them had clear ideas as to how this might happen. As a consequence, the history of spiritualist organisation is littered with argument and difference of opinion. The attempts at national organisation are described thoroughly by Geoffrey Nelson and Janet Oppenheim and do not need to be recounted here in detail.[94] What is relevant to note, however, is the way that some spiritualists actively sought to engage in proselytising, and that this took place across the country.

---

[93] *Medium and Daybreak* advertised Sunday services in London organised 'for the purpose of proclaiming the truth of spiritualism'. *Medium and Daybreak*, 8 Apr. 1870. *Light* claimed that there was no proper organisation for spiritualists, even in 1881, and sought to propose that spiritualists organised themselves to further the teaching. *Light*, 22 Oct. 1881.

[94] Oppenheim, *The Other World*; Nelson, *Spiritualism and Society*.

Thus as early as 1855 there were 'spirit-circles' in Yorkshire, gathering for meetings.[95] By the late 1860s groups of spiritualists in London were forming themselves into named 'associations' of 'spirit-circles' (the favoured term for groups of people holding séances) explicitly in order to work together to offer better access to the increasingly interested general public. They advertised their meetings and were open to anyone. In 1867 the East London Association of Spiritualists was formed offering a number of spirit circles for the curious to attend. Some association circles proved rather too popular, according to the *Spiritualist*:

> The pressure for admission to circles in London, where thoroughly good manifestations are obtained, is now very great. Séances in connection with the St John's Association of Spiritualists at Clerkenwell are overcrowded by the presence of strangers who are admitted as freely as possible, but the pressure and the unfavourable conditions militate against getting the best results.[96]

Three years later the same St John's Association discussed how to spread the message of spiritualism even further. Proselytising was underway elsewhere in the country. The *Spiritualist* noted that in Huddersfield the names and addresses of curious members of the public who had attended semi-public séances were taken; the local association then sent them cards following their attendance. The sending of cards had, apparently, worked well for encouraging return visits.[97] Another suggestion made at the same meeting by a Mr T. Weeks was that increased welfare and care of other spiritualists would encourage new members. Elsewhere it was thought helpful to offer information about spiritualism. In Lancashire, for example, the Lancashire Association for the Promotion of Spiritualism in New Districts was formed in 1875 to promote meetings and distribute literature. Across the country some spiritualists were thinking about co-ordinated strategies for spreading their message.

By 1873 members of some of the smaller local associations thought that the growth of spiritualism would be greatly assisted by the establishment of a national organisation. In August of that year the Psychological Society of

---

[95] There was even a 'conference' held in August 1855, although it was poorly attended due to bad communication between the various local circles. *Yorkshire Spiritual Telegraph*, Sept. 1855.

[96] *Spiritualist*, 3 Dec. 1869. The East London Association formed in 1867. The St John's Association formed in May 1868 with twenty-seven members and had grown to forty members by 1869. Séances were held on Thursday evenings at St John's Temperance Hall, Clerkenwell, with forty to sixty people in attendance.

[97] Ibid., 15 Apr. 1870.

Liverpool held a conference in the Islington Assembly Rooms, Liverpool, and from this conference emerged the beginnings of the British National Association of Spiritualists.[98] By the following year the *Spiritualist* newspaper was regularly listing the affiliated associations around the country, with their presidents' names and committee member lists. This offered the possibility for spiritualists to communicate more easily with one another, and reminded local groups that they were part of a larger and more impressive national association. Provincial societies existed in places such as Birmingham, Nottingham, Manchester, Lowestoft, Gateshead, Halifax, Cambridge, Darlington, Hull, Leicester and Durham. In London there were eight separate societies alongside the British National Association of Spiritualists, including the Marylebone Association of Inquirers into Spiritualism, which had been established earlier, in 1872.[99]

By the 1880s some spiritualist associations and societies were buying or building their own halls and meeting places in order to accommodate themselves and enquirers. There was, for example, a meeting house in Shakespeare Street, Nottingham, by 1881, which seated around a hundred people.[100] In Belper, Derbyshire, a large hall was built by a spiritualist, Mr W. P. Adshead, and in Sowerby Bridge, Yorkshire, a special hall was built for Sunday services.[101]

Not all attempts at encouraging followers and members were successful, often due to the infighting among spiritualist members. In Birmingham, initial attempts to bring spiritualists together in 1870 failed through 'sectarian differences' which caused division. The spiritualists who knew one another numbered fewer than a hundred.[102] In Walsall spiritualism was reportedly at a low ebb in 1873, with only about a dozen spiritualists in the town.[103] Concern was expressed in 1881 that spiritualists in Yorkshire were disunited and in need of organisation after a popular local medium was exposed as a fraud.[104]

Spiritualists grouped and regrouped themselves according to their differences and preferences. The British National Association of Spiritualists moved to premises in Great Russell Street, London, but experienced infighting and financial problems. In 1883 around a hundred spiritualists in London broke away from the British National Association of Spiritualists and

---

98 Ibid., 1 and 15 Aug. 1873.
99 *Light*, 8 Jan. 1881.
100 Ibid.
101 Britten, *Nineteenth Century Miracles*, 222.
102 *Spiritualist*, 15 Oct. 1870.
103 Ibid., 1 July 1873.
104 *Light*, 12 Feb. 1881.

formed themselves into the London Spiritualist Alliance. By 1890 there was some cohesion, when the Inaugural Conference of the Spiritualists' National Federation was held; in 1901 it became the Spiritualists' National Union Ltd. At its inception it had 42 affiliated societies; by 1917 it had 141. By 1939 the Spiritualists' National Union estimated that there were 520 affiliated societies, serving some 160,000 individuals.[105]

Despite their differences, spiritualist associations and organisations attempted to make the spreading of the spiritualist message more efficient and organised – although the infighting meant that they had only limited success. They tended to exist in the large towns across the country, where groups of like-minded people could more easily gather together in sizeable numbers. The presence of associations in towns rather than villages does not necessarily indicate a lack of spiritualism in the countryside; merely a lack of organised spiritualism.

Spiritualist associations were, of course, open to the sorts of people who wanted to join societies and committees and who, perhaps, needed companionship and encouragement in their spiritualist practice. Indeed, the sorts of activities organised by spiritualist associations would have been familiar to anyone who was or had been associated with a local church. One group of spiritualists in London, for example, held a fete in the People's Gardens, Old Oak Common, Willesden in August 1873. The fete included hand bell ringers, a band, a 'good tea' and bonfire at the end.[106] It was the sort of gathering that would have appealed to some spiritualists, but not to all.

Children and spiritualism

Children played a part in the growth of spiritualism as a movement, and as early as the 1860s some were being taught and trained in the ideas of spiritualism. Children, and their mediumistic gifts, were taken seriously, and parents were encouraged to develop the talents of their offspring – the modern spiritualist movement had, after all, begun with the adolescent Fox sisters. The leading spiritualist F. J. Theobald wrote of how his own children had displayed spiritual sensitivity and mediumistic powers.[107] It also became a matter of grave importance to spiritualists as to whether they allowed their children to attend ordinary church Sunday schools, where they might be

---

[105] Archbishop's committee on spiritualism, *Report*, 6.
[106] *Spiritualist*, 15 Aug. 1873.
[107] Theobald, *Homes and Work*, 1: 16–17.

misled in their beliefs, and they were, of course, keen to ensure the next generation of adherents.

The Children's Lyceum Movement published a monthly journal, *Lyceum Banner*, which included puzzles and stories for children as well as advice for leaders. In its first edition it cautioned parents: 'Conscientious spiritualists can not, will not, allow their children any longer to imbibe those false teachings and hurtful restrictions [at church Sunday schools] which are misleading and circumscribing to old and young alike.' Hence the formation of lyceums:

> This movement has a work which is second to none in its importance viz., to develop the innate latent powers of the rising generation, and instruct them in the facts, truths, and principles of Spiritualism, which are diametrically opposed to the doctrine of the fall of man and consequent curse. It teaches a gradual ascent in the scale of mental and moral development. Instead of an angry God and a Devil who is more powerful to destroy than God to save, it tells us of a Father of Love, who is too good to be unkind, and too wise to err, in the first acts of creation.[108]

In 1866 Alfred Kitson, of Hanging Heaton, Yorkshire, began the first 'lyceum' for spiritualists' children in Nottingham. He followed the pattern of the Lyceum Movement in America founded in January 1863 by Andrew Jackson Davis in Dodsworth Hall, Broadway, New York. The Lyceum Movement flourished in England and continued into the 1930s, offering an alternative to Sunday schools for spiritualist parents.

In the 1870s *Medium and Daybreak* offered progress reports from the lyceums, and gave an insight for interested adults. The children were placed into different groups or classes, depending on their age, and each group was named after a natural element, such as 'stream', 'fountain', 'sea', 'beacon', 'star' or 'lake'. The children wore coloured badges to denote their group and were taught from the age of four to fifteen.[109] These different 'grades' or groups might be seen as a reflection of the different 'spheres' in the afterlife: children were encouraged to progress through them over time.[110] Teachers in the lyceums were instructed, 'Do not make your lyceum too "schooly" or your groups too "classy". Be bright, cheerful, active.'[111]

---

[108] *Lyceum Banner. A monthly journal for the Children's Progressive Lyceum throughout the World*, Nov. 1890, pref.
[109] See, for example, *Medium and Daybreak*, 3 June 1870.
[110] Spiritualist teaching about progress through the spheres will be dealt with in chapter four, pp. 88–89.
[111] *Lyceum Banner*, Jan. 1891, 33.

The Lyceum Movement, or rather, as it became known, the Children's Progressive Lyceum, had forty-seven registered lyceums across the country by 1891. They operated in cities and large towns, such as London, Middlesbrough, Walsall, South Shields, Oldham, Nottingham, Beeston, Belper, Liverpool, Sunderland, Leicester and Burnley.[112]

By 1890 the movement had become an organisation with defined objectives and methods, all of which were outlined in the constitution. These objectives were said to be 'formed after the plans adopted in the Summer-land, [and] are heaven-born and angel-nurtured'. 'Summerland' was the spiritualists' favoured term for the afterlife.[113] The organisation expected children to learn poems and a catechism, and began testing them by examination. The results of examinations, with the children's names and lyceum name printed, were then published by the British Spiritualists' Lyceum Union. Handbooks and 'helps' were also published to explain difficult words and concepts.[114] Marching was encouraged in lyceums, as was callisthenics, in order to help children use their muscles and to become graceful.

The lyceums taught the principles of spiritualism in rhymes and stories as well as by catechism, and offered moral guidance for the earthly life; poems and songs encouraged the children to think about the afterlife in a positive manner. It is a matter for speculation as to whether the children enjoyed the callisthenics, learning the questions and answers or listening to the stories. There is scant evidence from the children themselves as to the appeal or otherwise of lyceums. The only clues come from the *Lyceum Banner*, which advertised a society that children could join, called 'The Golden Group'. This was operated by 'Aunt Editha', and offers an indication that at least some children were content to make a personal commitment to the Lyceum Movement. Children who took three pledges and wrote to her were entered in Aunt Editha's 'Roll'. The pledges were:

> *Love*: 'I promise to be loving, kind and thoughtful to all my pets – birds, animals or fishes, and never to neglect, tease or be cruel to them, and at all times to prevent unkindness in and to others, when in my power to do so,'
> *Temperance*: 'I promise to be temperate in all things. That I will abstain from all injurious foods, beverages, and intoxicating drinks,

112 Ibid., Sept. 1891, 160–61.
113 Ibid., Nov. 1890. For more on the term 'Summerland' see chapter four, p. 92.
114 See, for example, Alfred Kitson, *Helps to the study of the Lyceum Manual of difficult words and phrases (arranged in alphabetical order)* (Keighley, 1927).

making sobriety of conduct the aim of my daily life. I further promise to abstain from the use of Tobacco in any of its forms'

Purity: 'I promise to avoid all impurity of thought, speech or act, in myself and to discountenance it in others. I will not use profane or vulgar language, nor permit its use in my presence without rebuking those who use it.'[115]

The children were encouraged to write to Aunt Editha themselves and, month by month, their letters were published in the *Lyceum Banner*. The following is a typical example:

Dear Aunt Editha,
I belong to the Liverpool Lyceum and am a member of Stream Group. I want to join the Golden Group. I am eight years of age, and have a big black dog, of which I am very fond, whose name is Prince. Please put my name down with the rest. I remain your loving niece, Maggie Love.[116]

Like Maggie Love, a number of children were willing to make the pledges for the opportunity to be entered into Aunt Editha's Golden Group Roll, and the membership of the group increased over successive journals, reaching 291 children by October 1891.[117] There is no record of how many of the children educated through the lyceums attended séances and became committed spiritualists as adults, although, judging by the *Lyceum Banner*, those who were child members of lyceums were thoroughly grounded in the teachings of spiritualism.

Spiritualist newspapers

In addition to the attempts at creating a spiritualist organisation and the work with children a number of journals were published which offered advice to spiritualists, articles, opportunities for debate, and reports of lectures and séances. They were numerous enough and varied enough to appeal to people with different interests.

The *Yorkshire Spiritual Telegraph* was the first spiritualist newspaper to be printed in England, running from 1855 until 1857. It was printed in Keighley, which, as we have already noted, had been alive with spiritualism ever since David Richmond had shared his mediumistic talents there in 1853. The

---

[115] *Lyceum Banner*, Nov. 1890, 8–9.
[116] Ibid., Mar. 1891, 64.
[117] Ibid., Oct. 1891, 172.

Keighley Spiritual Brotherhood was quickly established, with members operating a printing press and circulating pamphlets and tracts for the dissemination of spiritualist teaching.[118] The newspaper's editors gave their reason for publishing as follows:

> Our object is to propagate a *Truth* which, though it has not been hid from the world, yet so few appear to have knowledge of it, that its bearing on mankind has been imperceptible. No good can arise from this truth so long as mankind are [sic] ignorant of its existence, and we presume that nothing can be more appropriate to establish it as a truth than a narration of plain ungarnished facts.[119]

It was noted by *The Times* in 1857 as purporting to record 'facts' alone.[120] The *Yorkshire Spiritual Telegraph* sought, *The Times* said, to offer encouragement to spiritualists and to enlighten all classes of people about the wonders of spiritualism, as the editors understood them.

The *Yorkshire Spiritual Telegraph* offered reports of séances, articles about the nature of the afterlife and communications from the departed. It suggested that the afterlife presented by the Churches was different from the place experienced by the dead. Instead of finding, as the Churches allegedly taught, that their eternal state was fixed, the dead discovered that there was possibility of spiritual progress. The newspaper thought that spiritualism had something to teach both the sceptics and the churchgoers in the area:

> Spiritualism is necessary then to teach the sceptic that there is an hereafter, and the religionist, that that hereafter is a state of progression; and we do not become infinite by shuffling off this clay or covering.[121]

The *Two Worlds* circulated initially from October 1858 until May 1859, but was re-launched in 1887, and is still active. The mission of the *Two Worlds* was to deal with what it called the various departments of social science, mental philosophy and physiology. It also included a condensed edition of the week's news and debates about homeopathy, teetotalism and vegetarianism – indicating interesting connections with discourses noted earlier. In later years it became aggressively anti-Church, suggesting that the Church had been responsible over the centuries for the persecution and torture

---

[118] Britten, *Nineteenth Century Miracles*, 199.
[119] *Yorkshire Spiritual Telegraph*, May 1855.
[120] *The Times*, 5 May 1857, pg. 6, col. C.
[121] *Yorkshire Spiritual Telegraph*, Mar. 1856.

of those who might now be designated as 'spiritualists', and referring to the Church's 'terrible' teaching on a literal hell.[122]

The *Spiritual Magazine* began in 1860 and continued for five years. It saw spiritualism as both a religion and the 'science of the future life'.[123] It was scholarly and had a religious tone, viewing spiritualism as a natural extension of Christianity, although it claimed to 'avoid all dogmatism'.[124] It attempted to portray spiritualism as reasonable, disliking too much emphasis on the séance phenomena and preferring instead to connect the ideas of spiritualism to Christianity, ancient philosophy, poetry and literature.[125]

The *Spiritualist* ran from 1869 until 1882. Initially it was published fort-nightly, although for a period of two and a half years (February 1870–November 1872) it was published monthly – financial reasons were cited. The ethos of the publication lay in its subtitle: 'A record of the progress of the science and ethics of spiritualism.' Its first edition contained a short history of spiritualism on the cover, beginning with the story of John Wesley at Epworth Rectory, thus establishing spiritualism's place in a serious and worthy history of religion. It followed with an article on 'The Philosophy of Death', which gave a brief description of what the post-mortem spiritual life was like, according to spirits, mediums, clairvoyants and seers.[126]

Initially, the *Spiritualist* offered a record of séances around the country, as well as lectures and meetings that had taken place, or were planned. By 1872 it was becoming increasingly fixated with the movements of the 'star' mediums: the Guppys, Florence Cook, Daniel Home, and Kate Fox and her husband Henry D. Jencken, a barrister and spiritualist. Reports were given of their séances and also their social engagements. Then, following the inaugu-ration of the British National Association of Spiritualists, it gave more of its reporting to the organisation of spiritualism around the country, although it never really lost its fascination with the famous mediums of the day.

The *Spiritualist* offered the possibility for individual mediums, as well as local associations, to advertise in its pages. Thus a randomly selected edition finds the following advertisements:

> Miss Lottie Fowler, the great American somnambulist and clair-voyante, whose reputation is well known throughout Europe and

---

122 See, for example, *Two Worlds*, 25 Nov. 1887 and 8 Mar. 1918.
123 *Spiritual Magazine*, Jan. 1860.
124 Ibid.
125 See, for example, the article by William Howitt, ibid., Nov. 1860.
126 *Spiritualist*, 19 Nov. 1869.

America, can be consulted on either medical or business affairs connected with the living and the dead. Hours 12 to 8 (Sundays excepted). Terms, One Guinea. Address, 21, Princes Street, Hanover Square, two doors from Regent Street.

Miss Godfrey, Curative mesmerist and rubber and medical clairvoyant, 161, Hampstead Road, London N.W. To be seen by appointment *only*. Terms, on application by letter.

Mr Charles E. Williams, Medium, is at home daily, to give private seances from 12 to 5 p.m. Private seances attended at the house of investigators. Public seances at 61, Lamb's Conduit Street, on Monday evenings, admission 2s. 6d. Thursday evenings 5s.; and Saturday evenings, for spiritualists only, 5s.; at 8 o'clock in the evening. Address as above.[127]

The *Medium and Daybreak* ran from April 1870 to May 1895. It was 'A weekly journal devoted to the history, phenomena, philosophy and teachings of spiritualism'.[128] True to its word, it devoted many articles to the phenomena associated with spiritualism, offering, for example, a report of the young American spiritualist, Jesse B. Shepard, who not only played the piano under the influence of the spirits, but manifested the voices of a variety of characters from history.[129] There were articles concerning the powers of crystals and phrenology[130] and magnetised portraits of an American healer, Dr Newton, believed to have curative powers and advertised for two shillings.[131]

The *Medium and Daybreak* included reports about the mediums the editors endorsed, but equally offered lengthy articles on the philosophy of spiritualism. It also attempted to portray spiritualism as a part of modern scientific discovery. The newspaper was occasionally conciliatory towards the Church of England, applauding Canon Wilberforce for what was seen as his sympathy towards spiritualism at the Church Congress of 1881.[132] In June 1870 it claimed a readership of three thousand.

---

[127] Ibid., 14 August 1874.
[128] *Medium and Daybreak*, 8 Apr. 1870.
[129] These included Mary Queen of Scots, who had trouble with her vocal chords as a result of her execution. Ibid.
[130] Ibid., 28 Apr. 1879.
[131] Ibid., 20 May 1870. Non-magnetised portraits were one shilling.
[132] Ibid., 4 Jan. 1895.

The *Christian Spiritualist* ran monthly from 1871 until 1875. Its first editor, a Unitarian minister, F. R. Young, explained at the outset that another journal was needed to encourage people to recognise that spiritualism was not unfriendly to Christianity. The second editor, Dr George Sexton FRS, claimed that he was a convert from secularism to Christian spiritualism.[133] A later, apparently unconnected journal of the same name ran weekly from 1925 until 1939. The editor was the 'Revd' J. W. Potter, who believed that many thousands of spiritualists had turned to Christ as their spiritual ideal. The newspaper, which was the organ of Potter's 'Society of Communion',[134] offered Bible passages analysed from a spiritualist perspective, guides to Christian spiritualist circles indicating which were the best hymns to use in services, and articles written by clergy sympathetic to spiritualism, some anonymously. By 1925 it was claimed that eighteen thousand copies of the newspaper were being circulated.[135]

Light commenced publication in 1880 and continues to the present day, being, according to its subtitle, 'a journal devoted to the highest interests of humanity, both here and hereafter'. It sought initially to deal with the philosophical and religious questions behind spiritualism, rather than merely reporting the séances and meetings held by spiritualists. By the 1890s, however, it was under the editorship of the Rev. William Stainton Moses (1839–92), a clergyman and spiritualist, who had led the London Spiritualist Alliance to break from the British National Association of Spiritualists in 1883. He was a prominent figure and a strong advocate of spiritualism, writing letters and pamphlets and signing himself as 'M.A. Oxon'.[136] He took the journal in a different direction when he became editor, making it the organ of the London Spiritualist Alliance and reporting more meetings from London than elsewhere. When he died in 1892 *Light* resumed its broader scope. It was sympathetic to the Church, informative and not overly reliant on reporting the more exciting phenomena associated with spiritualism.

These publications, and other smaller ones besides, appealed directly to spiritualists, but each publication was different in tone and content, which suggests a variety of interests and opinions among spiritualists themselves. Spiritualism was explored by those who wanted also to know about

---

133 *Christian Spiritualist*, July 1873. This is the point at which Sexton took over.
134 See chapter six, p. 174.
135 *Christian Spiritualist*, 30 Sept. 1925.
136 W. Stainton Moses was ordained by Bishop Wilberforce, and was entitled to his pseudonym, having attended Exeter College, Oxford. He held livings in Dorset and the Isle of Man before teaching at University College School, London.

phrenology and crystals; it was examined by those interested in matters concerning telepathy and human physiology. It was discussed by Christians, secularists, committee members of the British National Association of Spiritualists and those interested in reading news of their favourite mediums. In short, it was suggestive of the variegated nature of the audience for spiritualism, if even the journal readership was so varied.

Celebrity spiritualists

In the early years of spiritualism in England the most famous figures of the movement were the mediums.[137] Mrs Hayden, who arrived in Britain from America bringing spiritualism with her, was the first to be noted by newspapers.[138] Thereafter the male medium Daniel Douglas (sometimes Daniel Dunglas, or 'D. D.') Home (1833–86) became for a time the darling of the press, celebrated both for the spectacular psychic phenomena of his séances and his scandalous private life. In 1860 the *Cornhill Magazine* included an account of his séances, in an article entitled, 'Stranger than fiction'. In it the journalist and writer, Robert Bell (1800–67) described a séance with Home, at which Home levitated out of his chair and sat resting at the height of everyone else's head. He then moved, in a lying position, floating in front of the window, so that the light from outside revealed him to be moving feet first horizontally in the air. The author noted that it was dark in the room.[139] Most famously, in another levitation séance Home floated out of his chair and this time moved outside of the window, levitating at about sixty feet above the ground, in the presence of Lord Lindsay, the earl of Dunraven and Captain Wynne.[140]

The eminent chemist and science journalist, Sir William Crookes (1832–1919), investigated Home's séances and became convinced that his phenomena were objectively real. He watched as Home altered the weight of bodies, lengthened and shortened parts of his body and caused music to be played on instruments without appearing to touch them. A newly purchased accordion was thus placed in a cage: Home made it play.[141]

---

[137] Joseph McCabe provides many of the stories about the mediums. McCabe, *Spiritualism*. For a more recent account, see Oppenheim, *The Other World*, esp. 17–21.

[138] Hardinge Britten claims she was treated disgracefully by journalists. Britten, *Nineteenth Century Miracles*, 131–3.

[139] *Cornhill Magazine*, II (1860), 219–24. Bell was a friend of the editor, Thackery.

[140] For a full account of the floating Home as told by Lord Lindsay, see Dunraven, *Experiences in Spiritualism*, 151–60. For a shorter account see *Spiritualist*, 15 July 1871.

[141] William Crookes, *Researches in the Phenomena of Spiritualism* (London, 1874), 9–15.

Home was noted as much for the way that he courted fashionable society as for his séance phenomena. He moved from London in 1855 and went to Italy and travelled from there around the continent, returning to London in 1859. He became involved in scandal when Mrs Lyon, a wealthy but illiterate widow, sued him for money that she had given him under the 'guidance' of her late husband. Home, in séance, told her that her husband wished her to adopt Home as her 'son', to give him money for his birthday and to name him as a beneficiary in her will. Home was acquitted in trial of improper conduct, but the publicity tarnished his reputation. He retired from his work as a medium in 1872.[142]

In the 1870s many new mediums arrived on the spiritualist scene and their exploits as well as their séance phenomena were reported in the spiritualist and non-spiritualist press. They were thought especially impressive when performing 'manifestations' – here the medium would be shut in a cupboard or room away from the séance and in his or her place the moving figure of a 'spirit' would appear. Among the 'stars' were Mrs Agnes Guppy, a young widow who, as Miss Nichol, had been engaged as a companion to Mrs Frances Sims, the sister of Alfred Russel Wallace, where she discovered a talent for influencing objects – and other mediumistic skills. She married the wealthy 79-year-old Mr Guppy, enjoying a positive reputation as a medium after his death.[143] Florence Cook was an attractive young woman, who managed full body manifestations of spirits during trances. She was accused of fraud in December 1873 when William Volckman, a friend of rival medium Mrs Guppy (and later Mrs Guppy's second husband), caught her masquerading as the spirit of 'Katie King, the pirate's daughter' during a séance.[144] Rosina Showers, a popular medium from Teignmouth, Devon, was

Crookes' experiments with Home were dismissed by the Royal Society as inadequate, so he published them in the *Quarterly Journal*, which he edited.

[142] For an account of the Lyon case see McCabe, *Spiritualism*, 128–9. Home added 'Dunglas' to his name when he returned to England from America. Although evidence is sketchy, it was believed that his father William was the illegitimate son of Alexander, tenth earl of Home. See Peter Lamont, *The First Psychic. The Peculiar Mystery of a Notorious Victorian Wizard* (London, 2005).

[143] The marriage was seen as rather strange even among spiritualists. Georgiana Houghton wrote of it: 'What was my astonishment to learn from Miss Nichol that she was married to Mr Guppy! It did indeed seem to me the most incongruous union, irrespective of his being old enough to be her grandfather!' Houghton, *Evenings at Home*, 162.

[144] 'Katie King' made herself known at many séances. She was, allegedly, the spirit of Annie Owen Morgan, daughter of the seventeenth-century Welsh pirate Henry Owen Morgan, who was known in the spirit world as 'John King'.

the daughter of an army general. She was similarly dismissed as a fraud when caught pretending to be a spirit. David Duguid was a Scottish cabinet maker; James Morse (sometimes referred to as 'J. J. Morse') was a former bartender whose performances were regularly noted in the spiritualist press. Emma Hardinge Britten, a former actress, was not only a medium but also a writer, travelling the country and detailing instances of spiritualism for readers of the spiritualist newspapers.

The popularity of these figures, and others like them, was reflected in the spiritualist press of the 1870s. The exposure of so many mediums in the late 1870s and 1880s meant that there was some despondency among spiritualists at the time. McCabe notes that the only well-known mediums to escape exposure of fraud were William Stainton Moses and two American mediums, Emma Hardinge Britten and Cora Tappan. None of these were known to perform spirit manifestations, and they tended not to allow the public to observe their séances.[145] In ten years nearly every British and American medium had been exposed for fraud, although some managed to continue in their work for a time.

There were a few popular mediums at work in England after 1885, such as Mrs Leonora Piper from America and Eusapia Palladino from Italy, but it was not until the turn of the twentieth century that spiritualism rediscovered the appeal of charismatic enthusiasts.[146] Two eminent and well-respected men, in particular, not only became convinced of the veracity of spiritualism, but published books and gave lectures that connected with the general public far more than had the antics of the celebrity mediums.

The first of these was the writer Sir Arthur Conan Doyle (1859–1930). He first became interested in spiritualism, by his own account, in 1886, although the grief he experienced at the death of his wife Louisa in 1906 and his son Kingsley in 1918 may have further encouraged his desire to communicate with the spirits of the dead. In his lecture to a crowded audience in Worthing in 1919, Conan Doyle offered what might be described as a 'testimony' of his conversion to spiritualism. He was, as a medical student, influenced by the likes of Thomas Huxley, Herbert Spencer and Charles Darwin:

> I was a believer in Materialism. I believed that life ended in death. I could see no more reason why we could survive the death of our bodies than that the flame could survive the candle after it had burnt out, or the electric current could survive when you break the cell.

---

[145] McCabe, *Spiritualism*, 165–7.
[146] For an account of their work see McCabe, *Spiritualism*, 186 (Piper), 204 (Palladino).

Having these views you can well imagine that nothing in this world seemed more absurd than Spiritualism.[147]

He read about spiritualism in newspapers and initially thought it all very ridiculous, until he read the life of the American judge George Edmunds, who believed he was able to keep in touch with his late wife. 'The judge seemed an intelligent and God-fearing man.'[148] He also read a book by Alfred Russel Wallace, the eminent naturalist and evolutionary theorist, who was sympathetic to spiritualism. He attended a number of séances as he became more interested in the subject, but found them vague and not very striking. He read some books by Sir William Crookes, 'the greatest chemist, I suppose, in Europe in those days' and was further impressed. He became even more persuaded after reading about D. D. Home.[149]

Conan Doyle regarded the worthiness of these spiritualists as important. He was a scientist and as such became convinced by the words of eminent scientists and men of letters. He wrote in his chief work on spiritualism, *The New Revelation* (1918), that:

When I regarded Spiritualism as a vulgar delusion of the uneducated, I could affect to look down upon it; but when it was endorsed by men like Crookes, whom I knew to be the most rising British chemist, by Wallace, who was the rival of Darwin and by Flammarion, the best known of astronomers, I could not afford to dismiss it.[150]

He was disheartened that those scientists who derided spiritualism, such as Huxley, Spencer and Darwin, had not deemed it worthy even of investigation; he found this attitude unscientific.

He found that the opinions of Wallace, Crookes and Flammarion were corroborated by his own, more personal, experiments with spiritualism:

One thing that made a great impression on me was the automatic writing by a lady who was stopping with my family ... although she made many mistakes she none the less gave us such detailed accounts of extraordinary things that were going to happen that there could be

---

[147] Arthur Conan Doyle, *A Full Report of a Lecture on Spiritualism delivered by Sir Arthur Conan Doyle at the Connaught Hall, Worthing on Friday, July 11th, 1919, the Mayor of Worthing (J. Farquharson Whyte, Esq., J.P.) in the Chair.* Facsimile edition with an afterword by Richard Lancelyn Green (London, 1997. 1st pubd 1919), 1.

[148] Ibid., 2.

[149] Ibid., 2.

[150] Arthur Conan Doyle, *The New Revelation* (London, 1981. 1st pubd 1918), 13.

no doubt at all that her information was coming from some source beyond herself.[151]

Having spent time reading the evidence of scientists and attending séances for himself the moment of revelation came for Conan Doyle when he thought about what the point of the spiritualist phenomena might be. It was when he recognised the comfort that spiritualism gave to mourners that he realised what its purpose was:

> What I saw clearly was that all these phenomena were really nothing at all. They were sent as an alarm to the human race, something to call their attention, but nothing more; to shake them out of their mental ruts and make them realise that there was something beyond all this.[152]

He continued,

> We may call it puerile that tables turn round or chairs go up in the air. So it is, but if you saw it you would ask yourself 'My Goodness! What is this? What is it that makes them do these things?' and that would be the starting point of a line of thought which would lead you along on to the force that was behind.
>
> We are a materialist generation, and the great force beyond appeals to us through material things. But they were not meant to stop there; their object is to arrest our thoughts and make us go forward. If you heard a telephone bell ring you would not sit still and ask who rang the bell. The message does not fit in with any professed philosophy; it is a new thing and it is a unanimous thing. There may be differences in detail, but when it comes down to the facts, those facts are the same.
>
> A great body of information which has come to us is information which purports to have come from the dead. When I formed the opinion that this was true I saw at once the enormous importance of it. I thought nothing that I could do in connection with it would be too much trouble. Here were many people in this land needing consolation so badly; so many mothers who had lost sons and wives who had lost their husbands, Rachels mourning and without comfort. If only they could keep in touch with their dear ones what a comfort it would be.[153]

Conan Doyle set off around the country with proselytising zeal, offering

---

[151] Doyle, *Full Report of a Lecture*, 3.
[152] Ibid., 4.
[153] Ibid., 4–5.

lectures to interested listeners. His already considerable fame made him a popular lecturer. His passion for spiritualism was made attractive by his speeches and by the clarity and accessibility of his writing. Although his own conversion to spiritualism had occurred, according to his own account, in the 1860s, it was during the Great War that he took to speaking in public about what spiritualism had to offer. The choice of phrase employed above, of 'Rachels mourning' perhaps gives an insight into the motives behind his lectures. Spiritualism, Conan Doyle believed, had some comfort to offer the women bereaved of their menfolk during the war. Indeed, it had offered comfort to him after the loss of his wife and son. Traditional Christian teaching, as offered by the Church of England, was not, he thought, giving people sufficient comfort.[154]

Conan Doyle's contribution to spiritualism was immense. He brought to it the authority of one known by the public to be objective, trustworthy and serious-minded. As the writer of the Sherlock Holmes stories he spoke about spiritualism as one committed to intelligent rational enquiry; as a bereaved father and widower he had the voice of authentic grief. What he gave to his audiences was a testimony that spiritualism had, for him, revealed the reality of an afterlife; and it could do the same for others.

The second eminent preacher of spiritualism was the physicist, Sir Oliver Lodge (1851–1940). Perhaps less immediately popular than Arthur Conan Doyle, Lodge nevertheless became a well-known advocate of spiritualism. He wrote many books on psychic research and religion – according to a bibliography of his work he published 70 books or articles on the subject of psychic research, 73 on survival after death and 170 that could be classified as philosophy or religion. Given that the total of his published writings numbered 1,156, his work on spiritualism implies a significant interest.[155] Like Conan Doyle, Lodge was not a medium himself, and what he offered to interested readers was, superficially at least, a critical and unprejudiced scientific eye on the nature of spiritualism.

Lodge became interested in spiritualism in the early 1880s, when he was professor of physics at University College, Liverpool. He joined the Society for Psychical Research and, in 1901, became the society's president. It was, however, through the authorship of one book in 1916, *Raymond*, that he came to be established as the authoritative voice of spiritualism. In *Raymond* he wrote not only as an eminent scientist but also as a bereaved father. The

---

154 Doyle, *New Revelation*, 33–4.
155 Theodore Besterman, *A Bibliography of Sir Oliver Lodge* (Oxford and London, 1935).

combination of his scientific eminence and the eloquence of his simple bereavement made *Raymond* the bestseller that it quickly became.[156]

In *Raymond* Lodge describes himself as one already sympathetic to spiritualism. The death of his son Raymond during the course of the war had come as a shock to him and his wife, but Lodge believed he had already been warned. The medium Leonora Piper had given him the words of his friend and colleague in the SPR, the late Frederic Myers, telling him of a blow to come.[157]

Raymond was killed in battle on 14 September 1915. Lady Lodge sat with another medium, Mrs Gladys Osborne Leonard, on 25 September.[158] Both Sir Oliver and Lady Lodge sat with different mediums and received a number of communications from Raymond that were collected and presented in the book named after their son.

The book is divided into three parts. The first part is a description of Raymond's life, with some of the letters he sent home during the war and accompanying memorials from his brother and army colleagues. The second part describes the sittings with mediums and the communications received after Raymond's death. The third part contains some of Lodge's own thoughts and his conclusions of the evidence for communication with the dead.

In the first part Raymond Lodge appears as a likeable and much loved young man, who approached his time in the army with enthusiasm. The descriptions of the séances and communications in the second part are occasionally confusing or obscure. For example, in one instance Raymond communicates to his father a description of a photograph he sat for with army friends.[159] Lodge didn't know the photograph, and many pages are given to Raymond's description of how he is positioned in the picture, and the background and surroundings in it. The photograph is then sent to Lodge by a

---

[156] Although, at eleven shillings for a cloth copy, it wasn't cheap, and perhaps indicates a more moneyed readership. See, for example, the advert in *Light*, 6 Jan. 1917. Jay Winter claims *Raymond* was a 'bestseller', but notes that it was not entirely uncritically received. Winter, 'Spiritualism and the First World War', 189.

[157] This was known as the 'Faunus message'. A message came to Lodge through Mrs Piper said to be from Frederic Myers. It was: 'Myers says, you take the part of the poet and he will act as Faunus.' This was understood by Lodge as a reference to Horace, Odes II. xvii. 27–30, where Faunus protects the poet from a falling tree. Lodge with hindsight saw this as meaning that Myers would protect him from the blow of losing his son. Lodge, *Raymond: or life and death. With examples of the evidence for survival of memory and affection after death*, 4th edn. (London, 1916), 90–92.

[158] Ibid., 120.

[159] Ibid., 105–16.

friend and all becomes clear – a copy of the photograph is included in the book to enable readers to decide for themselves how closely Raymond's own description matches the actual picture. However, the conversations surrounding the photograph and Lodge's ruminations remain somewhat stilted, and it is difficult for the reader to appreciate quite why the photograph warrants so much attention.

Within the complicated and protracted descriptions of séances come some of the better known passages of the book. Raymond, through the mediums, articulated a desire to set his family's mind at rest by assuring them of his own well-being. He told them that he was well and, although initially saddened at being dead, found his new life interesting and uplifting. He did not want to be back on earth, except to offer comfort to his family by his communications.[160] The place where he found himself was similar to earth: he had a house and there were trees and flowers.[161] He was surrounded by old friends, including his father's friend Frederic Myers,[162] and there were many new people passing over from the earth as a result of the war.[163]

Lodge's critics derided some of the passages in the book as crude. Most famously Raymond described to his family how soldiers passing over were initially confused as to where they were and, as a result, looked for familiar objects and sought to satisfy familiar needs. One soldier wanted to smoke a cigar, although when one was offered to him, he decided he didn't really want it, and a friend smoked it instead.[164] Others wanted to drink: 'When they first come over they do want things. Some want meat, and some strong drink; they call for whisky sodas. Don't think I'm stretching it, when I tell you that they [the heavenly angels] can manufacture even that.'[165]

It was this passage more than any other that was criticised. In a lecture given at St Martin-in-the-Fields on 14 February 1917 Viscount Halifax, president of the English Church Union, launched a scathing criticism of *Raymond*, concentrating unashamedly on what he described as the more 'foolish' passages in the book, such as the one above.[166]

In response to such criticism Lodge wrote *Raymond Revised* in 1922. In answer to the eyebrows raised over the whisky he countered:

---

160 Ibid., 120.
161 Ibid., 184.
162 Ibid., 98.
163 Ibid., 185.
164 Ibid., 197.
165 Ibid., 197–8.
166 Viscount Halifax (Charles Lindley Wood), '*Raymond'. Some Criticisms. A lecture given at St Martin-in-the-Fields, February 14, 1917, with the addition of a preface* (London, 1917), 7.

My son is represented as saying that when people come over, and are in a puzzled state of mind, hardly knowing where they are, they ask for all sorts of unreasonable things; and that the lower kind are still afflicted with the desires of the earth ... Imagine an assembly of clergymen in some Retreat, where they give themselves to meditation and good works; and then imagine a traveller arriving, mistaking their hostel for an hotel, and asking for a whisky and soda. Would that mean that alcoholic drinks were natural to the surroundings and part of the atmosphere of the place?

The book says that in order to wean these newcomers from sordid and unsuitable though comparatively innocuous tastes, the policy adopted is not forbid and withhold – a policy which might over-inflame and prolong the desire – but to take steps to satisfy it in moderation until the newcomers of their own free will and sense perceive the unsuitability and overcome the relics of earthly craving; which they do very soon.[167]

In similar fashion Lodge upheld the accounts of games and songs offered in Raymond's conversation. He argued, 'It may be true that when spirits are the souls of men made perfect they may not have need of games, but if young fellows remain themselves then games and exercise will not seem alien to them, at least at first.'[168]

Raymond offered an image of a young man still playful and vital beyond the grave. Raymond appeared, to his family, to have remained very much himself. This was what lay at the heart of the book's popularity at a time when many young men were dying in war and being buried in foreign places away from their families. *Raymond* suggested that the dead continued beyond the grave, and were the same people they had been in life. They were perfected over time, but initially were recognisably the same people as when they lived. *Raymond* was reprinted five times in 1916, twice in 1917 and again in 1918. New editions appeared in 1918 and 1922. What appeared to appeal to the public at large was the simple humanity of the conversations and the possibility that the dead continued in the afterlife as they had always been. In 1919 at the Church Congress one speaker could assume that everyone in the hall, or nearly everyone, had read *Raymond*.[169] As late as 1947 the images supplied by *Raymond* were continuing to have an effect on the way that people spoke

---

[167] Oliver Lodge, *Raymond Revised* (London, 1922), 191–2.
[168] Ibid., 192.
[169] 'Or again, if you will read, as many of you in this hall have read, *Raymond*, you will realise the pitiableness of such communications.' J. A. V. Magee, *Church Congress at Leicester*, 114.

about the afterlife. A London Anglo-catholic clergyman noted of his congregation: 'They talk glibly about heaven and the angels and think their children are going to be little angels in a place where some frightful difficulties now besetting them just are not. Like Oliver Lodge and Raymond ... who was supposed to have said there was good whisky there. They hope there'll be good beer.'[170]

In 1860 the *Spiritual Magazine* wrote that, 'The gentle British public is constantly, from one source or another, hearing something about spiritualism.'[171] Indeed, spiritualism had, from 1852, found a place in private homes, where it was practised by the wealthy as well as the poor, and this fascination continued. People read about spiritualism in newspapers, where it was sometimes derided and sometimes promoted. They may have been one of the many who bought a copy of *Raymond*, or heard Arthur Conan Doyle speak. There were different aspects to spiritualism. Its external features: the séance phenomena, the scientific possibilities, the celebrity mediums attracted different people. Yet it was something they could also try at home.

However people encountered it, spiritualism quickly became, and remained, a part of the common culture, available to people of all classes and backgrounds. Importantly, then, the teachings of spiritualism, and especially the chief claim that it was possible to communicate with the dead, were widely known. Amid the flamboyance of the séance and the careful scientific experimentation, the communications of the alleged spirits, the descriptions of the afterlife and the injunctions to the living formed a crucial part of spiritualism. These teachings, by their nature, challenged what was understood to be traditional Church of England teaching about the afterlife. It is to the teachings of spiritualism that we now turn.

---

[170] Mass Observation, *Puzzled People. A study in popular attitudes to religion, ethics, progress and politics in a London Borough* (London, 1947), 32.
[171] *Spiritual Magazine*, Feb. 1860.

4

The teachings of spiritualism

In his comprehensive study of nineteenth-century theological controversies concerning eternal punishment and the future life Geoffrey Rowell offers a brief word concerning spiritualism:

> No discussion of nineteenth-century ideas concerning the future life would be complete without a mention of the spiritualist movement, even though this had little direct influence on the doctrine of more orthodox thinkers. Where it was valued, it was so largely because it appeared to offer empirical evidence for a future life, and where it was ignored, it was frequently on the grounds that the reported psychic phenomena were the result of satanic agency. In any case it cannot be pretended that the picture of the future life generally presented by spiritualism was other than banal.[1]

In spite of Rowell's scathing comments, this chapter explores precisely 'the picture of the future life' presented by spiritualism, offering a systematic account of the ideas and imagery used to imagine the afterlife by both alleged spirits and spiritualists. Such an account is necessary because, as has been said, historians of spiritualism have shown little concern for these ideas and images until now.

The previous chapter demonstrated how spiritualism became a part of people's lives, regardless of their class, gender or geographical location. The different expressions of spiritualism, the quiet home experiments, theatrical séances, earnest accounts in spiritualist journals, along with the lectures, books and newspaper articles, brought people of all types into contact with its discourse. As a consequence, the *ideas* of spiritualism – its claims and beliefs – and the *images* of spiritualism – the rich pictorial language it employed –

---

[1] Geoffrey Rowell, *Hell and the Victorians. A study of the nineteenth-century theological controversies concerning eternal punishment and the future life* (Oxford, 2000. 1st pubd 1974), 10.

were communicated to an audience far wider than merely those who claimed to be convinced by spiritualism, or who called themselves 'spiritualists'. Thus, however 'banal' they may be judged to be, these ideas and images are nevertheless of great significance to any account of spiritualism.

Spiritualists certainly thought they were important. Indeed, as one nineteenth-century adherent pointed out, spiritualism was more than simply 'spirit-rapping'; it was more than the sum of its séance phenomena. Calling spiritualists 'spirit-rappers' was, he argued, like calling Christians 'water-dippers' because they practised baptism.[2] Another spiritualist and clergyman, Fielding Fielding-Ould, writing in 1920, thought similarly: 'Physical phenomena are very interesting, and it is pleasant to have our sense of wonder stimulated; but the important part of spiritualism, and that on which it must stand or fall, is its teaching, and the teaching is pouring into the world daily through an immense and steadily increasing number of channels.'[3] In his lectures about spiritualism, Arthur Conan Doyle argued that the very purpose of the phenomena was to invite people to listen to the message of the spirits.[4] Even the vicar of Thaxted, Conrad Noel, although ambivalent towards spiritualism, agreed: 'It is the religion of spiritualism which ought to be given more attention than the phenomena.'[5]

Those who attended séances or lectures, or who read spiritualist literature, were invited to ponder images of a future life that had, it was claimed, been mediated to them through the spirits of the dead. If spiritualists believed that the spirits of the dead were indeed communicating with the living at séances and in meetings, then what the spirits had to say about their environment, about the nature of God, salvation and sin, was a matter of some consequence. The alleged spirits were, after all, describing what salvation, or at the very least, post-mortem survival, looked like.

Occasionally, attempts were made to gather up the communications of the spirits in order to distil from them a spiritualist 'theology'. Adin Ballou, writing in the 1850s and using only what he thought of as 'reliable testimony' from the spirits, presented an 'exposition' of spiritualism that included a doctrine of the Trinity, as well as the various stages of progress experienced by the soul beyond death.[6] William Stainton Moses, clergyman and spiritualist, writing in 1880 – a time when a number of mediums were being exposed

---

2   Howitt, *History of the Supernatural*, 15.
3   F. Fielding-Ould, *Is spiritualism of the Devil?* (London, 1920), 64.
4   Doyle, *Full Report of a Lecture*, 4.
5   Conrad Noel, *Byways of Belief* (London, 1912), 139.
6   Adin Ballou, *An Exposition of views respecting the principal facts, causes and peculiarities*

for fraud – expounded what he termed 'the higher aspects of spiritualism', namely the ideas that lay behind the séance phenomena.[7] He was anxious that many people were being put off spiritualism by the 'antics' of some mediums and that spiritualism was being depicted in some newspapers as an 'unclean silly thing'.[8] Instead, Moses attempted to offer a serious theology that was, he said, taught by the spirits.

In 1871 the medium Emma Hardinge Britten received the 'Seven Principles of Spiritualism' from the recently departed Robert Owen.[9] The British National Association of Spiritualists, founded in 1873, adopted these principles.[10] They were taught as part of the catechism to the children of the British Spiritualists' Lyceum and were noted by the *Report of the Archbishop of Canterbury's Committee on Spiritualism* in 1939. The principles were as follows:

1. The Fatherhood of God.
2. The Brotherhood of Man.
3. The communion of the spirits and the ministry of angels.
4. The continuous existence of the soul and its personal characteristics.
5. Personal responsibility.
6. Compensation and retribution hereafter for good or evil deeds done here.
7. The path of eternal progress is open to every human soul.[11]

Neither Britten nor, indeed, the spirit of Robert Owen offered expansion or explanation of these principles.

Apart from the accounts offered by Ballou, Moses and Britten, a theology of spiritualism has to be gleaned and compiled from a variety of sources. These comprise for the most part the writings of people who were convinced that the spirits spoke to them or, indeed, from communications allegedly from spirits themselves. A remarkably systematisable account, however, emerges out of a tapestry of different ideas, imagery and theological argument.

---

involved in Spirit Manifestations, together with interesting phenomenal statements and communications (London, 1852).

[7] William Stainton Moses, *Higher Aspects of Spiritualism* (London, 1880).

[8] Ibid., 4.

[9] Robert Owen (1771–1858), socialist and philanthropist, had come to believe in spiritualism in 1853 when in America. *ODNB*.

[10] This became the London Spiritualist Alliance in 1884, but the Spiritualists' National Union, founded in 1901, also took these as its principles, and maintains them to the present day.

[11] See Britten et al., *The Lyceum Manual*, No. 139; Archbishop's committee on spiritualism, *Report*, 6.

By their critical comments, the opponents of spiritualism offered a presentation of the same images and ideas. Some of these have been included in the following account because people both sympathetic and antipathetic to spiritualism read them, and through them were similarly able to gain an impression of spiritualist teachings.

The ideas about the afterlife presented by spiritualists altered remarkably little over the period under consideration. Critics argued that spiritualism was incoherent and inconsistent, but this was not a reasonable judgement.[12] There were strands of thinking found in the *Yorkshire Spiritual Telegraph* in 1855 that could also be found in the *Christian Spiritualist* in the late 1920s.

Spiritualists themselves admitted occasional discrepancies and contradictions.[13] There were some minor disagreements among the spirit communications concerning the different 'levels' of the afterlife, and it is clear that the importance of the person of Jesus became a focus for more serious disagreement as time went on. However, in general there was little diversity in the teaching of spiritualism, so it is possible to present an account of what any person encountering spiritualism would have learned about the nature of the afterlife.

A theology of spiritualism

It may seem rather obvious to state, but it was death, the physical end to mortal life, that brought an individual to the point of entry into the afterlife. Rather than being an abrupt single moment of ending or beginning, however, death was regarded in spiritualist teaching as a seamless movement of 'transition', 'passing over' or 'passing on' into the next life; merely a junction along a person's life rather than a terminus. Spiritualist newspapers contained personal columns entitled 'Births, marriages and transitions'.[14]

Indeed, some claimed that there was no 'death' at all, but that there was one life lived out in two stages or 'phases', and that the life in the 'earth-phase' was but a preparation for the life to come.[15] Once a person died there was no interruption before their spirit's entry into the next life. Contrary to what

---

[12] R. H. Benson, *Spiritualism* (London, 1911), 8. Even Benson, having criticised spiritualism for inconsistency, had to admit that the dogmas were becoming more coherent by 1911.

[13] Ballou, *Spirit Manifestations*, 53.

[14] See, for example, *Two Worlds*, 18 Jan. 1918.

[15] See Robert Dale Owen, *The Debatable Land between This World and the Next* (London, 1871), 123. Robert Dale Owen was the son of Robert Owen. Stainton Moses also argued that life had two stages, the progressive and the contemplative. William Stainton Moses, *Spirit Teachings* (London, 1883), 16.

spiritualists characterised as the Church's teaching, there was no period of 'slumbering in the grave' before the spirit rose to a new life. Instead of sleeping or waiting after death for a final resurrection, the spirit of the dead person passed immediately and seamlessly into the afterlife.[16]

Importantly, spiritualists taught that beyond death the personality of the individual continued intact. 'Death destroys not', wrote Robert Dale Owen, 'in any sense either the life or identity of man.'[17] The testimony of the spirits was that the departed still possessed the same intelligence, memory, character and tastes as in life.[18] This meant that when spirits communicated with the bereaved they were recognisable; sitters at séances commented on the way that they recognised the personality and sense of humour of their departed friends when the spirits spoke to them. The continuation of the individual personality indicated, according to spiritualists, that personal characteristics, not just personal faith, were of significance in the next life.

Writing just after the Great War, Oliver Lodge claimed that the recently departed young soldiers remained true to their character and temperament after death. The majority of people at point of death were, he argued, neither saints nor devils and, indeed, 'ecclesiastical teaching has grievously erred in leading people to suppose that the act of death converts them into one or the other'. Youths 'shot out of the trenches' although 'fine fellows' were unlikely to become saints at once. If there was such a thing as personal survival, he thought, then something of the personal identity must survive.[19]

If death was the seamless transition of the individual spirit from one world into the next, then it was a positive transition because it brought the individual to a place where profound happiness and new spiritual growth began immediately. The afterlife could thus be approached with hope and confidence rather than fear. Even the very moment of death could be neared without anxiety because it was, spiritualists taught, a painless process. Whatever illness, physical decline or pain brought a person to the point of death, the moment itself was gentle and tranquil. This was something agreed upon by communicating spirits.[20] The peacefulness of death was particularly emphasised during the

---

[16] The 'slumbering' was a characteristic of Luther's theology of death, which claimed that the soul slept at death, waiting for the General Resurrection and Judgement at the end of time. See Robert Dale Owen, *Footfalls on the boundary of another world* (London, 1860), 352; also Charles Tweedale, *Present Day Spirit Phenomena and the Churches* (Chicago, 1920), 5.

[17] Owen, *Footfalls on the boundary*, 353.

[18] According to Sir Oliver Lodge, in Sir Arthur Keith et al., *Where are the dead?*, 11.

[19] Lodge, *Raymond Revised*, 193.

[20] This was so according to Conan Doyle, *Full Report of a Lecture*, 7. A female spirit

First World War, with the spirits of dead soldiers informing mediums of how easy death in battle had been for them.[21]

The comforting information that the point of death was painless was further underlined by the revelation that the moment of death was also extremely social. The spirits told of how, as a person came increasingly close to the point of death, the deathbed became surrounded not only by living family members and friends, but also the spirits of departed friends and relatives, who offered encouragement during the transition into the next life. According to an article in the *Spiritualist* that was why the dying so often spoke of seeing departed friends around their bed.[22] At the moment of death the spirit was taken from the body of the dead person by the spirit friends and 'guided over' to the new life. Unless a person was unfortunate enough to undergo a death that was particularly sudden or violent, the passing into the next world was merely a gradual diminishing of the old earthly life and a slow awakening into something new. In 1869 the *Spiritualist* claimed that spirits, mediums, clairvoyants and seers agreed closely in their descriptions of the human body approaching death:

> The vital forces first quit the feet and lower extremities of the body, and those who have the power of spirit vision see a luminous haze forming above the head and connected with it by a shining cord. Gradually, as the vitality of the body diminishes, the cord above assumes a distinct shape and the spirit form of the departing individual is seen lying in a state of insensibility above the prostrate body. At last the spirit awakes to consciousness, the silver cord connecting it with the body is severed and the new-born spirit quits the house in company with spirit friends and relatives who awaited its arrival.[23]

Another departed spirit, communicating in 1917, said that his death had felt like 'weight slipping away'. Feeling himself gradually free of his body he had watched himself lying on the deathbed until the 'cord of light' had snapped and separated him from earthly existence.[24]

Once the departed spirit reached its destination it began to acclimatise to the new surroundings, in a place known variously as 'Summerland' or the

---

communicated, 'I did not feel any pain in "dying"; I felt only great calm and peace.' Stead, *After death*, 1.
[21] See, for example, *Two Worlds*, 29 Nov. 1918.
[22] *Spiritualist*, 19 Nov. 1869.
[23] Ibid.
[24] J. S. M. Ward, *Gone West. Three narratives of after-death experiences* (London, 1917), 29.

'Spirit World' or 'Spirit Land'. Some spirit communications presented this acclimatisation as being like waking up after a good and refreshing sleep. Mabel Corelli Green, a young woman who died in 1921, communicated to her bereaved mother that, initially, she needed sleep. She described how she was taken to the 'Hill of Rest' and to a 'bower of roses' where everything was peaceful, soothing and beautiful. She slept for a time before being woken by a 'shining and radiant figure' whom she mistook for Jesus, but who was, she later discovered, another spirit.[25] A young child spirit communicated that, 'I awoke in the beautiful gardens of the Spirit Land, where all the happy spirits suited to my capabilities were thronging around me.'[26] The images of spirits resting, waking up and then surveying the new surroundings added to the depiction of death as a gradual and gentle process.

Some spirits, however, described the incremental awareness of their new situation in terms of bewilderment rather than refreshed awakening. They did not always know where they were. Thus the young child from the 'Spirit Land' mentioned above commented that at first, 'I was not absolutely conscious that I had passed the gates of death'.[27] The spiritualist and clergyman George Vale Owen admitted that some departed spirits did not realise that they had died, but said that this was because they awoke to a place that appeared similar to the earth they had left.[28] According to Oliver Lodge those who arrived in the afterlife were often 'puzzled' and 'hardly knowing where they are'. Again, the reason for this puzzlement seems to have been due to confusing similarities between the new life and earth.[29] Quickly, however, confusion turned to joy in finding the familiar things of life and home around them. The spirit of a dead soldier communicating through automatic writing claimed that, 'at first all souls are deeply impressed with earthly habits and ideas'.[30] Resemblances with earthly life included, as we have seen, the availability of meat, cigars and whisky sodas.[31]

The seemingly earthly nature of the afterlife was, however, simply the spirit's introduction into his or her new situation. The physical landscape of the afterlife, and familiar substances like food and drink, assisted the passage

---

[25] Mabel Corelli Green, *Life in the Summerland. Given from the Spirit World through inspirational writing to her mother, Corelli Green* (London, 1922), 7–8.
[26] 'F. J. T.', *Heaven opened, or, Messages for the bereaved from our Little Ones in Glory* (London, 1870), 7.
[27] Ibid.
[28] G. Vale Owen, *The Life beyond the Veil*. 2 Vols (London, 1926. 1st pubd 1922), 1: 107.
[29] Lodge, *Raymond Revised*, 191.
[30] Macfie, *From Heaven to Earth*, 31.
[31] Lodge, *Raymond*, 197–8.

between life and death. As they grew used to the new life they were 'weaned' from previous tastes and desires.[32] The spirits told of how, as they looked about them, they gradually realised that they were in a different place. Many of the communicating spirits emphasised the sheer beauty of their surroundings. Around them lay 'earth made perfect'.[33] One spirit communicated that, 'Lo! I was in the most exquisite scenery imaginable.'[34] There were many vivid descriptions of the landscape, of which the following, given by a spirit at a séance in the Spiritual Library, Holborn, is typical:

> When I recovered consciousness after the change I found myself in what you would call a beautiful garden. I was lying on a bank by the side of a stream: the stream gave forth a gentle musical sound, and I think it was that which brought me to consciousness again … It was a gentle sloping bank: on the top of the bank was a broad plain, and above me were flowers distributed into beds; there was a broad path of dazzling whiteness that went right across the greensward to a house beyond. This house was enshrouded with trees … On the lawn in front of the house were little bowers of the branches of the tree, with flowers much like your rose, but more beautiful …[35]

Spirits communicated an intensity of colour, light, sound and smell in their surroundings:

> I lay where I was brought by the spirit, on the couch of flowery essence, yielding forth refreshing and supporting perfume, and my ear was aroused to spirit life by thrilling songs of welcome and love. Oh! I did not wish for earth![36]

> I was *bathed*, as it were in floods of melody and joy. The sweet voices of my lost ones were near me, uttering words of welcome … I lay on a couch of rest which was in the most beautiful garden, and was, itself, formed by living flowers and fruits, and canopied over by a graceful vine. I stretched forth my hand to gather these fruits and flowers and as my touch came near them did I receive nourishment and strength, by the aromal essence that was at once infused into my spirit-life in all its senses, of tasting, hearing and smelling as well as seeing.[37]

---

[32] Ibid., 192.
[33] Owen, *Life beyond the Veil*, 1: 17.
[34] Ward, *Gone West*, 29.
[35] From a report in *Spiritualist*, 31 Dec. 1869.
[36] 'F. J. T.', *Heaven opened*, 7.
[37] Theobald, *Homes and Work*, 2: 55–6.

The spirits spoke of encountering long departed friends and family members, recognising them in their spiritual bodies.[38] They found their loved ones altered by their time in the afterlife. 'All traces of earthliness, sadness, weakness and pain, being removed; and all that was to my earthly eyes very lovely in form was added to infinitely by the purity and heavenly atmosphere in which they have of late been trained.'[39] The spirits found themselves in spiritual bodies, which were either a replica of their earthly bodies, or else distinct forms that corresponded to their spiritual identities.[40] Over time they became more refined; old people bent over by life were 'straightened out'[41] and the higher, purer, spirits were represented as beings of light and airiness.

However inadequately, the spirits tried to convey that they had found something more than simple beauty in the afterlife. They attempted to express this by using vivid imagery of colour and light. Thus George Vale Owen's departed mother spoke of how the spirits' clothing altered its tint depending upon where the spirits were and the depth of their spiritual quality.[42] Others spoke of their surroundings having an 'atmospheric hue',[43] of 'life and colour interwoven with all the most beautiful ideals you can picture',[44] of everything having 'an acute brightness, and yet blending into a harmony of mellowness'.[45] The physical landscape was important, but what made it truly beautiful was something the spirits recognised as profoundly 'other'. By having to use earthly language in order to communicate with the living something of the profound spiritual significance of it all was lost. The spirits were conscious of this and often commented on it.[46]

If death was a dynamic transition or 'passing over' to new and vivid life, then beyond death the dynamism certainly continued. Once present in the next life a spirit was expected to progress; spirits were not in the afterlife merely to wonder at and enjoy the beautiful surroundings, but to develop in spiritual knowledge. There were some minor variations in the way that this growth was described but, most commonly, spiritual progress was expressed as a physical

---

[38] Stead, *After death*, 38.
[39] Theobald, *Homes and Work*, 2: 57.
[40] Adin Ballou argued that the forms were the human spirit made recognisable; Ballou, *Spirit Manifestations*, 55. Arthur Conan Doyle thought they were replicas of earthly bodies. Doyle, *Full Report of a Lecture*, 7.
[41] Doyle, *Full Report of a Lecture*, 8.
[42] Owen, *Life beyond the Veil*, 1: 27–30.
[43] Theobald, *Homes and Work*, 2: 56.
[44] Green, *Life in the Summerland*, 9.
[45] Macfie, *From Heaven to Earth*, 17.
[46] See, for example, Green, *Life in the Summerland*, 14. 'Earthly language is inadequate to describe it all.'

movement 'upward'. Spirits were expected to 'rise'. The afterlife was stratified into 'spheres' or 'realms' and a spirit was understood to have progressed when it rose upward through these different realms.

There was some disagreement among spirits and spiritualists as to the exact number of spheres. One of the earliest accounts of the spheres of the spirit world came in the *Yorkshire Spiritual Telegraph* in 1855, when the spirit of Professor Hare communicated that there were seven spheres, of which the earth was one. In the afterlife, 'Boundaries are not marked, but spirits know when they are passing from one sphere to the next. The spheres are represented as having a gradation on constitutional refinement. Elevation is determined by a moral specific gravity, in which merit is inverse to weight. There are six subdivisions in the spheres, so thirty-six gradations. The lower degrees are of vice, ignorance and folly, the upper being virtue, learning and wisdom.'[47] Adin Ballou claimed that there were seven 'circles', inferior to the heavenly circles, with unspecified numbers of degrees in each circle.[48] One communicating spirit declared that there were twelve spheres;[49] another thought six, subdivided.[50] Most spiritualist accounts of the afterlife did not offer a number, simply stating that there were spheres or realms to be passed. In fact, an exact number appeared to be less important than the simple imagery of realms or spheres and the strong emphasis on the spirits' vocation to progress upwards through them.

Although there was little agreement as to the precise number of spheres, there was, however, an unspoken assumption that the afterlife was more broadly divided into three sections or classes. The communicating spirits tended to speak from a place ranked somewhere in the middle section.[51] Thus their descriptions of the afterlife, as a place of rest, beauty and 'earth made perfect', were really only accounts of the middle spheres as they experienced them.

This did not prevent them from speaking about the other realms of the afterlife. Some communicating spirits professed knowledge of life in both the

---

[47] *Yorkshire Spiritual Telegraph*, August 1855. This is Professor Robert Hare, MD, of Pennsylvania University, who wrote about spirit manifestations in his earthly lifetime.
[48] Ballou, *Spirit Manifestations*, 55.
[49] *New Spiritualist*, 27 Sept. 1922.
[50] Ward, *Gone West*, 36. A diagram is included in this account.
[51] This was countered by the spirit of 'John King', who appeared in many fashionable séances in the 1860s and 1870s. 'King', otherwise known as the Welsh pirate Henry Owen Morgan, claimed that communicating spirits were from the lower spheres – those spheres nearest to the earth. The spirits returned to communicate with the living in order to work off their sins and further their progress to heaven. Once there, they would not return to earth. *Medium and Daybreak*, 6 Jan. 1871.

lower and upper realms, although they tended to acknowledge that this was only partial comprehension. Most spirits suggested that a degree of interaction took place between the spheres. Thus a newly arrived, middle-ranking, spirit might be taken by a higher spirit 'guide' to observe the lower or higher regions, but these visits appeared to be made for the purposes of educating the middle-ranking spirits and did not happen frequently. The middle-ranking spirits observed that spirits from the higher spheres also visited those in the very lowest spheres in order to guide and educate them, thus enabling them to rise into the middle realms.[52] Or else the middle-ranking spirits might assist the new arrivals at the 'border'.[53] A few accounts, however, suggested that interaction between the spheres was minimal, and that spirits remained within their own realm. Indeed, the afterlife might be a place where people moved towards like-minded others, and where, as one spiritualist described it, 'a man can elect his friends and gravitate to his own congenial social sphere'.[54]

The communicating spirits were not able to offer such full descriptions of the higher and lower spheres as they were of the middle realms, but they were certain of one thing: that hell, as a separate place, did not exist. One departed spirit said: 'I find that there is no hell, and I am very glad that there is none; I find that all people, no matter what they are, have good in them which will be brought out soon, and that knowledge gives me pleasure.'[55] Not only that, the doctrine of eternal punishment, characterised by spiritualists as being traditional Christian teaching, was 'almost always explicitly denied'.[56] The idea of eternal punishment was abhorrent, according to the spirits. God was a loving parent and could not punish throughout eternity without any hope of reformation or progression.[57]

This was not to say that wicked deeds in earthly life went unpunished in the afterlife. There were certainly spheres of the afterlife that were 'lower' and 'darker' and these were described as places of punishment, of 'darkness' and 'grossness'.[58] There were even regions of 'torture'.[59] According to the spirits, the individuals who found themselves in the lower spheres were those whose

---

[52] Owen, *Life beyond the Veil*, 1: 31; Green, *Life in the Summerland*, 20.
[53] Mabel Corelli Green wrote of how her brothers helped those crossing over: Green, *Life in the Summerland*, 21. The soldier communicating with McLaren Post Macfie claimed that some spirits were 'detailed off' to receive new arrivals: Macfie, *From Heaven to Earth*, 31.
[54] *Medium and Daybreak*, 27 May 1870.
[55] *Spiritualist*, 31 Dec. 1869.
[56] Benson, *Spiritualism*, 9.
[57] *Two Worlds*, 9 Dec. 1887.
[58] Owen, *Life beyond the Veil*, 1: 107.
[59] Ward, *Gone West*, 203.

earthly lives had been full of bad or immoral deeds.[60] They were described as obstinate people who refused to grow in love and understanding, and thus remained where they were – in a place of punishment.

These spirits were not consigned to places of punishment by God, however, but found themselves in the lower regions by 'self-banishment'.[61] This was, according to one account, a permanent situation.[62] The vast majority of spirits, however, claimed that even these lower spheres offered opportunity for an individual to undo the misdeeds of life and rise higher. Indeed, murderers and suicides could work themselves out of the lowest spheres in time, and progress was made as the individual spirit acknowledged and remedied his or her defects.[63] No one, however slow in responding, could fail to be drawn upwards towards the divine laws and the heavenly mansions.[64]

Although the idea of a separate, everlasting, inescapable hell was abhorrent to spiritualists, the imagery of the 'traditional' hell, of darkness, torture, chaos and personal torment, was however readily employed to describe the lower regions of the afterlife. In using such language spiritualists attempted to communicate that the consequences of earthly sin were serious; they were not advocating loose living on the grounds that all people ended up in the same afterlife. Punishment for sin was not the vindictive act of an angry God, but it was the inevitable consequence of earthly sin, and was not pleasant.[65] By referring to the lower regions as 'hell', spiritualists reminded people that the afterlife was not only a place of light, beauty and joy, and an individual would certainly be called to account for evil deeds in the earthly life. Thus 'hell', or at least its imagery, was 'necessary', according to spiritualist and archdeacon, Thomas Colley.[66]

If the spirits were unanimous that hell as a separate entity did not exist, they occasionally disagreed as to whether the higher realms alone constituted a

[60] A murderer found himself in such a sphere and described it as 'hell'. Ibid., 200.
[61] According to Archdeacon Thomas Colley, *Sermons on Spiritualism at Stockton* (London, 1907), 16.
[62] Owen, *Life beyond the Veil*, 1: 31.
[63] Moses, *Higher Aspects of Spiritualism*, 88; Ward, *Gone West*, 261. The murderer began to rise once he began to pray.
[64] Houghton, *Evenings at Home*, 9; Charles Drayton Thomas, Cambridge University Library, *SPR Archive*, MS 58/4/15; Ballou, *Spirit Manifestations*, 56. One spirit who claimed to have died 2,500 years ago said that he had spent time in the lower regions and taken a long time to work up to the highest spheres. *Spiritual Truth*, 27 Sept. 1922.
[65] Moses, *Higher Aspects of Spiritualism*, 88; *Yorkshire Spiritual Telegraph*, Aug. 1855.
[66] Colley, *Sermons*, 16.

distinct 'heaven',[67] or whether the whole afterlife as they currently experienced it was, in fact, to be designated 'heaven'.[68] In the latter case, the higher planes were described as being more *holy* than those the spirits currently inhabited, but nevertheless this suggested that the afterlife existed as some sort of spiritual continuum. There were also differences of opinion as to whether residence in the higher spheres meant a necessary cessation of communication with the other spheres and with the earth. Some spirits suggested that a spirit remained fixed in the higher spheres once he or she had reached them, and either lost the desire to hold on to earthly or material things,[69] or else was unable to communicate – as no medium was spiritually skilled enough to transmit the messages.[70] Others said that the earth was never beyond their thoughts.[71]

When it came to naming the middle spheres, where most of them found themselves, the spirits tended to prefer 'Summerland' or 'spirit land' to describe their location. Such phrases suggested neither that the spirits of the dead had reached immediate perfection (in heaven), nor that they were in hell, nor even undergoing some sort of purgation. They were in a place that was different from the locations named in traditional Christian teaching, a tangible land that was full of sunshine as well as spirits. In *Raymond Revised*, however, Oliver Lodge tried to connect the afterlife with a more traditional name. He claimed that the 'paradise' offered by Jesus to the penitent thief at the crucifixion was akin to the 'Summerland' of the spiritualists.[72] Paradise was not heaven, the place of perfection; it was a different place – but a place, nevertheless, where Jesus, on the cross, had assumed he would be after his death. Robert Dale Owen referred to the middle-ranking afterlife as 'hades',[73] as did the spiritualist vicar of Brockenhurst, Arthur Chambers.[74] 'Hades' was a pre-Christian term for the afterlife, but one adopted in early Church traditions.[75] Lodge, Chambers and Owen managed to identify within the Christian

---

[67] William Stainton Moses thought that 'heaven' was separate, a place that the spirits reached when they moved from a life of progress to contemplation. *Spirit Teachings*, 16.

[68] George Vale Owen subtitled his two-volume work 'The Highlands and Lowlands of Heaven', suggesting a continuation rather than separation of the spheres. *Life beyond the Veil*.

[69] Macfie, *From Heaven to Earth*, 31.

[70] Moses, *Spirit Teachings*, 12.

[71] Owen, *Life beyond the Veil*, 1: 107.

[72] Lodge, *Raymond Revised*, 193.

[73] Owen, *Footfalls on the boundary*, 356.

[74] Arthur Chambers, *Our Life after Death, or, The teaching of the Bible concerning the Unseen World* (London, 1894), 44.

[75] Hades was the Greek translation of the Jewish 'Sheol' found in the Septuagint. See chapter five for further explanation of hades, p. 122.

tradition the names for the afterlife that had no connection with judgement. 'Paradise' and 'hades' were places that, for them, simply implied the next stage after death. They were part of an ancient Christian tradition and might have provided Christian spiritualists with a better way of connecting their teaching with Christian doctrine than non-Christian phrases like 'Summerland' and 'spirit land'. It was these non-Christian terms, however, that proved more popular among spiritualists.

Whatever the afterlife was called, what was common to all spirit accounts was the teaching that a spirit entered the afterlife in a sphere that was conducive to its spiritual calibre at the moment of death. Adin Ballou said that, 'If a person is spiritually in a certain sphere at death, in that sphere he finds himself the moment he resumes his consciousness in the spirit world, with kindred spirits.'[76] Arthur Conan Doyle claimed that the spirits taught that 'when you die it is on your own spiritual development at that moment that you take your place in the next world'.[76] Another spiritualist writer, Charles Drayton Thomas, claimed that his dead father had told him that what determined one's sphere on arrival in the afterlife was the habit of one's thought in life.[78] A spirit named only as 'H. J. L.' told of how the dead joined the 'set' to which they belonged according to their beliefs and actions.[79] The spirits therefore advised that the living pay attention to their spiritual health in their earthly lifetime. 'Struggle continually, therefore in your path of life, that you may lay the seeds of goodness and virtue which will blossom up here more abundantly as you have sown upon earth, and which sowing, plentifully or scarcely, will gain you a higher or lower place upon the pyramid.'[80]

Spirits progressed upward through the spheres by increasing their enlightenment. It was the *raison d'être* of the spirit to rise, and thus progress. As William Stainton Moses put it, 'This is the one desire of the spirit. More progress! More knowledge! More love! Till the dross is purged away and the soul soars higher and yet higher towards the Supreme.'[81] They achieved this by spending their time in good works, right-thinking and learning, but acknowledged that the path upward was not always pleasant, as they needed to seek forgiveness for wrongs in order to move.

Indeed, sometimes a spirit would be forced to 'tarry along the way',[82] as

---

76 Ballou, *Spirit Manifestations*, 55.
77 Doyle, *Full Report of a Lecture*, 10.
78 Thomas, *SPR Archive*, MS 58/4/1–7.
79 Ward, *Gone West*, 2.
80 Macfie, *From Heaven to Earth*, 17.
81 Moses, *Spirit Teachings*, 26.
82 Macfie, *From Heaven to Earth*, 31.

some sort of purgatorial process took place. An angel told one spirit, who was expecting judgement and punishment for her misdeeds in life, that she was her own judge, and would move up through the spheres only by reviewing her life and confessing her sins. She found, to her delight, that in consequence she understood more of the love and mercy of God.[83] Another spirit, finding himself in the lowest sphere, progressed upward by acknowledging God and praying for forgiveness.[84] Individual spirits who confessed the sins that had held them back in life gained the spiritual strength to rise through the spheres, and experienced an 'awakening'.[85] The awakened spirits would become increasingly uncomfortable and out of place in their environment and, crying out for light, would be directed upwards to a brighter sphere until, gradually, that sphere likewise became too dark for them in their enlightened state and they continued upwards yet again.[86] God, emphatically, did not judge the individual nor decide his or her eternal destiny. The individual's life and spiritual maturity were the deciding factors in how quickly the spirit progressed, and each person was the arbiter of his or her own destiny.

The communicating spirits agreed that every spirit was expected to rise up the spheres in time, even if some, through their obstinacy, refused to do so. Although the upward movement was expected, Thomas Colley sounded a note of warning: spirits who, by their base nature, became uncomfortable with heavenly spiritual surroundings did *not* rise, but declined into the lower realms.[87] Adin Ballou agreed that without conforming to God's laws a spirit could not progress, but obscured and debased himself. It was possible to sink down through the spheres on one's own account, but a spirit only rose up through the spheres when given permission to do so, having 'qualified' to move as a result of spiritual progress.[88]

Even allowing for the possibility of spirits falling into lower realms as well as rising up through them, the dynamic of the afterlife, according to spiritualists, was one of perpetual upward progress. No future scene of judgement was, therefore, imagined; nor was there any place for the 'Parousia', or Second Coming of Christ – certainly none was ever mentioned. Spiritualists were not millenarians. Progress was made by the individual in the afterlife

---

[83] Owen, *Life beyond the Veil*, 1: 121.
[84] Ward, *Gone West*, 261.
[85] Thomas, *SPR Archive*, MS 58/4/13.
[86] Owen, *Life beyond the Veil*, 2: 63.
[87] Colley, *Sermons*, 16.
[88] Ballou, *Spirit Manifestations*, 56–7. The spirit of 'the officer' indeed fell into the lowest regions by continued depravity before beginning to rise through prayer and confession. Ward, *Gone West*, 200–261.

until such time as that spirit was sufficiently enlightened to enter the highest realms. There was no single moment hoped for when God would bring about the final days and the righteous would collectively enjoy eternal felicity. Instead, the individual made slow and steady progress towards personal spiritual fulfilment.

Although the progress of each spirit was brought about by individual effort, the communicating spirits taught that they were assisted in their progress through the afterlife by beings called, variously, 'spirit guides', 'angels' or 'guardians', as has already been noted. Angels, or guides, were particularly present to take care of those who had died as babies or children. According to the *Two Worlds*, angels carried babies 'to the bright spheres', regardless of whether they were baptised or not.[89] Some thought that the higher spirits were the spirits of dead children, as children were deemed to be already more spiritually pure than adults. According to Stainton Moses children did not pass at once to the higher spheres because the value of the earth experience could not be neglected and needed to be taught them. However, the absence of worldly contamination meant that they rose rapidly through the spheres.[90]

Newly arrived children found themselves surrounded by their favourite pets and games.[91] In some instances, adolescent spirits, like Mabel Corelli Green, became involved in teaching the spirit children. Mabel was delighted to do this, as she had loved children in life, and they needed to be taught in the ways of earth, in reading and writing and games, before being taught in the spiritual life.[92] Loving adoptive parents in the spirit world brought up stillborn babies and young children – knowledge of which, it was hoped, brought comfort to bereaved parents.

Whether the spirit was a child or an adult, however, its status at the initial point of entry into the afterlife had little to do with confessed religious belief. The communicating spirits were universally certain of this. The outward confession of a Christian faith counted for nothing if the inward spiritual life did not reflect this.[93] A strongly professed faith was not discouraged; indeed,

---

[89] *Two Worlds*, 9 Dec. 1887.
[90] Moses, *Spirit Teachings*, 25.
[91] Theobald, *Heaven opened*, 9–10.
[92] Presumably they all spoke English. Green, *Life in the Summerland*, 18.
[93] Although every person of faith might agree with this, what the spirits communicated was that a reliance on conviction without action was wrong. Thus the spirit of Martin Luther communicated that he had erred by stressing the importance of faith over works. What mattered most, he found in the afterlife, was good works. *Yorkshire Spiritual Telegraph*, June 1855.

one spirit taught that people ought to go to church 'occasionally',[94] but of far greater significance for the placing of a spirit in a particular sphere was the righteousness of the life that had been lived. So some spirits found, to their surprise, on entry to the afterlife that Christ did not meet them with a 'well done'.[95] A spiritualist lecturer taught that, 'When you come to the spirit life you will find you will not be asked, "What have you believed?" but, "What have you done?"'[96]

This led some spirits to conclude that the teaching offered by the Church regarding eternal salvation had been misleading. One female spirit, communicating in 1869, claimed that she had initially been concerned that no one was singing hosannas to the Lamb, as she had expected. 'I did not find the throne of God, or the Lamb or angels singing, yet had anybody said anything against that belief in the flesh I should have thought them very wicked.' She continued: 'Creed and dogmas have little influence for good on the spirit life; it is by actions that we know each other. Your thoughts and actions here govern your state upon entering the spirit life; if you have been good and noble here you will find the home for the good and noble awaiting you on the other side. If you were not good and noble you cannot at first pass into that state, as it would be unnatural, and it is only by patient working that you will rise to gain wisdom.' She found that her wayward son entered the afterlife at the same sphere as she had done herself because he had been truer to his inner nature than she had been and 'had not artificially fettered himself with creeds and dogmas'.[97]

The *Yorkshire Spiritual Telegraph* had reached a similar conclusion in 1856. Whereas the Church, it said, had taught that an individual's eternal and unalterable condition was determined by an act of faith, even made in the last dying moments of life, the spirits taught that eternal happiness was attainable in knowledge and duty, rather than faith and prayer. This had come as a shock to many recently departed spirits: 'Thousands have waked up in the Spirit-world, and for the first time discovered their awful mistake.'[98] The spirits stressed that a person's actions throughout their whole earthly life and the reality of their spiritual maturity were of far higher importance in the spirit world than a confessed faith.[99]

---

[94] Macfie, *From Heaven to Earth*, 27.
[95] Owen, *Life beyond the Veil*, 1: 129.
[96] Lecture given at the Mechanics' Institute, Openshaw, by a Mrs Green of Heywood, reported in *Two Worlds*, 9 Dec. 1887.
[97] Report of a spiritualist meeting at the Spiritualist Library, in *Spiritualist*, 31 Dec. 1869.
[98] *Yorkshire Spiritual Telegraph*, Mar. 1856.
[99] Indeed, Stainton Moses was highly critical of what he saw as one Christian tradition, which

The value of good actions continued in the afterlife, where spirits were expected to be active in their progress through the spheres. There was a sense of busyness about the spirit world, as spirits engaged in good works. The spirit 'Julia' was told to 'endeavour to be as useful as I could'.[100] Some cared for newly arrived spirits, or children. Far more were engaged in communicating with those on earth, in order that the living might understand the eternal importance of a good and noble life, or be comforted in bereavement. Indeed, as one critic of spiritualism pointed out, in years past people had contented themselves with the idea that their departed loved ones worshipped God, but now believed them to be busying themselves with the affairs of the world.[101] The higher spirits exercised themselves by teaching and encouraging those in the middle and lower spheres. Life beyond death was 'full of interest and occupation'.[102] There was 'nothing supine about the rest and joy they have entered'.[103] People developed interests in new areas of music, drama or science. The afterlife, as presented by the spirits, was not a place of passive faith; instead it was a life of earnest seeking after truth, work, prayer and duty, and both the living and the departed were advised to love and honour God and help brothers and sisters onward in the path of progress.

Alongside the busyness there was worship in the afterlife. However, the communicating spirits chose not to dwell on the nature of worship, or else they suggested that worship was an activity more fitting to the higher, rather than the middle-ranking, spirits. It took place, but it did not feature excessively in their accounts, and some spirits did not mention worship at all. George Vale Owen found that it was not his departed mother, communicating from the middle spheres, who shared details of spiritual worship with him, but a spirit called Zabdiel from a higher plane. Zabdiel spoke of angels in robes, heavenly music, gorgeous cathedral-like architecture and uplifting liturgy, but there was little indication that this was observed often by spirits in the middle or lower spheres, or even that they participated in it.[104]

Mabel Corelli Green told her mother of a 'beautiful' temple where lovely worship took place and the 'cherubs' sang, but it seemed to play only a minor

---

allowed a deathbed confession of faith to expiate a lifetime of wickedness. Moses, *Spirit Teachings*, 75.

[100] Stead, *After death*, 2.

[101] A criticism made in the *Literary World*, but reported in the *Medium and Daybreak*, 18 Aug. 1871.

[102] Doyle, *New Revelation*, 41.

[103] Lodge, *Raymond Revised*, 194.

[104] Owen, *Life beyond the Veil*, 2:27.

part in her life in the Summerland.[105] It was the higher spirits, the angelic beings, who had managed to leave behind earthly needs, who worshipped, being more heavenly minded and closer to God. Adin Ballou likewise placed the virtues of religious aspirations, worship, study, self-examination and contemplation only in the realms of the higher spheres.[106]

God was present in the afterlife, according to most spirits, although, interestingly, not all of them mentioned him. In some instances God was described as an all-pervading spirit or 'force' towards which the spirits climbed as they moved through the spheres;[107] in other cases God was the Supreme Spirit, or Father of the spirits, and distinct from their own progress.[108] The communicating spirits could speak of God made present in Christ walking among them, conversing with them and leaving 'his mark' on them.[109] Or else God was described as a sort of 'vibrating force' or 'magnetic ray' that offered strength to all of the spirits.[110] God was infinite spirit, all life, all love, all wisdom and all power. He was the centre of light and love.

A few further aspects of God's nature emerged. It was clear from the spirits' communications, for example, that God was considered to be loving and merciful. It was also emphasised that the God of the spiritualists did not punish unnecessarily. God's justice was reforming rather than retributive, and he was not to be understood as a being enthroned in heaven receiving the homage of the elect and torturing the lost.[111] Words such as 'fear' and 'dread' were not to be connected with God, who sought to be loving and endearing to all.[112]

Beyond these vague thoughts, however, being in the nearer presence of God did not enable the spirits to reveal much more about his nature to the bereaved and the curious at séances. Stainton Moses thought that this was because, although they understood more of his ways, no spirit would pretend to have seen God.[113] However, such a lack of information, and even lack of speculation from the inhabitants of the afterlife, is a little surprising, even assuming the integrity of the communications; and reveals either that the spirits thought it unnecessary to speak of God, assuming a common belief in his existence and common understanding of his nature, or else that there was a

---

[105] Green, *Life in the Summerland*, 14.
[107] Ballou, *Spirit Manifestations*, 57.
[106] Macfie, *From Heaven to Earth*, 31; Benson, *Spiritualism*, 9.
[108] Ballou, *Spirit Manifestations*, 53.
[109] Theobald, *Homes and Work*, 2: 59.
[110] Green, *Life in the Summerland*, 8, 14.
[111] Moses, *Spirit Teachings*, 54.
[112] Macfie, *From Heaven to Earth*, 27.
[113] Moses, *Higher Aspects of Spiritualism*, 82.

decidedly anthropocentric concern among the spirits of the dead. Or perhaps spiritualists were simply content to offer, as one critic put it, only 'a vague kind of Theism'.[114] Whichever was the case, God was, judging by the communications, strikingly unimportant to the life of middle-ranking spirits.

A few spiritualists were keen to make clear that the God of the Summerland, even if only vaguely described, was nevertheless the Christian God. The Christian spiritualist Thomas Shorter, for example, when offering a description of a séance, made it clear that prayer should begin the proceedings.[115] Adin Ballou attempted to maintain a Trinitarian theology, given that the divine being was manifested in history as Father, Son and Holy Ghost. Yet his description of Jesus of Nazareth as having been brought into the world with 'especial fitness' to receive the spirit of God 'in perfect purity and fullness' was a world away from the traditional Christian doctrine of the eternal co-existence of the Son with the Father.[116] As Viscount Halifax asked with regard to the Jesus of the spiritualists, 'Is such a record in any way consistent with what we believe of Him who is Very God of Very God, equal to the Father, and by Whom the world was made?'[117]

Indeed, Jesus proved problematic for spiritualists. In the first place, they struggled to suggest how he might be divine. He could be the highest and best of men, but fell somewhat short of divinity. The spiritualist and clergyman Fielding Fielding-Ould claimed that a number of spiritualists were Unitarian in their thinking about God. He himself argued that Jesus was divine, but then, rather demolishing his own argument, he went on to say that Christ's divinity was subordinate to that of God the Father.[118]

Some argued that those spirits who called him the Son of God did so because he was the one true great medium, who conversed not only with the departed spirits but also with the centre of the Godhead.[119] Yet still he was revered for his life's work, rather than his divinity. As the spirit communicating with Stainton Moses expressed it, 'no spirit more pure, more godlike, more noble, more blessing and more blessed, ever descended to your earth. None more worthily earned by a life of self-sacrificing love the adoring reverence and devotion of mankind.'[120]

114 Benson, *Spiritualism*, 9.
115 Shorter, *Confessions of a Truth Seeker*, xvi.
116 Ballou, *Spirit Manifestations*, 53.
117 Halifax, *'Raymond'. Some Criticisms*, 8.
118 His criticism of Unitarian spiritualists did not prevent him from sounding like a Unitarian himself, or even an Arian. Fielding-Ould, *Is spiritualism of the Devil?*, 68–9.
119 F. J. Theobald, *Spirit Messages relating to the nature of Christ's person* (London, 1884), 6.
120 Moses, *Spirit Teachings*, 90.

In the second place, they found his exclusivity difficult. Spiritualism suggested that *all* spirits were capable of progressing through the spheres towards God and reaching spiritual perfection. If Jesus, who had appeared on earth in human form, was unique in being at the heart of God's divine life, then this teaching was nullified. No spirit would ever reach perfection if that divine life was reserved for Jesus alone.

So, instead, Jesus was presented as the spiritualists' ideal. The *Christian Spiritualist* wrote in 1925 that Christ was the model for life, claiming that no finer human being accomplished a greater work in his lifetime.[121] Mrs Mabel St Clair Stobart thought that he was a spiritual example for others, who stood in a long line of spiritual teachers including Moses, Pythagoras, Socrates, Lao-Tzu, Mohammed, Swedenborg and Krishna.[122] Not all spiritualists agreed with this view. Robert Dale Owen, for example, thought that those who saw Jesus as only one of many great teachers in history would, ultimately, see the error of their thinking.[123] Yet the exclusivity taught by Christianity was, some claimed, even a cause of concern for Christ himself. Thus Stainton Moses said, 'We do not dishonour the Lord Jesus – before whose exalted majesty we bow – by refusing to acquiesce in a fiction [i.e. his divinity] which He would disown, and which man has forced upon his name.' Men had taken his name and turned it into a 'battleground for sects', a sight which he looked upon 'with sorrow and pity'.[124]

Additionally, the Christ of the creeds bore little resemblance to the Jesus revealed by the spirits. According to them he was more human and understandable in reality than Christian teaching had suggested.[125] Jesus' teaching had been, originally, essentially simple and this plain teaching was revealed to spirits in the afterlife. One spirit declared himself astonished at how the Church had distorted the simple teachings of Jesus over the centuries into complicated and unnecessary doctrines.[126] Another, asked by an enquirer about the divinity of Christ replied, 'Why do you trouble yourself with these scholasticisms?'[127]

In particular, spiritualists disliked the doctrine of atonement, the belief that the death of Jesus had, in some way, atoned for the sins of the world and opened the way to salvation for all believers. The doctrine of atonement was

---

[121] *Christian Spiritualist*, 5 Aug. 1925.
[122] M. St Clair Stobart, *The Either–Or of Spiritualism* (London, 1928), 193.
[123] Owen, *The Debatable Land*, 175.
[124] Moses, *Spirit Teachings*, 90.
[125] Doyle, *Full Report of a Lecture*, 9.
[126] Macfie, *From Heaven to Earth*, 11.
[127] Stead, *After death*, 48.

therefore dismissed and criticised. According to Arthur Conan Doyle, too much stress had been laid on Christ's death and not enough on his life and teachings. People did not understand such things as 'redemption from sin' and phrases like 'cleansed by the blood of the Lamb'; still less did they understand why they needed to believe in them.[128]

Where this 'distorted' Christianity had taught that those without belief were without salvation, being damned and lost, spiritualism taught instead that every soul had potential to rise up to the glory of God. The 'true grandeur' of the Christian faith and the 'true lessons' lay in the way that Christ came to earth to give an example of life, preaching 'easy tolerance for others, broad-minded moderation, gentle courage and annoyance with bigoted people'. There was no mention of atonement or redemption and his teaching was 'essentially simple' and offered an example for life.[129]

Spiritualists claimed that the true Christian faith was simple and pure. This meant that spiritualism was not a heterodox religion, they argued, but a pure and undistorted form of Christianity, and thus represented a return to an earlier primitive Christianity. Indeed, there was much to suggest that by removing the unnecessary doctrine of atonement, along with hell and the fear of death, spiritualism would encourage a revival in the religious life of the country.[130]

In summary, at its heart spiritualist teaching was simple: the progress of the soul, the love of God, the removal of the fear of death and the importance of good actions in life. This teaching had implications for the life on earth, as well as the afterlife. Far from advocating an uncritical universalism where, because all people received salvation in the next life, behaviour in this world mattered little, spiritualism stressed the importance of spiritual development in the present. The spirits taught that, although there was no hell and no eternal damnation, every individual entered the afterlife in the spiritual condition that they left the earth and progressed from that point. God did not judge them, but every action in life, for good or ill, had eternal consequences and sins would need to be dealt with. The higher the realm at entry, the less punishment and sorrow for sin was required and the more rapid the progress towards spiritual perfection. Thus in life each person was called to grow in spiritual knowledge and self-knowledge, to exercise a duty in culture and bodily purity, to live a life of charity, duty, progress, order and truth.[131] Prayer was believed to be important as a means of strengthening the inner spirit. Church attendance,

---

128 Doyle, *New Revelation*, 34.
129 Ibid., 34.
130 W. H. Evans, *Spiritualism. A Philosophy of Life* (Manchester, 1926).
131 Ibid., 85.

although not condemned, was only half-heartedly encouraged.[132] Instead, as we have seen, it was important to live a good, active and virtuous life in preparation for the life to come, to cultivate the habits and actions of a faithful life, rather than merely speak the words of a 'fitful faith'.[133] The progress of the spirit could begin in this life and did not need to be postponed until the next. A spirit advised, 'Live well in the world of clay, that ye may live happy in the world of spirits.'[134]

It was intimated, even by some of those who maintained their Christian faith as spiritualists, that those of other faiths found a place in the Summerland. Worship in the heavenly realms took place in different temples and people were free to worship God in their own way.[135] Spiritualism was a means of bringing vitality to all creeds while being inimical to none.[136] It proposed no separate Church and had no creed or ordained ministers. Instead, according to Robert Dale Owen,

> It spreads silently through the agency of daily intercourse, in the privacy of the domestic circle. It pervades, in one or other of its phases, the best literature of the day. It invades the Churches already established not as an opponent but as an ally. Its tendency is to modify the creed and soften the asperities of Protestant and Romanist, of Presbyterian and Episcopalian, of Baptist and Methodist, of Unitarian and Universalist. Its tendency is to leaven with invigorating and spiritualizing effect, the religious sentiment of the age, increasing its vitality, enlivening its convictions.[137]

Spiritualism had something to commend it to everyone: sensuous demonstrations at the séance, wisdom in spirit teachings and decisive evidence of the continued presence of the departed for those who suffered bereavement. In addition, according to its adherents, it communicated to people, in the flesh

> numberless affectionate and intelligent assurances of an immortal existence, messages of consolation and annunciations of distant

---

[132] No spirit suggested that church attendance was important for one's eternal destiny. McLaren Post Macfie said that people should go to church occasionally and take communion occasionally, but that it was better to look to the product of God's handiwork in nature, the sunshine and flowers and commune with God directly in the heart. Macfie, *From Heaven to Earth*, 27.

[133] Moses, *Spirit Teachings*, 160.

[134] *Yorkshire Spiritual Telegraph*, May 1855.

[135] Owen, *Life beyond the Veil*, 2: 117.

[136] Charles Maurice Davies, *Unorthodox London, or, phases of religious life in the Metropolis*, 2nd edn (London, 1874: 1st pubd 1873), 303.

[137] Owen, *Debatable Land*, 175–6.

events unknown at the time, but subsequently corroborated; predictions of forthcoming occurrences subsequently verified, forewarnings against impending danger, medicinal prescriptions of great efficacy, wholesome reproofs, admonitions and counsels, expositions of spiritual, theological, religious, moral and philosophical truths appertaining to human welfare in every sphere of existence, sometimes comprised in a single sentence, and sometimes in an ample book.[138]

Antecedents of spiritualism

As was observed in chapter two, modern spiritualism, with its phenomena and séance paraphernalia, did not appear out of thin air; neither did the theology of spiritualism. Although spiritualists claimed that what they learned about the afterlife had been taught to them by the spirits of the dead, spiritualist theology had antecedents. Occasionally these antecedents were acknowledged and even revered, especially by those who consciously sought to place spiritualism within the wider context of Christian history. More often, spiritualists remained quiet about roots of the teaching, not least because they claimed simply to have received it from the spirits. The advocates of spiritualism, especially those writing in the later part of the period, were far more likely to emphasise its presence in the Bible,[139] the plausibility of the physical phenomena and the names of eminent people who were already associated with it.[140] Other influences were not openly acknowledged and sometimes have to be deduced.

Earlier spiritualist writers were comfortable enough noting the precursors of the physical aspects of séance phenomena. Unusual phenomena in history were, they claimed, messengers of the spiritual outpouring of modern spiritualism to come. Tracing the history of spirit manifestations across the world in the nineteenth century, Emma Hardinge Britten noted that 'the wonderful preaching epidemic in Sweden, the obsessions in Morzine, the uprising of Mormonism, Shakerism, the gift of tongues amongst the Irvingites and the great revivals in Ireland are all unmistakable fruits of the same mighty

---

138 Ballou, *Spirit Manifestations*, 11–12.
139 For example G. R. Dennis, *The Quest of the Unseen. Spiritualism in the Light of Christianity* (London, 1920), 27–9. Dennis argued that St Paul placed mediumship among the list of spiritual gifts and that Jesus' conversations with Moses and Elijah at the Transfiguration were conclusive proof of the biblical sanction for spiritualism.
140 Conan Doyle was impressed by the spiritualism of the eminent scientist Alfred Russel Wallace and the numbers of clergy sympathetic to spiritualism. See Doyle, *New Revelation*, 13; *Our Reply to the Cleric*, 7.

contagion of spiritual forces, surging through an age specially prepared for their reception'.[141] To modern readers the connection between spiritualism and some of these other eccentric spirit manifestations may seem unflattering. Indeed, the association between spiritualism and religious mania in Sweden in 1841, accusations of demon possession and miraculous healing in 1850s France, and the strange behaviour of 'Mother' Ann Lee and her Shaker followers was something that later, more reserved spiritualist writers, like Conan Doyle and Stainton Moses, tried to avoid.[142] Yet Britten saw in these strange occurrences something of the fervour and excitement she noted as present in her experiences of modern spiritualism around Britain and in America.

Writing at a time when perhaps he was feeling persecuted himself, the medium Daniel Douglas Home found connections between the physical manifestations of spiritualism and the spiritual gifts of those condemned or persecuted as heretics by the Church. He recognised those with spiritual gifts, like Joan of Arc. He also noted the fifteenth-century Italian Dominican Giralmo Savonarola, who preached against the excesses of the Church, and the Waldensians, a group committed to preaching the simple teaching of Jesus and living a life of poverty in the twelfth and thirteenth centuries.[143] Home also found spiritualism present in the lives of John Wesley and Emanuel Swedenborg, as well as Zoroastrians, Brahmins and figures in the Old Testament.

On other occasions spiritualist writers found precursors to the physical phenomena of the séance in accounts of the miraculous and unexplained. In 1863 William Howitt, for example, in *The History of the Supernatural in all ages and nations*, offered a comprehensive two-volume account of miraculous events from the beginning of time in the Bible, Greek and Roman literature, and the stories of Ancient Egypt. From the more recent past he cited, as has been noted, 'knockings' at Rushton Hall near Kettering in 1584, 'drumming' and knocks at Mr Mompesson's house in Tedworth in 1601 and the familiar account of 'knocking' at Wesley's Epworth parsonage in 1716.[144]

The strange occurrences at the Epworth parsonage (where a rapping sound

---

[141] Britten, *Nineteenth Century Miracles*, 91.
[142] Moses despaired that spiritualism was so often 'silly' when presented by its own enthusiasts. *Higher Aspects of Spiritualism*, 4; Conan Doyle encouraged people to look beyond the flying furniture of the séance. *Full Report of a Lecture*, 4.
[143] D. D. Home, *Lights and Shadows of Spiritualism* (London, 1877), 113–26. At the time of this book's publication Home had been retired for five years. *Lights and Shadows* contained harsh condemnations of many of his fellow mediums and exposures of their fraudulence.
[144] Howitt, *History of the Supernatural*, 2: 172–200.

imitated the knock at the gate of John Wesley's father and responded to the word 'Amen') provided the advocates of spiritualism with perhaps one of their most reliable and orthodox forerunners. Offered by Emma Hardinge Britten, William Howitt and Robert Dale Owen as both an indication and confirmation of the 'rapping' phenomenon to come with modern spiritualism, the story of Epworth parsonage also appeared on the cover of the first edition of the spiritualist newspaper the *Spiritualist* in 1869. The newspaper thus attempted to establish its credentials as a serious religious newspaper by making a connection between a well-known example of unexplained phenomena occurring in the home of someone of unimpeachable religious character and the new unexplained phenomena of spiritualism.

The early spiritualist writers saw precedents for the spiritual manifestations of the séance in the unexplained, the miraculous and the unusual incidents of the distant and recent past. They were less likely to identify theological ante-cedents for spirit teachings, but if they did they tended to look towards Emanuel Swedenborg.

Emanuel Swedenborg (1688–1772) was born the son of a Swedish Lutheran bishop. In the early part of his life he was a talented scientist, engineer and mathematician, but by the time he reached his late fifties he had become increasingly drawn by spiritual and religious matters. In London between 1749 and 1756 he published a series of eight volumes entitled *Arcana Caelestia* (Secrets of Heaven), which he claimed came from teaching he had received as he visited the afterlife. He gave a systematic account of his theology in *De Nova Hierosolymae et Ejus Doctrina Caelestia* (The New Jerusalem and its Heavenly Doctrine) in 1758 and in the same year he published his most famous work, *De Caelo et Ejus Mirabilibus et de Inferno* (Heaven and its Wonders and Hell).[145]

Swedenborg did not enjoy recognition for his religious works in his own lifetime and the New Jerusalem Church, based on his teachings, that was founded after his death never managed to be anything other than small and obscure. He became more fashionable with the rise of modern spiritualism in the 1850s.[146] His life and teachings excited some spiritualists and he was held

---

[145] Biographical and bibliographical details can be found in Emanuel Swedenborg, *The New Jerusalem*, transl. John Chadwick (London, 1990); Arthur Edward Waite (et al.), *Three Famous Mystics* (London, 1939); and Colleen McDannell and Bernhard Lang, *Heaven. A History* (New Haven, 1988), 181–5. For the best assessment of Swedenborg's ideas of the afterlife, see Bernhard Lang, 'Glimpses of heaven in the age of Swedenborg' in E. J. Brock (ed.), *Swedenborg and his influence* (Bryn Athyn, Pa, 1988), 309–38.
[146] Members of the Swedenborgian New Jerusalem Church wanted little to do with

up as a forerunner of spiritualism by, for example, Robert Dale Owen and by one of spiritualism's critics, Joseph McCabe.[147] This was principally because he received visions of the afterlife while still awake, and spiritualists thought that this was similar to what happened to trance mediums.

Much, although not all, of what Swedenborg revealed as a result of his visions corresponded with the teachings of the spirits about the nature of the afterlife, according to spiritualism. So, for example, he claimed that there was only a thin veil between the earthly and heavenly realm, and that at death a person went straight to the afterlife – there was no sleeping or waiting for judgement and no rupture between life and death.[148] He taught that the after-life was a place of love and reunion, where the spirits actively engaged in work and did not stand around in passive adoration of God.[149] Little children who died were cared for by angel women who had loved children in the earthly life.[150]

In addition, and most controversially for his time, he claimed that God did not judge the individual; each person decided where he or she spent eternity by their response made to divine instruction.[151] In the next life each person found themselves alongside people of a similar spiritual character, but there was also the possibility of movement upward towards perfection and towards God by virtue of spiritual development and education.[152] Heaven for Sweden-borg was, as it was for spiritualists, a sensual and beautiful place where society was ordered on similar lines to that of earth[153] and where the outward aspect of a person reflected their inward spiritual nature. This nature was revealed gradually from the moment of death as the interior life of each indi-vidual was revealed for what it truly was.

Where Swedenborg differed from the spiritualists was in his insistence on the presence of a hell in the afterlife, from which no one could escape. According to his visions, those who loved only themselves and who had no

---

spiritualists, however, believing that the phenomena of séances debased the visions of their founder. See Davies, *Unorthodox London*, 166–74. Also *Medium and Daybreak* 15 Apr. 1870 for a spiritualist response to the criticism of Swedenborgians.

[147] Owen, *Debatable Land*, 123–6; McCabe, *Spiritualism*, 13.

[148] Swedenborg, *Heaven and its wonders, and Hell from things we have seen* (London, 1937. 1st pubd 1758), 46:447. [Swedenborg's works are divided into chapters and verses, so that text can be found whichever translation is being used]

[149] Swedenborg claimed that spiritual employment was either ecclesiastical, civil or domestic and that the Kingdom of Heaven was a 'kingdom of uses'. Swedenborg, Ibid., 41: 387.

[150] Ibid., 37: 332.

[151] Ibid., 57: 545.

[152] Ibid., 6: 44; 17: 158.

[153] Ibid., 42: 396, 402.

potential for spiritual growth were consigned to hell, a place of fire, which Swedenborg identified as the fire of self-love. In this presentation of the after-life there were three 'layers': an immediate place of instruction, a heaven and a hell. Only those in the place of instruction could move towards perfection and heaven; those who found themselves in hell remained there for eternity.

There were few other theological references made in spiritualist teaching. Robert Dale Owen claimed that Joseph Butler's *Analogy of Religion, Natural and Revealed* (1736) presented life as perpetual progress through experience.[154] One critic saw the visions of the sixteenth-century German mystical writer and shoemaker Jacob Boehme in spiritualism, although Boehme's vision of heaven was quite distinct from the visions offered in spiritualism.[155]

Beyond this, however, most spiritualists relied on presenting the theology as purely and simply what the spirits of the dead had revealed to them. There were credible theological connections that they ignored. The early Christian writer Origen (c. 185–c. 254), for example, had taught that the punishment of the wicked was not eternal and that all things would be restored to God.[156] Gregory of Nyssa (d.394) similarly envisaged the eventual purification of the wicked.[157] And Catherine of Genoa (1447–1510), in her treatise on purgatory, argued that this was a place where souls were made fit for the presence of God.[158] It was perfectly possible for spiritualists to look back into the history of the Church and find connections between established Christian teaching and the musings of the spirits, but they chose not to do so. By contrast, Frederic Farrar, canon of Westminster Abbey, preached a controversial series of sermons in 1877 arguing that God's mercy extended beyond the grave and repudiating the traditional imagery of hell. Without hesitation he drew on Early Church Fathers, such as Athanasius, Jerome, Irenaeus, Origen and Gregory of Nyssa, to support his teaching.[159]

---

154 Robert Dale Owen claimed that Butler's *Analogy* preceded spiritualist teaching on the possibility of progress after death; *Debatable Land*, 123–6. See also Henry Scott Holland, *The Optimism of Butler's 'Analogy'* (Oxford, 1908).
155 This was the view of Dr Thornton expressed in the Church Congress of 1881 at Newcastle. See also John Joseph Stout, *Sunrise to Eternity. A study in Jacob Boehme's Life and Thought* (Philadelphia, 1957).
156 For an explanation of Origen's teaching on restoration, see the classic, and still standard, text, J. N. D. Kelly, *Early Christian Doctrines*, 5th edn (London, 1977. 1st pubd 1958), 473–4.
157 Ibid., 483.
158 'J. M. A.' [John Marks Ashley], *The Treatise of S. Catherine of Genoa on Purgatory newly translated* (London, 1878).
159 F. W. Farrar, *Eternal Hope. Five Sermons preached in Westminster Abbey, November and December 1877* (London, 1892. 1st pubd 1878), 84–5. Farrar became dean of Canterbury in 1895.

Spiritualists did not make the connections between their teaching and the teachings of the great saints of the Church. Given the concern that some of them had to ensure that spiritualism was taken seriously by people of faith, this was most likely a conscious decision, although, it must be said, not an 'openly' articulated decision. Gradually, and with increasing confidence, they interpreted the Bible in a spiritualist manner and located the teachings of the spirits in the texts of the scriptures. This work was done, in particular, by clergymen who were also spiritualists, who sought to make clear that spiritualism was contributing something of significance to Christianity.

Spiritualism did not, though, fit neatly into any existing Church tradition. It was not explicitly Anglican, nor, indeed, was it always explicitly Christian. Having no clear organisational structure, no written creed or articles of faith and no appointed 'experts' meant that the teachings of spiritualism could be adopted and used by anyone, from any background or opinion. Some Anglican clergy found themselves drawn to it – for different reasons.

In order to understand more fully the reasons why some Anglicans became spiritualists, and how the images and ideas of spiritualism were drawn into the Church of England's teaching about the afterlife, it is important now to focus attention on the Church itself. Spiritualists were fond of characterising orthodox Christian teaching as presenting a static afterlife: the eternal destiny of an individual was fixed at death. The 'traditional' afterlife was lacking in love and possibility of progress; it was full of fear, judgement and the imagery of hell. This was a caricature, and it was probably employed because it suited some spiritualists to portray the Church in such a dismal light. In reality, of course, the Church's teaching was much more layered and complex.

5

The Church of England and the departed
c. 1850–1900

The teaching of communicating spirits was, according to convinced spiritual-ists, strikingly different from what they characterised as the 'traditional' teaching of the 'orthodox' Churches. Whereas spiritualism offered a vision of the afterlife as a place of beauty, love and peace, the Churches, it was claimed, taught people about a 'fearful place' beyond the grave.[1] Death, argued spiritu-alists, according to this 'traditional' teaching, was followed by a period of 'slumbering'[2] before human beings rose from their tombs for the final day of judgement, after which those deemed unfit for heaven were punished and tormented for all eternity in a place of 'unmitigated misery'.[3] Divine judge-ment of an individual was made purely on the evidence of the earthly life; and, even though judgement day was at an indeterminate point in the future, an individual's eternal state was fixed at point of death, with the result that some left the world irrevocably damned and finally lost.

In the spiritualists' presentation of 'traditional' teaching, God was a Being 'enthroned on high where he receives the homage of the elect and enjoys the torture of the lost'.[4] The chief tormentor of the lost souls, the Devil, appeared to be more powerful than God.[5] God himself was rendered even more monstrous, according to spiritualists, by the 'crude' doctrine of atonement, whereby the salvation of a 'sin-stained' humanity was purchased by the sacri-fice of Christ on the cross, offered to an 'angry God':

> You have been taught in the creeds of the orthodox churches to believe in a God who was propitiated by the sacrifice of his Son, so far

---

1 *Spiritualist*, 31 Dec. 1869.
2 Owen, *Footfalls on the boundary*, 352.
3 Ballou, *Spirit Manifestations*, 55.
4 Moses, *Spirit Teachings*, 54.
5 *Lyceum Banner*, Nov. 1890, preface.

as to allow a favoured few of His children to be admitted into an imagined heaven, where for ever and ever more, with monotonous persis-
tence, their occupation should be singing His praise. The rest of the
race, unable to gain admission to this heaven, were consigned to a hell
of indescribable torment, perpetual, endless and intolerable.[6]

Spiritualists were particularly scathing about what they characterised as the
defining element of this orthodox teaching: that an individual could only be
saved for eternity by believing in Christ's atonement. This made Christ's
atonement merely 'a store of merit laid up by the death of this incarnate God
on which the vilest reprobate may draw at his death, and gain access to the
society of God and the perfected'[7] – which seemed to spiritualists both wrong
and unfair:

> The idea of an unutterable and unalterable state of eternal bliss or
> eternal woe is what we have been taught in the churches; such eternal
> and unalterable condition being determined by an act of faith. This
> hath very naturally led men to believe that they could accomplish their
> salvation in a few hours, sometime before they departed this life. Such
> false teaching makes virtue appear like an useless ornament.[8]

Of course, it suited spiritualists to caricature the Churches' teaching as
harsh, judgmental, violent, unfair and therefore unattractive. By contrast, they
taught that the afterlife was gentle and beautiful; it included the possibility of
spiritual progress, and excluded eternal torment. Such caricaturing of
orthodox traditions was nothing new; like reformers, radicals and liberalisers
before them, they took swipes at 'orthodox' teaching and made this part of the
presentation of their own alternative.

In criticising the teaching of the *Churches*, spiritualists did not criticise
Church of England teaching specifically, but the teaching of all 'orthodox'
Churches. This meant that they could include in their attack, for example,
imagery such as that in the work of a Roman Catholic priest, rather appropri-
ately named Father Furniss, whose books were influential beyond the Roman
Catholic Church. His book for children, *The Sight of Hell* (1861), included
smoke, fire, darkness, torment and even the 'dreadful sickening smell' of
death.[9] The 'sinners' tormented in hell were not excessively wicked people,
but ordinary adults and children. One story told of a young girl living in hell

---

6 Moses, *Spirit Teachings*, 75.
7 Moses, *Higher Aspects of Spiritualism*, 104.
8 *Yorkshire Spiritual Telegraph*, Mar. 1856.
9 J. Furniss, *The Sight of Hell* (London, 1861), 9.

wearing a dress and bonnet of fire, condemned because, in life, she had gone to the park to show off her new clothes rather than attend church. There was a man buried in a narrow burning coffin because he had loved money, and a girl condemned to walk over a hot floor for eternity, who in life had kept bad company, against the wishes of her parents.[10]

Furniss claimed that the punishments lasted for the duration of eternity. In answer to the question of exactly how long eternity lasted, he gave the following response:

> Think of a great solid iron ball, larger than the heavens and the earth. A bird comes once in a hundred millions of years and just touches the great iron ball with a feather of its wing. Think you that you have to burn in fire until the bird has worn away the great iron ball with its feathers? Is this eternity? No ... How long then will the punishment of sinners go on? For ever, and ever, and ever![11]

From a different Church tradition, the popular Baptist preacher and writer Charles Spurgeon (1834–92) offered a poem to illustrate, as Furniss had in his stories, both the terrifying nature of hell and the dreadful length of its duration:

> 'Forever' is written on their racks
> 'Forever' on their chains
> 'Forever' burneth in the fire
> 'Forever' reigns.[12]

The question remains as to how accurate the spiritualists' caricature was when applied specifically to the Church of England's teaching about the after-life. Although rather crude, it was not without substance. An examination of the theological debates which took place in the second half of the nineteenth century reveals a slow but significant movement away from what the Church had, itself, widely understood as 'traditional' teaching. But academic theological debates provide only part of the story; in liturgy, sermons and hymnody – those aspects of the Church of England with which ordinary people had more contact – the language and imagery remained set within a traditional framework.

---

[10] Ibid., 17–20.
[11] Ibid., 24.
[12] In Joseph Bland, *The Keys of Hell: Who holds them, and why, and when will they be used?* (Birmingham, 1884), 20.

Theological and legal debates

Christian theologians inevitably begin by turning to the Bible as the foundation for their work. The New Testament, in particular, offers a pattern for the nature of the afterlife: the moment of death is followed by a period of sleep until a final resurrection. The Bible is unclear and imprecise, however, about exactly how and when these stages happen, and so three broad interpretations have developed over the centuries.

The first of these posited a conscious and active intermediate state between death and final resurrection. Rooted in St Paul's words that the dead were 'at home' with the Lord,[13] this account envisaged the dead as actively waiting together for the return of Christ at his Second Coming, rather than simply sleeping. By the late second century, with Christ having not returned, this had become instead a period of purification, rather than mere waiting. In 1336, however, Pope Benedict XII, in his Bull *Benedictus Deus* declared that those who had no need of purification entered directly into heavenly bliss. No longer was the whole of creation, living and departed, waiting for the Coming of Christ, being purified in the meantime; instead, the afterlife had become individualistic and each soul was separately on its journey towards heaven. The prayers of the faithful helped; meaning some souls reached heaven sooner than others.

The more specific idea of 'purgatory' was confirmed as doctrine by the Roman Catholic Church at the councils of Lyons (1274), Florence (1439) and Trent (1545–63), although the nature and duration of the purgatorial process were never defined. The roots of the medieval doctrine of purgatory lay in the teaching of St Augustine (d. 430), who taught that an individual was judged by God at death and, the eternal fate being fixed, made to endure purifying pain for a time. St Thomas Aquinas (d. 1274) added that after death, even for those judged ultimately worthy of heaven, there was punishment for small sins, a punishment which was, nevertheless, greater than the greatest pain on earth. The prayers of the living no longer simply helped the souls on their way to heaven, but were also thought to assuage their purgatorial punishments.

During the sixteenth century the Protestant reformers challenged the idea that the soul was purged and aided by prayer in the intermediate state. They argued that if individuals were saved from sin by the death of Christ, then it was faith in Christ alone, rather than the prayers of the living, that made a person fit for heaven. Taking another strand in St Paul's teaching, namely that

---

[13] II Corinthians v. 6–7; Philippians i. 21.

the dead were 'woken up' only at the final resurrection, Martin Luther (d. 1546) taught that in the intervening time between death and resurrection the soul slept.[14] Instead of being active, the soul was passive; it did nothing because there was nothing to be done. The eternal state was already fixed, the soul had been judged, and so it slept until the last day and awoke to the sound of a trumpet. This period, although of indeterminate duration, would appear as only a brief moment to the soul, but the soul was definitely asleep. John Calvin (d. 1564) suggested in the *Psychopannychia* (1542) that the soul, although resting, was conscious.[15] Placed in either heaven or hell, the soul was thus aware of the bliss or the horror that would eventually come, although still unable to alter its destiny.

The theological systems that developed after the deaths of these two reformers, Lutheranism and Calvinism, shaped much of what the spiritualists characterised as 'traditional' teaching. Lutheranism insisted that salvation was found 'sola fide' (through faith alone).[16] Calvinism, especially in its stricter form, placed strong emphasis on the omnipotence of God, and on absolute predestination: God willed the bliss of the righteous, but also the punishment of the damned. God even predestined the sin that led to the damnation of the individual.[17] Thus 'traditional' Protestant teaching about the afterlife suggested that it was a confessed faith in the earthly life alone that led to ultimate salvation, and that God's judgement was irrevocable.

The third, and most widely held, understanding of what happened after death was rooted in Jewish apocalyptic tradition, rather than New Testament writing. At death the individual soul was judged and sent immediately to its eternal place in either hell or heaven. The language of 'sleep', in this instance, served as a metaphor for death. There was no intermediate state: at the point of death the individual stepped out of earthly time and into an eternity of either bliss or hell.[18]

The Early Church teaching had envisaged all departed souls awaiting

---

[14] I Corinthians xv. 52. For a good explanation of Luther's eschatology, see Bernhard Lohse (transl. Roy Harrisville), *Martin Luther's Theology. Its history and systematic development* (Edinburgh, 1999), 325–9.

[15] Calvin argued that the soul was immortal; it was aware of its state after death. See T. H. Parker, *Calvin. An introduction to his thought* (London, 1995), 122–6.

[16] As Luther himself had done. See Alister McGrath, *Luther's theology of the cross. Martin Luther's theological breakthrough* (Oxford, 1985), 174.

[17] For an explanation of 'double predestination', see Alister McGrath, *A Life of John Calvin. A study in the shaping of Western Culture* (Oxford, 1990), 208–18.

[18] For an account of this third strand of thinking, see Christopher Cocksworth, *Prayer and the Departed* (Cambridge, 1997), 12.

judgement for an unspecified period; judgement did not take place at death. From the Middle Ages onwards death became the point of judgement, and the judgement fixed the eternal state of the individual. What was then disputed was what happened to the individual in the intervening period between death and resurrection: a mitigated hell, or painful purification, unconscious sleep, or conscious awareness of what was to come? Or else, the soul was immediately relocated to heaven or hell following judgement at death, in which case there was no possibility of purgatory or any post-mortem spiritual change.

By the mid nineteenth century these distinct strands of thought had converged, leading some to criticise what they saw as confusion in the teaching of the Church. Thus the spiritualist Robert Dale Owen, writing in 1860 and quoting the (London) *National Review*, claimed that most people believed that the spirit did not rest in the grave, but passed immediately at death to a new condition of being. The Church of England was by contrast, he thought, confused:

> The opinion has gained adherents and disputes the ground with the more material one, that it [the spirit] rests in sleep with the body, to await one common day of awakening and judgement; and so confused are the common impressions of the subject that you may hear a clergyman, in his funeral sermon, deliberately give the impression to both in one discourse, and telling you in the same breath that my lady lately deceased is a patient inhabitant of the tomb, and a member of the angelic company.[19]

Elsewhere theologians, as well as ordinary clergymen, were criticised as being 'vague' regarding the future life. The positivist writer Frederic Harrison, contributing to the *Nineteenth Century* in 1877 said, 'They know that their own account of the Soul, of the spiritual life, of Providence, of Heaven, is daily shifting, growing more vague, more inconsistent, more various.'[20]

Perhaps part of the 'vagueness' and 'shifting' lay in the fact that theologians were simply reflecting the different strands of teaching represented above. The impression was held, though, that clergy of the Church of England had, at some point in the past, been clearer in which strand of teaching was favoured. Philip Almond has observed that at the Reformation the Church of England widely adopted the Calvinist idea of the soul waiting in a static but

---

[19] Owen, *Footfalls on the boundary*, 10.
[20] *Nineteenth Century*, Vol. I (1877), 833.

conscious state after death.[21] By the seventeenth century, however, teaching about this 'static' state was being questioned largely, although not entirely, from outside the Church of England. Cambridge Platonists, such as the independent minister Peter Sterry (1613–72), began to explore the possibility of post-mortem repentance.[22] The nonconformist Jeremiah White (1629–1707), influenced by Sterry, noted that in the biblical story of Dives and Lazarus, Dives began to show remorse and concern for his brothers, thus suggesting the possibility of change and repentance after death.[23] In the eighteenth century Unitarians such as David Hartley (1705–57), Joseph Priestley (1733–1804) and Thomas Belsham (1750–1829) questioned the idea that a God of love could create depraved human beings and then condemn them to a predestined eternal torment. Post-mortem punishment was necessary, they thought, but it was reformatory, rather than retributive, and allowed for the possibility of repentance and, ultimately, salvation. Such opinions influenced some in the Church of England, meaning that the 'traditional', or Calvinist, teaching was increasingly challenged, although, importantly, not publicly.[24]

The first significant *public* criticism of the Church of England's 'traditional' understanding of the afterlife in the mid nineteenth century came from Frederick Denison Maurice (1805–72), an Anglican clergyman with a Unitarian father. Maurice not only questioned the traditional idea of hell, but he also acknowledged the fear generated through the Church's doctrine of the atonement, the nature of eternity and the necessity of the eternal torment of the wicked. In doing so, he also offered an insight into the 'traditional' understanding of the afterlife that was criticised by spiritualists and others.

In 1853 Maurice, professor of theology at King's College London, published his collection of *Theological Essays*. In his essay 'Atonement' he argued that some teachings, common to Roman Catholics and Protestants, were an 'outrage' to the conscience. One such was the doctrine of penal substitution, whereby God the Father, demanding a penalty for human sin, laid the guilt of all upon Christ, who became the 'substitute' for human beings. This generated, he argued, a 'fearful amount of insincere belief' and,

---

21 Philip Almond, *Heaven and Hell in Enlightenment England* (Cambridge, 1994), 38.
22 Ibid., 74.
23 D. P. Walker, *The Decline of Hell. Seventeenth Century Discussions of Eternal Torment* (London, 1964), 113.
24 Leading Geoffrey Rowell to conclude that by the end of the century Unitarianism was waning because the 'liberalism of its theology, if not the detail of its arguments, had become the property of almost all the major denominations'. For Rowell's account of the influence of Unitarianism, see *Hell and the Victorians*, 33–61.

more crucially for Maurice, it came not from any Christian creed or revelation, but from a 'theology of consciousness' which modern enlightenment thinking had substituted for the Bible. The problem was that belief in the doctrine of atonement had become a test of faith. It had become a means of consigning the unbelievers to doom and thus it had generated fear of torment, when the very point of it, argued Maurice, had been to assure human beings that they, in Christ, had been reconciled to God, despite their sin.[25]

In his essay 'The Judgement Day', he noted that judgement was, according to traditional opinion, an event in the distant future. The vivid imagery associated with judgement was, he thought, used to terrify people into moral behaviour in their earthly life. However, he countered that, 'if the popular notion on this subject is thought necessary to produce terror in the minds of thieves and vagabonds, I own that I am ideal enough to think that the constabulary force is a more useful, effectual, and also a more godly instrument'.[26]

In contrast to a judgement day taking place some time in the future, Maurice argued that, because for the Christian Christ was ever present, then the Christian lived every day in a constant state of judgement. 'It is impossible, without violating the law of my being ... that I should separate myself from Christ ... wherever I am, whatever I am doing, he must be there.'[27] Christ had become connected with human beings at the Incarnation and was present as saviour and judge at all times, and not just at some indeterminate moment beyond death.

In his essay 'Eternal Life and Eternal Death', he challenged the prevailing definition of eternity, arguing that it was a qualitative description of God, rather than a noun of duration. Why, he asked, did people say of eternal punishment that it was without end, when the word 'eternal' used of God meant without beginning as well as without end?[28] Eternal life, promised to the saved, could not be 'a mere future prize'.[29]

The prevailing notion that eternity was connected with future duration was again, he argued, a product of enlightenment thinking rather than Christian teaching. The Fathers of the Early Church had understood eternity to be an attribute of God, and eternal life to mean true knowledge of God. Eternal death had been, in early Christian thought, the loss of that knowledge of God, rather than endless punishment. The influence of the philosopher John Locke (1632–1704), among others, had meant that teaching that had been complex

---

[25] F. D. Maurice, Theological Essays (London, 1957. 1st pubd 1853), 113.
[26] Ibid., 217.
[27] Ibid., 207.
[28] Ibid., 304–5.
[29] Ibid., 309.

or inexplicable had been cast aside in favour of something more simplistic. The result was that 'eternity' had come to mean 'everlasting'.[30]

Maurice contended that the Church needed to recover what he understood as the true sense of 'eternal life'. Eternal life was knowledge of God and eternal death was the loss of that knowledge. As such, eternal life and eternal death could be understood and experienced in the present, and not just as rewards or punishments in the future.[31] If eternal life was only a state in the future then it was robbed of its reality and power for the present.

Controversially, in 'The Resurrection of the Son of God from Death', he suggested that beyond death it was possible for an individual to progress. Citing Bishop Joseph Butler's *Analogy of Religion* (1736) as his authority, he claimed that death 'does not change the substance of the human creature, or any of its powers or moral conditions, but only removes that which had crushed its substance, checked the exercise of its powers, kept its moral conditions out of sight'.[32] Death could not be, he thought, the climax of a human life beyond which no growth could occur. Death, rather, removed the obstacles and offered 'perpetual growth in the knowledge of God and in the power of serving him'.[33]

Maurice was criticised for his essays from various quarters and was subsequently dismissed from King's. The college council considered that his words regarding the future punishment of the wicked and day of judgement were 'of dangerous tendency', and calculated to 'unsettle the minds' of King's students.[34] He was charged by Richard William Jelf, the principal of King's, with throwing 'an atmosphere of doubt' over the word 'eternal', and of conveying a general notion of ultimate salvation for all.[35] The second charge Maurice strenuously denied. Universalists, he argued, understood time and duration in the same manner as did those who clung to the prevailing tradition. They simply believed that after a particular period of time, the punishment of the wicked would stop and all would be restored to God. By contrast, Maurice understood punishment to be an individual's decision to remove him- or herself away from the love of God. 'I have desired, and hope always to desire

---

[30] Ibid., 316.
[31] Ibid., 323.
[32] Ibid., 137.
[33] Ibid., 137.
[34] Frederick Maurice, *The life of Frederick Denison Maurice chiefly told in his own letters. In two volumes*, 2nd edn (London, 1884), 2: 191.
[35] F. D. Maurice, *The Word 'Eternal' and the Punishment of the Wicked. A Letter to the Rev. Dr. Jelf, Canon of Christ Church and Principal of King's College* (Cambridge, London printed, 1853), 4.

for myself and for all men, that we may never cease to be punished by God till we cease to punish ourselves by rebelling against him.'[36] Yet despite recognising that some may, through their own rebellion against God, be separated from him, he stressed the idea that an individual continued in spiritual growth beyond death, allowing for the possibility of repentance and restoration.

Charged with casting doubt over the word 'eternal' Maurice took the opportunity to develop his thinking further. He examined the Greek word for eternal, 'αἰώνιος', and the different translations that had been made of it. The root of the word, αἰών, meant, he claimed, a period of time that was circular, rather than linear; it had a sense of completion; it meant yesterday, today and tomorrow. With this sense of completion about it, it raised human beings out of ordinary notions of time as linear duration. The Saxon translation ('everlasting') was inferior; it could not convey what the word meant.[37] St Athanasius, the upholder of orthodoxy against Arianism in the fourth century, had used αἰώνιος to describe the eternal generation of God the Son, so to translate that word simply as 'everlasting' or 'endless' was, Maurice thought, to miss the sense of the quality of eternity as a living principle.[38] From the New Testament, he pointed out that the words of the First Epistle of John concerning eternity maintained a sense of the present (Christ *was abiding* in men, this *is* eternal life, eternal life *was manifest*) rather than the future.[39] Along with his contention that post-mortem repentance was possible, it was this re-assessment of the word 'eternal' that was taken up by later theologians.

Maurice's work, and the controversy that it raised, was important for three reasons. In the first place, Maurice, an academic and clergyman, criticised the Church of England's teaching about the afterlife. His representation of this teaching, although less crude, was not unlike that of the spiritualists, which suggests that their caricature was at least partially accurate. Maurice criticised Church teaching as overly wedded to a doctrine of penal substitution. He characterised this teaching as guaranteed to inculcate a sense of fear of future torment, rather than faith. He claimed that the Church taught that the terrible judgement day was in the distant future, but that in the meantime, beyond death there was no possibility of repentance, change and forgiveness.

Secondly, Maurice's work challenged two 'traditional' ideas about the afterlife: that it was static and that eternal life was a reward in the future. Maurice suggested instead that the afterlife was dynamic, with the possibility

36 Ibid., 19.
37 Ibid., 4–5.
38 Ibid., 9.
39 Ibid., 11.

of spiritual growth and ultimate salvation. His detailed analysis of the word αἰώνιος encouraged people to think about the afterlife in terms of quality rather than duration, and eternal life as the soul's state in the present rather than simply a future reward. Thirdly, although his essays were unlikely to be read by many beyond academic circles, Maurice, an ordained clergyman and professor, made his criticisms of the Church's teaching in public and brought a theological controversy into the arena of common culture. The newspapers, according to his son, 'teemed with articles on the subject of "King's College and Mr. Maurice" ',[40] and a supportive letter to Maurice from F. J. Furnivall told of how in Oxford 'thousands' were taking a deep interest in his book.[41]

Maurice was not the only clergyman who was criticised for rethinking traditional ideas in public. In 1862 the Court of the Arches suspended Henry Wilson (1803–88) from his living for a year for his contribution to the theologically liberal *Essays and Reviews* (1860). In his essay Wilson, a Broad Churchman, had, as well as advocating an historical and critical approach to scripture, declared his hope that beyond death there would be possibility for individuals to continue to develop spiritually. He was concerned less for those already 'ripe' for entering a 'higher career', but with those 'germinal' souls, the mass of mankind who appeared to be on the 'verge of that abyss'. He offered his hope that such as these 'infants ... as to spiritual development' might ultimately be restored to the care of God the 'Universal Parent'.[42] Wilson was condemned by the court, specifically for teaching what was contrary to the sense of the Athanasian Creed, the final lines of which read:

> And they that have done good shall go into life everlasting: and they that have done evil into everlasting fire. This is the Catholick faith: which except a man believe faithfully, he cannot be saved.[43]

Wilson appealed against the judgement, and in 1864 the court found in his favour, claiming that there was nothing in the Formularies of the Church of England that could require them to condemn a clergyman for hoping that the wicked would ultimately be pardoned.[44]

In response, 11,000 clergy signed a declaration claiming the eternal punishment of the wicked to be part of Christ's teaching in the Bible. Opinion

---

[40] Maurice, *The life of Frederick Denison Maurice*, 2: 210.
[41] Ibid., 2: 203.
[42] H. B. Wilson (ed.), *Essays and Reviews* (London, 1860), 206.
[43] The Athanasian Creed follows the order for Evening Prayer in the Prayer Book. The rubric instructs that the creed shall be recited at various named feast days at matins in place of the Apostles' Creed.
[44] Rowell gives a good account. Rowell, *Hell and the Victorians*, 118–23.

about the creed remained divided. Five years later, at the Canterbury Convocation in 1869, the bishop of Ely, Edward Harold Browne, presented a petition to the Upper House calling for the rubric above the creed to read 'may' be said or sung rather than 'shall'. The petition was signed by 35 clergy and laity. In response the bishop of Gloucester and Bristol, Charles Ellicott, presented a petition asking that no alterations be made to the creed; it was subscribed by 3,500 signatures gathered by the Church Union.[45] In 1871, the creed still under discussion, the bishop of Lincoln, Christopher Wordsworth, expressed concern that the bishops' debates might 'stir up' in the minds of the public the teaching about the eternal punishment of the wicked. The debates in Convocation ceased in 1873, only to re-emerge in 1917.

Even eight years after the Wilson judgement, the words of Edward Goulburn, the dean of Norwich, summed up the consternation of some clergy at what they saw as the undermining of traditional belief, and the possibility of religious error that its removal would bring:

> Even now the eternity of the punishment of the wicked is, despite the plain declaration of Holy Scripture, stoutly denied by some. So that the errors which this creed condemns can by no means be said to be exploded in modern times. And in sweeping it away from use, or letting it lie dumb in our Prayer Books, we shall be demolishing a bulwark against religious error which we cannot afford to lose.[46]

A letter to the *Church Times* the following year claimed that the widespread 'hatred' of the creed was due to 'two forms of mischief', summed up as 'Christ is not God' and 'Religious error does not affect man's future condition'.[47] Such strong criticism of Wilson, and the court's eventual judgement, suggested deep anxiety that traditional belief was being undermined. Concerns were expressed that the Church was losing hell as a moral sanction and, more importantly, that people's future salvation might be in jeopardy if the Athanasian Creed, and the clauses it contained, were unimportant. Criticisms of Wilson also revealed that a publicly articulated belief in the eternal torment of the wicked, and in the rightness of that torment for those in 'religious error', was as widespread as spiritualists claimed.

It was not only Broad Church clergymen who challenged 'traditional' teaching about the afterlife. Thomas Rawson Birks (1810–83) was the

---

[45] *Chronicle of the Convocation of Canterbury*, 15 June 1869.
[46] Edward M. Goulburn, *Two Discourses by the Dean of Norwich on the Athanasian Creed* (London, 1872), 52.
[47] *Church Times*, 7 Feb. 1873.

evangelical vicar of Holy Trinity Cambridge. He had been critical of *Essays and Reviews*, and of what he saw as the challenges to scripture made by the new biblical scholarship. Despite his evangelical credentials, in 1867 he wrote *The Victory of Divine Goodness*, in which, without explicitly suggesting a doctrine of universal salvation, he offered a hope that all people would be saved.

Traditional evangelical teaching had, he argued, represented God as an impossible judge and salvation as impossible, robbing the Gospel of its 'glad tidings'.[48] He criticised what he saw as the prevailing view: 'No impressions are more frequent and usual, in religious circles and even beyond them, than that good men, when they die, go at once to heaven, or pass into glory. These statements occur perpetually in hymns and religious works, as if they were the plainest and most fundamental part of the Gospel.'[49] Instead, he argued that there was an intermediate state, which was characterised by a sense of expectation but which was also a period of sleep.

After this period, and at the final judgement, Birks thought that the love of God would prove so overwhelming that even the wicked would, at that moment, turn and be saved. Birks was not advocating purgatory, nor suggesting that individuals 'progressed' or grew spiritually in the intermediate state, but rather that the inherent grace of God would change them ultimately. 'Will they not be saved, in a strange, mysterious sense, when the depth of their unchangeable shame and sorrow finds beneath it a still lower depth of Divine compassion, and the creature, in its most forlorn estate, is shut in by the vision of surpassing and infinite love?'[50]

Although steeped in the language of the Bible, Birks was unable to justify his thinking from biblical texts, and suggested instead that this 'truth' had been deliberately hidden 'for wise reasons', but could be deduced by 'humble and reverent hearts'.[51] He was criticised for his opinions, and felt it necessary to resign as honorary secretary of the Evangelical Alliance.[52]

Another evangelical, Andrew Jukes (1815–1901), was ordained deacon in 1842. He left his orders to become a Baptist and had a congregation in Hull for a time, but moved to London in 1868 and returned to Anglicanism, although he was never ordained priest. In *The Second Death and the Restitution of All*

---

[48] T. R. Birks, *The Victory of Divine Goodness* (London, 1870. 1st pubd 1867), 5.
[49] Ibid., 55.
[50] Ibid., 191.
[51] Ibid., 64.
[52] He noted criticisms from Mr Grant, editor of the *Morning Advertiser*, and Mr Baxter, a solicitor and politician. Ibid., 199.

Things Jukes appeared to advocate a form of purgatory. The Bible, he argued, which was the first point of appeal in all controversies,[53] contained evidence of trial and perishing beyond death, as well as blessing and restitution. The common conclusion to this apparent contradiction was that some were saved and some were not. The 'approved teaching' of Christendom was that the restitution of all things was not the same as the reconciliation of all men to God.[54]

He went on to suggest that all people, both the righteous and the sinners, would at death pass through some sort of 'fiery trial'.[55] Judgement would enable individuals to recognise that they were in need of grace, leading to their repentance. Their flesh, or sinful nature, would be destroyed in order to give them life. The elect would pass through this judgement or ordeal faster than sinners, but they would be the 'first fruits' of salvation, rather than the only ones to be saved. Any objection to the ultimate salvation of sinners he likened to the mean-spirited reaction of the older brother to the return of the prodigal son.[56]

For Jukes and Birks the only possibility for salvation lay with God: whether he chose to save individuals by grace, or by testing them in a fiery trial. By contrast, the liberal clergyman, Frederic William Farrar (1831– 1903), a few years later hinted that post-mortem spiritual development lay within the potential of the individual. In November and December 1877, when he was rector of St Margaret's and a canon of Westminster Abbey, Farrar preached a series of sermons in the Abbey concerning the nature of the afterlife. As Maurice had done before him, Farrar examined the word αἰώνιος and similarly concluded that it was to be understood as 'eternal', describing a quality of God, rather than 'everlasting', meaning endless, when applied to the future life. He analysed the three words used in the Bible that were commonly translated by the one English word 'hell', and suggested that 'tartarus' (II Peter ii. 4) meant an intermediate place where the dead dwelt before judgement. 'Hades' (Acts ii. 27, 31) was similar to 'sheol' in the Old Testament and was, again, a place where the dead dwelt before judgement. Finally 'gehenna', the word most commonly employed by Jesus, was the Jerusalem sewer, where the unburied corpses of criminals were thrown. It was not a place of endless torment.[57] 'Hell' in its 'traditional' interpretation, with vivid images of

---

[53] Andrew Jukes, *The Second Death and the Restitution of All Things* (London, 1869), 17.
[54] Ibid., 20–6.
[55] Ibid., 83.
[56] Ibid., 99.
[57] Farrar, *Eternal Hope*, xxxix–xlii.

torment, could not be found in the New Testament. Phrases that had been meant as metaphor had, he argued, been 'crystallised' into creed.[58]

He criticised what he claimed was the common conception of eternal torment: 'that at death there is passed upon every impenitent sinner an irreversible doom to endless tortures, either mental or material, of the most awful and unspeakable intensity'.[59] There was, he argued, nothing in scripture to prove that the everlasting fate of an individual was fixed, irrevocably, at death. Punishment for sin beyond death might be there to teach the impenitent but the possibility of progress, or 'amelioration', also lay beyond the grave.[60] Rather than using 'proof' texts for his teaching he argued that it was founded 'not on two texts in St Peter, but on what seems to me to be the general tenor of the entire scriptures, as a result of the love of God in Christ'.[61] He cited the Early Church Fathers, such as Origen, Clement of Alexandria, Athanasius, Jerome, Ambrose and Irenaeus, all of whom, he argued, supported the possibility of spiritual growth beyond death.[62]

Farrar was criticised for his sermons. Edward Bouverie Pusey (1800–1882) wrote *What is of faith as to everlasting punishment?* (1880) in response. In a lengthy and scholarly work, citing evidence from the Old and New Testaments as well as the Jewish Targums, Pusey criticised the tenor of Farrar's argument. He accused Farrar of caricaturing 'common opinion' regarding hell as a place of physical torment, where the vast mass of mankind existed for endless duration, in an irreversible situation.[63] This was, he said, rigid Calvinism, rather than Church of England teaching and Christ had never given any indication as to the proportion of saved and lost.[64] Instead, the Church, 'as it has been beautifully said, has its long list of saints; it has not inserted one name in any catalogue of the damned'.[65]

Yet, importantly, Pusey conceded ground to Farrar, agreeing that it was impossible to know what had happened to those who had died outside the state of grace, even suggesting that post-mortem purification might assist them. This would, he argued, be a 'preparation' of souls, transforming their wills to the will of God, where they would be comforted by angels and prayers.[66] In other words, the afterlife was dynamic rather than static, and there might,

---

58 Ibid., 74.
59 Ibid., xxii.
60 Ibid., lii.
61 Ibid., xiv.
62 Ibid., 82.
63 E. B. Pusey, *What is of faith as to everlasting punishment?* (London, 1880), 6.
64 Ibid., 11.
65 Ibid., 14.
66 Ibid., 125.

therefore, be possibility for repentance and grounds for hope, but that the possibility of purification lay in the control of God, rather than the individual.

Others were outraged by Farrar. Charles Childe, the rector of Holbrook, near Ipswich, criticised the 'flashy and superficial rhetoric', and claimed it marked a daring assault on biblical truth.[67] An anonymous writer thought *Eternal Hope* to be 'a mass of verbiage with scanty meanings'.[68] Robert Paterson, curate of Ramsgate, criticised Farrar's 'overuse' of poems and quotations, but also thought that *Eternal Hope* treated sin too lightly; this had implications for morality:

> Men are ever too prone to regard sin as a trivial thing, and to put off preparing to meet their God. Dr. Farrar's views as regards the future destiny of the unsaved would not help to turn the tide in the right direction. Indeed, they carry with them the germs of far-reaching evil.[69]

He concluded that *Eternal Hope* was a 'castle in the air' for the impenitent. 'Almighty God forbid any poor hell-deserving sinner should trust to it.'[70] But others, like the nonconformist Joseph Bland from Kidderminster, thought that Farrar's words would be a help for the poor, who found it hard to believe in eternal torment when they experienced such torment in the present.[71]

By 1889, the publication of another collection of essays, *Lux Mundi*,[72] had made it clear that, in liberal academic circles at least, theological opinion concerning the afterlife and the nature and duration of eternity had changed significantly over the course of forty-five years. In the essays, written by younger High Church thinkers, the earlier debates received hardly a mention. Indeed, the only consideration of the afterlife came in Robert Lawrence Ottley's essay concerning Christian ethics. Ottley rooted his ideas about the afterlife in a consideration of the ethical nature of God's being. Although denying that there was any scriptural basis for universalism, Ottley argued that beyond death there was hope for every individual. 'We find warrant in

---

[67] C. F. Childe, *The Unsafe Anchor, or 'Eternal Hope' a false hope. Being strictures on Canon Farrar's West Minster Abbey Sermons* (London, 1879).

[68] Anon, *A critique of Canon Farrar's 'Eternal Hope'* (London, 1878).

[69] Robert Paterson, *Canon Farrar's 'Eternal Hope'. A Review of his Five Sermons preached at Westminster Abbey, November and December 1877* (London, 1878), preface.

[70] Ibid., 49.

[71] Bland, *The Keys of Hell*.

[72] *Lux Mundi* was a collection of twelve essays edited by Charles Gore. Each essay was themed around the importance of the Incarnation and took contemporary science and biblical criticism into account in the course of the theological arguments.

scripture for the belief in an intermediate state in which the imperfect character may be developed, ignorance enlightened, sin chastened and desire purified.' He continued, 'We cannot think that helpless ignorance or inevitable poverty of character will finally sever a human soul from God.'[73]

Ottley maintained that it was possible for an individual to be eternally separated, by rebellion, from God beyond death, and that God would, indeed, judge people at an appointed hour in the distant future. But in the intermediate time, and in an intermediate place, there was possibility for spiritual progress and inclusion in the company of the Kingdom of God, the perfect moral community. Individuals were called to be holy, and that call continued beyond death, as did the possibility that an individual could reject the call.[74] Significantly, Ottley's words assumed that post-mortem spiritual progress or deterioration was the responsibility of the individual, rather than God: it was the individual who chose, even after death, to rebel against God, or turn towards him.

When spiritualists attacked the Church of England's 'traditional' teaching they attacked the same teaching that Maurice, Wilson, Farrar and Birks recognised. By the end of the nineteenth century, however, liberal opinions had changed the balance of theological debate – so much so that Ottley could, without causing controversy, suggest post-mortem spiritual progress, minimise the existence of hell and emphasise the desire of God to save all people. By 1915, the Bampton lecturer Hastings Rashdall could even, publicly and without fear of reprisal, describe Jesus' own teaching as 'latent Universalism'.[75] 'Traditional' teaching was certainly in evidence, according to Anglican critics, but so too, and increasingly, was the alternative teaching that they themselves were offering.

This changing theological landscape regarding the afterlife was reflected in two significant court cases in the mid and late nineteenth century. These were not matters of theology or Church discipline, but concerned Church property. They are significant because both required legal opinion to be given regarding the state of the departed in the afterlife and both concerned the relationship between the local church and its parishioners. In order to offer opinion, the judges concerned were required to draw upon the tradition, theology and

---

[73] Charles Gore (ed.), *Lux Mundi. A Series of Studies in the Religion of the Incarnation* (London, 1890 edn), 515.
[74] Ibid., 477.
[75] Hastings Rashdall, *The Idea of Atonement in Christian Theology. Being the Bampton Lectures for 1915* (London, 1920), 437. See chapter seven, p. 185.

practice of the Church of England as laid down in law. The results of the two cases also suggest that this period did not mark a simple theological transition from 'traditional' thinking to a more liberal approach: the reality was more complex.

In 1838 a Roman Catholic lady, Mrs Woolfrey, had inscribed on her husband's tombstone in Carisbrooke parish churchyard the words, 'Pray for the soul of J. Woolfrey', with the added reminder from the Apocrypha, 'It is a holy and wholesome thought to pray for the dead.'[76] Parishioners were allowed to challenge additions or alterations to church fabric or additions to the churchyard if they thought the changes unsuitable. The chancellor of Winchester diocese received letters concerning the Woolfrey tombstone and the case was tried, initially in the Court of the Arches, as a criminal suit. The onus was on the incumbent, who was opposed to the wording, to prove that Mrs Woolfrey had acted unlawfully by causing an inscription to be made 'contrary to the articles, canons and constitutions, or to the doctrine and discipline of the Church of England'.[77]

The question, which was eventually argued at Doctors' Commons, turned then on whether words that invited prayer for the departed were necessarily unlawful. The incumbent, John Breeks, argued that they were unlawful on three grounds: firstly, they were connected with the doctrine of purgatory and therefore contravened Article XXII of the Articles of Religion. Secondly, he claimed that such prayers were inconsistent with the doctrine of the Church of England. Prayers for the dead had been omitted from the second Edwardian Prayer Book as being inconsistent with the doctrine of a reformed Church. Thirdly, he claimed that prayers for the dead were contrary to Article XXXV, referring to the Book of Homilies. The third part of the homily concerning prayer contained the words,

> Let these and such other places be sufficient to take away the gross error of purgatory out of our heads; neither let us dream any more, that the souls of the dead are any thing at all holpen by our prayers.

The court, presided over by Sir Herbert Jenner, dean of the Arches, found that in answer to the first argument, prayers for the dead were offered by the Church long before the doctrine of purgatory. It was therefore impossible to claim that prayers for the dead were necessarily connected with a doctrine of

---

[76] II Maccabees xii. 46.
[77] For a full account of this and the following case, see *Re Parish of South Creake, All England Law Reports, [1959] Vol. 1*, 197–208, at 200–203.

purgatory.[78] In answer to the second argument, the court found that there was no express prohibition of prayers for the dead in the second Edwardian Prayer Book; it merely omitted prayers for the dead. In answer to the third argument, Jenner concluded that the Book of Homilies did not state that prayer for the dead was unlawful, but only that it was useless. Prayers for the departed would have no effect on their condition and the practice was discouraged.

In conclusion, Jenner's opinion was that there was no prohibition against such prayers. The framers of the articles of the Church had had ample opportunity to declare their illegality, had they wished to, but had not done so. The authorities of the Church of England discouraged the practice, but did not make it illegal.[79]

Breeks v. Woolfrey might have remained an insignificant matter between a parishioner and incumbent, but for the fact that Jenner's extremely scholarly judgement became so frequently cited. It appeared in correspondence between archbishops of Canterbury and clergy concerning inscriptions desired by parishioners for tombstones. Archbishop Tait, for example, cited the case in 1871 when he wrote to a clergyman in Margate about wording on a tombstone.[80] In 1884 Archbishop Benson referred a confused clergyman in Grayford to Breeks v. Woolfrey to assist him in dealing with requested inscriptions.[81]

Interestingly, archbishops also cited Breeks v. Woolfrey in answer to more general concerns about prayers for the dead. In 1870 Tait received a number of letters criticising him for suggesting at a clerical gathering in Greece that the Church of England did not sanction prayers for the dead. One correspondent, Alexander Forbes, the bishop of Brechin, pointed out that Breeks v. Woolfrey had ruled that they were not prohibited, even if not encouraged. Tait responded that he knew the case and had taken this into consideration.[82]

Frederick Temple, in 1900, sanctioned prayers during the war in South Africa, provoking criticism from evangelical members of the Church Association. The Association's president, the duke of Devonshire, criticised the prayers for adding a petition explicitly for the departed.[83] Temple replied that

---

[78] It was argued that the primitive church prayed for the dead from the third century. Although some scholars claimed that purgatory was introduced in the fifth or sixth century, it wasn't declared as doctrine until the council of Florence in 1439.
[79] *Re Parish of South Creake*, 202.
[80] Tait to Mr Bateman, 17 Feb. 1871. *LPL: Tait Papers*, Vol. 172, fols. 90–92.
[81] Benson to Mr Smith, 5 Aug. 1884. *LPL: Benson Papers*, Vol. 15, fols. 174, 185.
[82] Tait to Forbes, 10 Oct. 1870. *LPL: Tait Papers*, Vol. 167, fols. 298–300.
[83] The petition read: 'For all those who have fallen in the true faith of Thy Holy Name, that they may enter into the rest which Thou hast prepared for them that believe in Thee'. *LPL: F.*

such prayers were discouraged but not prohibited, and cited Breeks v. Woolfrey as the authority.[84]

It is interesting to note that Temple chose to cite Breeks v. Woolfrey in 1900 when it was no longer the only legal opinion on the subject. In 1894 the Court of the Arches considered the case of Egerton v. Odd Rode. In this instance John Egerton, the Anglo-catholic incumbent of Odd Rode, Stoke-on-Trent, wished to erect a memorial window including the inscription, in Latin, translated to the effect, 'Of your charity, pray for the soul of [H. F.] ... deceased ... and for the soul of [J. H. C.] ... deceased'.[85]

In this instance the chancellor, the Revd Dr Espinell Espin, disputed Jenner's earlier judgement. He argued that, Breeks v. Woolfrey notwithstanding, not only had prayers for the dead not been restored to the second Prayer Book of Edward VI, but they had remained omitted from further revisions to the Prayer Book in 1603 and 1661. More importantly, the chancellor went on to suggest that in the 'popular mind' prayers for the dead were 'unquestionably' associated with the doctrine of purgatory. A bequest made for such prayers to be offered was therefore, 'void by the common law of the realm as superstitious'. He concluded his judgement against the inscription:

> Though in private such prayers may be offered, as comfortable to the ways of the Primitive Church, certainly from the second century and downwards; and however deeply we do sympathise with sentiments of affectionate respect in the bereaved ... it does not seem to belong to a court of the first instance to do what the formularies of the Church have abstained from doing; it is not for me here to authorise directly the setting up in a place of public worship of an inscription demanding the prayers of the worshippers for the souls of certain persons who have departed this life.[86]

To the mind of Archbishop Temple in 1900, however, Breeks v. Woolfrey remained the chief legal authority. It was cited as the authority again when prayers for the dead were issued during the war in 1917.[87]

It is interesting that by the end of the century Breeks v. Woolfrey, which suggested prayer was possible, maintained precedence over Egerton v. Odd

---

Temple Papers, Vol. 42, fol. 97. The petition was optional and only included in the fifth of five litanies.

[84] Temple to duke of Devonshire, 8 Mar. 1900. Ibid., Vol. 42, fol. 339.

[85] *Re Parish of South Creake*, 202.

[86] Ibid., 203.

[87] See chapter seven, p. 199.

Rode. Regardless of the legal issues, prayer for the dead implied a dynamic, rather than a static afterlife. Although the Book of Homilies had suggested that prayers from the living did not affect the state of the departed and were therefore useless, they were, as Espin pointed out, associated with purgatory in the 'popular' mind. Thus it is significant that two archbishops (Temple and Davidson during the war) chose to endorse a practice which strongly suggested to the 'popular' mind not only the possibility of post-mortem spiritual progress, but also the efficacy of prayers. It is equally significant that bishops and archbishops gave advice to clergy and laity by turning to legal opinion, rather than theology. This suggests that either they were unwilling to articulate their own theological position on the state of the departed, or that they thought that Breeks v. Woolfrey offered a legitimate as well as an adequate response to traditional teaching – which they would surely have otherwise had to uphold.

Thus in the second half of the nineteenth century the balance of theological academic debate shifted away from the 'traditional' ideas, expressed in penal substitution, the everlasting punishment of the wicked and the eternal state being fixed at the point of death. Instead there was a reappraisal of the nature of eternity, a minimising of hell's torments and the possibility of an active spiritual development for every individual beyond death. The citing of Breeks v. Woolfrey over the period reflected the fact that this theological change was not confined to academic circles, but was also taking place in the arena of episcopal pastoral advice. This theological shift was significant, but was by no means consistent, as the criticisms levelled at Maurice, Wilson and Farrar, and the legal opinion of Espin, reveal.

The Church of England's teaching, however, was unlikely to reach many ordinary parishioners through academic debate and legal judgement. In order to assess how accurate the spiritualists' criticisms of Church teaching were it is also necessary to turn to the places where people most often encountered such teaching.

Liturgy, sermons and hymns

The Prayer Book burial service, in particular, was the rite that, given its nature, necessarily included reference to the dead. It may reasonably be assumed that the majority of the English population who experienced bereavement were acquainted with this rite to some degree.

Three quarters of the burial service is composed of scriptural passages, after which the service concludes with four prayers, one of which is the Lord's Prayer. The service begins with a reading from either, or both, psalms thirty-nine and ninety. The former is a psalm of penitence; the psalmist recognises the limitations and sorrows of the earthly life and puts his hope in God. The latter, similarly, contrasts the finite nature of human existence with the eternal nature of God. Following the psalms, St Paul's teaching on the nature of resurrection from I Corinthians xv. 20–58 is read. After this the funeral party moves to the graveside, if the readings have been read in church, and as the 'corpse' is 'made ready to be laid into the earth'[88] words from Job xiv are read (Man that is born of a woman hath but a short time to live). This is followed by words addressed to God as a prayer, but offering a cautionary note to the living (In the midst of life we are in death ... O holy and most merciful Saviour, deliver us not into the bitter pains of eternal death ...Thou knowest, Lord, the secrets of our hearts ...).

After the committal and before the prayers there is another verse from scripture, from the Book of Revelation: 'I heard a voice from heaven, saying unto me, Write, From henceforth blessed are the dead which die in the Lord: Even so, saith the Spirit, for they rest from their labours.'[89]

In the prayers that follow three theological points may be discerned: firstly that death is a positive event for a Christian, not so much because they move to a better state but because they are released from a sinful world. Thus in the third prayer the minister says, 'We give thee hearty thanks, for that it hath pleased thee to deliver this our brother out of the miseries of this sinful world.'

It is assumed that the deceased has gone from the sinful world, and is either in a better place, or else at least in a state where sin is no longer possible.

Secondly, sin and judgement, although not referred to explicitly, pervade the prayers. Phrases referring to the sinful nature of human life include references to 'our vile body' (taken from I Corinthians xv) and, again, 'the miseries of this sinful world'. That judgement will come to all is assumed. Hope is expressed that 'we may be found acceptable' in the sight of God and that Christ may say, 'Come ye blessed children of my Father, receive the Kingdom prepared for you from the beginning of the world.'

Thirdly, there is an affirmation of faith in the 'General Resurrection at the last day', but little certainty about whether the deceased will be part of the elect. There is also, despite a reference to the soul's 'sleep' in God, a possibility that the righteous already enjoy a state of blessedness. So, in the third prayer the minister affirms,

---

[88] The deceased is referred to as 'the corpse' in the rubrics and is not mentioned by name at all.
[89] Revelation xv. 13.

> Almighty God with whom do live the spirits of them that depart hence in the Lord, and with whom the souls of the faithful, *after they are delivered from the burden of the flesh, are in joy and felicity* [my italics],

which suggests immediate bliss. But in the final collect he prays,

> We meekly beseech thee, O Father to raise us from the death of sin unto the life of righteousness; that, when we shall depart this life, *we may rest in him*, as our hope is this our brother doth; and *that at the general Resurrection at the last day, we may be found* acceptable in thy sight and receive that blessing, which thy well-beloved Son shall then pronounce to all that love and fear thee [my italics],

which suggests a time of restful waiting.

Thus according to the Prayer Book burial service, familiar to most adults in England, the world was a place of sin and temptation from which the departed person had been relieved. The righteous rested from the labour of life, either enjoying joy immediately, or sleeping until the final day. The certainty of judgement pervaded the text. There was no mention of 'heaven', nor indeed of hell, only the promise of rest, perfect consummation and life for the righteous. There was no guarantee that the departed individual was one of the elect and no prayer that he might be made so; only a hope that he was among the saved. However, the tone of the service – and the final prayers in particular – suggested that the rite was concerned to deal with the spiritual life of the living, rather than speculate on the state of the departed – in general or in particular.

Apart from the burial service, and the final clauses of the Athanasian Creed, the only other significant place in the Prayer Book where the dead were mentioned was the order for Holy Communion. At the end of the prayer for the Church 'militant here in earth', the minister prays,

> And we also bless thy holy Name for all thy servants departed this life in thy faith and fear; beseeching thee to give us grace so to follow their good examples that *with them we may be* partakers of thy heavenly kingdom [my italics].

The emphasis in this prayer, as in the burial service, is on the lives of the living and the nature of God rather than the state of the dead. God is blessed for the dead, and their good examples are to be remembered in order that the living might themselves be counted as righteous.

The language of the Prayer Book suggested that God was to be both loved and feared in the earthly life, because this life had eternal consequences. As will be seen in chapter seven, in the 1920s the proposed alterations to the

131

Prayer Book suggested much more of a dynamic afterlife, the possibility of spiritual progress, and an ongoing fellowship between the living and the dead. In the second half of the nineteenth century, however, the Church's liturgy offered only the certainty of judgement and a call to a righteous life in the present.

The Church's public teaching about the departed was also to be found in funeral sermons or, more commonly, as John Wolffe has noted in *Great Deaths* (2000), memorial sermons.[90] Wolffe argues that there was 'a substantial minority of preachers who specifically addressed the nature of the afterlife' in these sermons.[91] Of course, even if a substantial minority of preachers addressed the nature of the afterlife, then a sizeable majority did not.

In fact, one of the most striking characteristics of memorial sermons in the period 1850–1900 is the lack of teaching about the afterlife. Instead sermons echoed the Prayer Book: reminding the living of the need to live a Christian life, and that judgement would follow their own deaths. Such teaching was not confined to any one Church tradition. Thus, following the death of the Prince Consort in 1861, John Howes, the High Church preacher at St Mary the Less, Cambridge, chose to call the congregation to repentance for the lax morals of the nation.[92] In 1872, Henry Fox, evangelical curate of St Ebbe's, Oxford, after the funeral of the rector's wife, chose not to speak of the dead but 'to speak a word in season to the living'. He cautioned his audience, 'When we hear of a sudden death we should ask ourselves whether we are prepared to meet our God.'[93]

Across the period, sermons about the death of an individual, whether a known Church member or a member of the royal family, were occasions for preachers to remind hearers of the need both to lead a moral life and hold fast to the Christian faith with the future judgement in mind. The eternal significance of a righteous life was made clear in phrases such as 'Ye shall perish',[94] 'The Son of Man hath shut the door, they, who were not ready are not

---

[90] As Wolffe points out, such sermons were normally delivered after the funeral, either at a special service or on a Sunday near to the date of the funeral. John Wolffe, *Great Deaths. Grieving, Religion and Nationhood in Victorian and Edwardian Britain* (Oxford, 2000), 58.

[91] Ibid., 62.

[92] John George Howes, *Sermon preached in the parish church of S. Mary the Less, before the Corporation of the Borough of Cambridge on Monday, December 23, 1861* (London, 1861).

[93] Henry Fox, *The funeral sermons preached in St Ebbe's Church, Oxford on Sunday, Sept. 8, 1872, on the occasion of the death of Catharine Louisa, the beloved wife of the Rev. Edward Penrose Hathaway, Rector of St Ebbe's* (Oxford, 1872).

[94] W. A. Soames, *Funeral Discourses preached at Greenwich on Sunday, November the 21st, 1852 upon the public funeral of Field-Marshal the Duke of Wellington* (London, 1852), 8. Soames was prebendary of St Paul's and rural dean and vicar of Greenwich.

known'[95] and 'Are we ready? Are our lamps burning? Shall we come forth from the valley of the shadow of death into the land of everlasting peace and joy and glory?'[96]

Even at the end of the century, funeral sermons offered the preacher the opportunity to call his hearers to examine their lives. In 1898 the dean of Christ Church, Oxford, Henry Liddell, and author and fellow of the college, Charles Dodgson, died within a few days of each other. In his memorial sermon the bishop of Oxford, Francis Paget, reminded his hearers of the judgement that would one day befall them all:

> We must try to imagine, so far as our faltering imagination goes, what it will be some day to stand before Him Who requireth truth in the inward parts; to bring our life, our character, bare and unsheltered into His Presence; to know, at last that nothing, absolutely nothing can be hid from Him; and to feel then that we must be tried by that Light which now God calls us, for His Love's sake, to welcome with simplicity into our souls, that it may guide and rule us day by day, till it bring us where the pure in heart see Him.[97]

Some sermons appeared designed to inculcate a sense of foreboding or even fear of the future. Without explicitly detailing what the eternal consequences for lack of faith or righteousness of life would be, some preachers managed to convey that God's judgement against an individual would lead to a terrible outcome. As one preacher suggested, if the Son of Man found 'open rebellion and indifference' in a person then, 'instead of loving recognition there will be a glance from the throne reproachful and terrible; from the fury of that glance there will be no hiding place; from the wrath of the Lamb no covering; it will then be too late to cry for mercy when it is the time of judgement'.[98]

---

[95] R. S. Beloe, *Be ye Ready. A sermon preached in the parish church of Holton on the occasion of the death of his Royal Highness the Prince Consort (22 Dec 1861)* (London, 1861), 15. Beloe was rector of Holton St Peter, Suffolk.

[96] Henry Law, *The Smitten Nation. A sermon preached in the parish church of Weston-super-Mare on Sunday, December 15, 1861, immediately after the announcement of the lamented death of his Royal Highness the Prince Consort* (London, 1861), 7. Law was archdeacon of Wells and became dean of Gloucester in 1862.

[97] Francis Paget, *The Virtue of Simplicity. A sermon preached in the Cathedral Church of Christ Church, Oxford on Sunday, January 23, 1898* (Oxford, 1898). Francis Paget (1851–1911), bishop of Oxford; Henry Liddell (1811–98), lexicographer and dean of Christ Church; Charles Dodgson (pseud. Lewis Carroll) (1832–98), author and mathematician. *ODNB*.

[98] Beloe, *Be ye Ready*, 15.

The stirring up of a sense of foreboding could have been a conscious rhetorical device designed to move hearers to either greater faith or more moral lives. Thus the vicar of Winkfield, Charles John Elliott, preaching in 1851 after the death of Sunday School teacher Mrs Ellis, spoke of her pure motives in ministering to the poor and to children, and invited his congregation to consider their own guilt and 'half-heartedness'.[99] They were invited to fix their affections on heaven, as Elliott told them: 'Beware, I beseech you, how you trifle with present convictions, or make light of present warnings, or break through holy resolutions. Much, very much, hangs upon the decisions of this day.'[100] John Ward Spencer, the incumbent of Wilton, Taunton, used the death of the Prince Consort to derive a lesson of 'timely instruction for the living', urging people to 'flee from the wrath to come by hiding ourselves in a sure place of refuge'.[101] The event of a death, being an opportunity to reflect on human mortality and divine judgement, offered the preacher a chance to stir up his congregation.

In a sermon preached at the village church of Whatley on an ordinary Sunday, Richard William Church reminded his hearers of the God 'whom we shall meet with when we are dead, either to be with him in the light of heaven, or to live cast away from his presence, in the outer darkness, with the worm that never dies'.[102] The real motivation behind these words came later in the text. Church's reminder of God's judgement was followed by comments of concern about the smallness of his congregation and the irregular attendance of worshippers. He cautioned that although regular church attendance was not a means of salvation, it was a 'true and sad sign against a man having the beginnings of the power of God when he is careless and seldom worshipper'.[103]

A few sermons did, however, turn from encouraging the living to contemplate their own future judgement and instead speculated on the state of the departed individual. It was rare for a minister to suggest that an individual was, or would be, consigned to hell, although it happened occasionally.[104]

---

[99] Charles John Elliott, *A sermon preached at St Peter's, Cranbourne, on Sunday, May 11, 1851, on the occasion of the death of Mrs Conyngham Ellis* (London, 1851), 5.

[100] Ibid., 20.

[101] J. W. Spencer, *Christian Sorrow for the Pious Dead. A sermon preached in Wilton Church on Monday, December 23rd, 1861* (Taunton, 1861).

[102] R. W. Church, *Village Sermons* (London, 1892), 108. These sermons (undated) were preached at Whatley between 1852 and 1871. Richard William Church (1815–90) was influenced by Newman and the Tractarians when he was a student at Oxford. He became dean of St Paul's Cathedral in 1871.

[103] Ibid., 115.

[104] *Chronicle of the Convocation of Canterbury*, 12 Feb. 1866. In 1866 the bishop of Oxford

More often sermons suggested, with varying degrees of certainty, that the individual was either in heaven now, or else would have been judged righteous by God and therefore would be in heaven ultimately. There was considerable ambiguity in sermons about when the rewards of a positive judgement would be enjoyed.

Richard Lynch Cotton's sermon to the community of Worcester College, Oxford, following the death of John Hayward Southby in 1861, was inscribed 'to the parents of the lamented subject of this discourse in hope that it may strengthen their consolation and increase their joy in contemplating *the present and eternal* happiness and glory of their departed son'. [my italics] In his sermon Cotton, the college provost, suggested that there were two 'tests of heirdom' of the Kingdom of Heaven, namely faith in Christ and the Christian spirit which flows from faith (i.e. good works). Given that the subject of the text was blessed in both of these, Cotton concluded that he was therefore 'one of the blessed'.[105] The speaker was clear that his rewards were enjoyed in the present. Grief was mitigated, therefore, by 'the contemplation of the glory and felicity which he *is now* enjoying'. [my italics][106]

Similarly, a sermon preached by the evangelical curate Henry Elliot Fox suggested that his rector's late wife was already enjoying heaven. The grieving congregation were to imagine 'another voice speaking to you today, beloved, – a voice mingled with yours in your prayers and praise but one little week ago, – a voice *now joining* with the far higher hymns of heaven'. [my italics][107] A memorial sermon preached by James Hessey at Gray's Inn in 1861 suggested that God had rewarded the young man who had died, because he had trusted in God in his lifetime. 'His looking for God in holiness has now been realized. His glimpses of God's power and glory have issued in seeing God face to face. His lips *now* praise God more cheerfully than ever. His hands *are now* lifted up in more complete adoration.'[108]

The words preached by Charles Ranken Conybeare to St Mary's Church,

---

informed the Upper House of Convocation of a clergyman in his diocese who had buried three parishioners, but refused to read the burial service over them 'as if they were his brothers and sister'. The 'whole parish' agreed with his actions. It appears that the woman had two lovers. One of the lovers killed her and the other man – and then drowned himself.

[105] R. L. Cotton, *A sermon preached in Worcester College Chapel on the occasion of the lamented death of John Hayward Southby Esq.* (Oxford, 1861), 7.

[106] Ibid., 15.

[107] Fox, *The funeral sermons preached at St Ebbe's Church, Oxford*, 7.

[108] James Augustus Hessey, *A sermon on the occasion of the death of Rev. William Henry Hart MA, Demy of Magdalen College Oxford and Chaplain of Grey's Inn: preached October 13, 1861 in Grey's Inn Chapel* (London, 1861), 12.

Itchen-Stoke, in 1881 were printed in order that those who were mourning 'may find in them some slight hint of comfort'. In the text he claimed immediate recompense for those who died in Christ, with a strong hint of spiritual growth:

> When we lie down to die we know that we are going whither Christ has gone before, to our Father, because to His Father. We know that the souls of those who love God, *immediately* after death here, live there with Christ, safe for ever; all weary labour ended, the glad work of serving Him with new and growing powers begin; enabled more and more to know God and all His works with fuller knowledge, and to see God as He is.

He claimed that beyond death the soul would be clothed with a spiritual body, and that there would be 'no more parting, pain, anxious fears'; the dead would be 'united for ever with those who, with us have loved the Lord'.[109]

By contrast, some preachers were keen to maintain that there was a pause between death and the heavenly bliss to come beyond the General Resurrection. Thus Edward Denison, bishop of Salisbury, preaching on Easter Day 1850 in Salisbury Cathedral following the death of Dean Francis Lear, maintained the teaching of St Paul in I Corinthians xv and the distinction between the period of rest and the heavenly joy to come. The soul of the deceased, 'God's faithful servant', delivered from 'the burthen of the flesh', was in joy and felicity but very definitely *rested* in hope of the resurrection, but 'shall *hereafter* be raised in glory, when this corruptible shall put on incorruption and this mortal immortality'.[110] The bishop confidently added, 'Our friend and brother lived in Jesus, and therefore he now *sleeps* in Jesus.' [my italics][111]

John Spencer, incumbent of Wilton, similarly affirmed the separation of 'the blessed state of the pious dead', which was sleep, from the heavenly bliss that awaited the righteous after the General Resurrection. Sleep was a positive state for the dead because it meant both rest from the labour of life and freedom from possible temptation. Sleep was also an indicator of the coming resurrection: when people went to sleep they did so in the hope of rising again, to find Christian friendships renewed. 'We ought therefore as Christians, not to sorrow as others who have no hope, for them which are asleep, seeing that

---

[109] C. R. Conybeare, *Those things which God prepared for them that love Him. A Sermon preached at St Mary's, Itchen-Stoke, Aug. 21, 1881* (Oxford, 1881), 8.
[110] Edward Denison, *Sorrow and Consolation: A sermon preached in the cathedral of Salisbury. Easter Day 1850* (London, 1850), 6.
[111] Ibid., 14.

we trust that they sleep in Jesus and in a better state with Christ than if they were alive; and though death has meant a separation, for a time, between us and them, and between their souls and their bodies, yet these shall meet again.'[112]

For the most part, the small number of sermons that commented on the present state of the departed did not speculate on the landscape of the afterlife as spiritualists did. It was enough to suggest that the dead individual was with God, serving God, adoring God, or else sleeping in anticipation of bliss. In the few instances when the preacher strayed into the realms of speculation, the visions of the heaven were rooted in biblical imagery. Heaven was the place of the great multitude, of realms of light, of the presence of God the judge of all and the glory of the inheritance of the saints.[113] John James, evangelical canon of Peterborough Cathedral, preaching in 1861, taught that those who had lived a virtuous life in a 'spirit of humble trust' would find that 'higher services' awaited them after death. Heaven would be 'an unbounded sphere of activity' in the company of the angels. The citizens of heaven would be engaged forever in the presence of their Saviour.[114]

In a similar way, memorial sermons tended to shy away from descriptions of hell. Although the tone of the sermon might be of judgement and dread, the eternal consequences of a wicked faithless life, as John Wolffe has noted, were not spelled out.[115] This might have been, in part, due to pastoral considerations. It would have been pastorally difficult for a preacher to focus the weight of a funeral or memorial sermon on the nature of hell and the consequence of an ungodly life with bereaved family and friends present. The absence of hell in such sermons would suggest that the spiritualists' critique of Church teaching as presenting the afterlife as a place of fear and hellish torment was somewhat exaggerated. However, sermons given in ordinary church services, as distinct from funeral sermons, were another matter.

In ordinary Sunday sermons, clergy guided congregations in how they ought to think, believe and behave. These sermons did, at times, affirm a literal hell and endless punishment. Even where they did not explicitly and luridly speculate about the nature of hell, they noted a 'traditional' belief.

The controversy concerning the Athanasian Creed in the early 1870s, for example, gave rise to sermons, preached to ordinary congregations, that

---

112 Spencer, *Christian Sorrow for the Pious Dead*, 11.
113 Cotton, *A sermon preached in Worcester College Chapel*, 4–5.
114 John James, *A sermon on the lamented death of his Royal Highness the Prince Consort preached in the cathedral Church of Peterborough (22 Dec 1861)* (London, 1861), 13–14.
115 Wolffe, *Great Deaths*, 62.

upheld the traditional teaching that God condemned the wicked to everlasting torment. As has been noted, the dean of Norwich preaching at Maddermarket, upheld the inclusion and regular use of the creed in 1872. The eternal torment of the wicked was part of traditional belief.[116] In the same year the congregation at Bramshall Church in Staffordshire heard an exposition of the Athanasian Creed in two sermons from David Smith, the curate of Shenstone, which advised them that,

> Creeds should not (and the creeds of the Church of England do not) descend to points of inferior moment. They are made to embrace only such truths as are undeniably revealed in the Bible and have the plainest reference to the Divine way of salvation. On these subjects there cannot, with safety to men's souls, be differences of opinion.[117]

The creed which condemned the wicked to 'everlasting fire' was the true faith. Cartaret John Fletcher, High Church rector of St Martin's, Oxford, although taking a different view of the creed, noted what he saw to be the 'prevailing belief' that the Father would cast all but a few elect and righteous people into a pit of fire to suffer endless torments. He denounced this as 'portentous error'.[118]

At the beginning of Lent, R. W. Church took the question of the Philippian gaoler to St Paul in Acts xvi. 30, 'What must I do to be saved?', to lead into a sermon of warning about the future life. He encouraged his congregation to think about the degree of their faith. 'The return of this season of Lent reminds us, once more, as it has often done so before, how necessary it is to ask it [the same question].'[119] He posed the rhetorical question, 'Where shall I end? With God, or with the Devil?' He used sentences from the Bible to spell out the consequences of not being saved. 'Now also is the axe laid unto the root of the trees: every tree therefore which bringeth not forth good fruit is hewn down and cast into the fire.' 'On the ungodly He shall rain snares, fire and brimstone, storm and tempest; this shall be their portion to drink.'[120]

He went on, making use of the Devil. The Devil, their tempter now, would be their accuser as they stood before God's judgement seat:

---

[116] Goulburn, *Two Discourses by the Dean of Norwich on the Athanasian Creed*, 52.

[117] D. Smith, *A brief and simple exposition of the Athanasian Creed; two sermons preached in Bramshall Church, Staffordshire on Sunday mornings, May 26th and June 2nd, 1872* (London, 1872), 4.

[118] C. J. H. Fletcher, *Divine Punishment in This Life and the Next. A Sermon preached at St Martin's, Oxford, Sunday December 8th, 1872* (Oxford, 1872), 4.

[119] Church, *Village Sermons*, 48.

[120] Ibid., 55.

> Every oath you swear, every lust you give way to, every drunken riot you fall into, every lie that you tell, every act of spite or revenge that you commit ... every theft or dishonesty, or unfair dealing you are guilty of – all are marked down against you; and at the end the devil is ready to meet you with the black list and number of your sins.[121]

It was time to answer the question, what are you going to do to be saved? For some this would be, he argued, a turning point. 'God is calling them now. He is calling them to make up their minds whether they will choose Him, or take their chance of everlasting damnation.'[122] And, in case his congregation thought that they would leave repentance to the hour of their death, he cautioned that a late repentance was seldom a true repentance.

The hell-fire teaching criticised by spiritualists was not explicit in the Church of England, but it was certainly present and implicit. The 'prevailing belief' about the consequences of an unrighteous life included biblical imagery of worm, fire and devil, as well as words and phrases like 'damnation' and 'everlasting torment'.

Preachers occasionally spoke of heaven. Following the imagery used by St Paul, R. W. Church spoke of heaven as the 'prize' to which a Christian ran, a life of 'endless service' with the angels where all would wear 'the incorruptible crown'.[123] Elsewhere, heaven was compared with an endless church service. God had set the church building in the midst of the people as 'a witness and figure of heaven'. It was there that people could glimpse what lay in store. 'If only we thought of what we were doing, we should see that we are practising here on earth what will be our life in heaven, – we are rehearsing the songs which we hope to sing with the redeemed in heaven.'[124] Heaven was the 'grand realm of light and glory, where all is joy and triumph and peace'.[125] More commonly, people encountered Christian teaching about heaven, not from the Bible, but in hymns.

Congregations in the second half of the nineteenth century were singing more published hymns as part of their Sunday worship than they had in earlier years, and these presented Christian ideas and images of the afterlife to churchgoers in a vivid way. Hymn singing had, until the mid nineteenth century, been controversial. The practice had been encouraged and developed by nonconformist Churches and spread among evangelicals in the Church of

---

121 Ibid., 55–6.
122 Ibid., 57.
123 Ibid., 202.
124 Ibid., 110.
125 Cotton, *A sermon preached in Worcester College Chapel*, 12.

England. For a time, therefore, it was associated more with the evangelical tradition and was unconnected with the traditional liturgical patterns and seasons of the Church.[126] By the beginning of the nineteenth century the prejudices against hymn singing were wearing away, assisted by the posthumous publication of Reginald Heber's *Hymns written and adapted to the Weekly Church Services of the Year* (1827).[127] The fresh attention paid to the medieval Church by scholars of the Oxford Movement, and by people such as John Mason Neale (1818–66) and Edward Caswall (1814–78), led to English translations of ancient hymns. Several of John Keble's poems from his popular work, *The Christian Year* (1827), were used as hymns.[128]

With the development of more efficient printing, hymn-books began to appear in the 1840s and 1850s, and in 1861 *Hymns Ancient and Modern* was published. The book took seriously the way in which hymn singing might be incorporated into the liturgical year, and the regular services of the Church of England. Thus the index of the hymn-book, as well as giving the names of composers and details of the hymns' metre, provided suggestions of hymns for occasions such as 'Quinquegesima', 'Sunday next before Lent', 'Whitsuntide' and 'Rogation Days', as well as suggestions for morning, noonday and evening services. It also suggested hymns fitting themes such as 'the divine attributes', 'his redeeming work', 'the holy church' and 'the life of pilgrimage'.

An appendix was added to the hymn-book in 1868, and a second edition was published in 1875, with supplemental hymns in 1889. This edition was reprinted 'many times' until a new edition was published in 1904.[129] It was popular because it was comprehensive, including new compositions alongside translations of ancient hymns, hymns translated from Reformation German and popular hymns by Charles Wesley and Isaac Watts.[130]

The hymn 'Now the labourer's task is o'er' by John Ellerton (1826–93), a parish priest noted for his hymn writing, included lines, repeated at the end of

---

[126] The Prayer Book made no provision in its rubrics for the possibility of hymns. It was permissible to sing the psalms and the canticles, for example the 'Te Deum Laudamus' at Matins. The only occasions when singing was mentioned came in the services of Matins and Evensong, where, after the final collect, comes the rubric, 'In quires and places where they sing here followeth the anthem'. This suggests that anthem singing was not universal.

[127] Reginald Heber (1783–1826) was bishop of Calcutta.

[128] John Keble (1792–1866). *The Christian Year* ran to 96 editions in Keble's own lifetime. By 1873, when the copyright expired, 305,500 copies had been sold.

[129] 'Many times', according to the bibliographical note to the new edition of 1924, itself a reset edition of 1889 with the supplement of 1916.

[130] For a good introduction to hymnody, see J. R. Watson, *An annotated anthology of hymns* (Oxford, 2002).

each of the five verses, which suggested that the faithful soul was resting in sleep:

> Father, in thy gracious keeping
> Leave we now thy servant sleeping[131]

In another of his hymns the words, addressed to God, affirmed with the Prayer Book that the departed were 'set free' from the world of flesh, and not dead; but rather, in the repeated refrain, were 'living unto thee'.[132]

John Mason Neale's original hymn and Catherine Winkworth's translation of a German hymn both drew on the biblical imagery of Christ the Lamb and the Good Shepherd to suggest that the departed individual was safe with God:

> The lamb is in the fold, in perfect safety penn'd
> The lion once had hold, and thought to make an end:
> But one came by with wounded Side,
> and for the sheep the Shepherd died.[133]

> (For a child)
> Tender shepherd thou hast still'd
> Now thy little lamb's brief weeping
> Oh, how peaceful, pale and mild,
> In its narrow bed 'tis sleeping.
> And no sigh of anguish sore
> Heaves that little bosom more.[134]

Four different translations by Neale of St Bernard's hymn described the heavenly realms, and each version ended

> O sweet and blessed country, the home of God's elect!
> O sweet and blessed country that eager hearts expect!
> Jesu in mercy bring us to that dear land of rest
> Who art, with God the Father, and Spirit ever blest.[135]

The four translations contained ever more vivid descriptions of the heavenly realms. The third version followed the imagery of the heavenly city in the Book of Revelation; the final version included both the Revelation image of the serene daylight of the heavenly city and 'pastures' – a rural image not found in the Book of Revelation:

---

131 *Hymns Ancient and Modern* (1924 edn.), No. 401.
132 Ibid., No. 608.
133 J. M. Neale, ibid., No. 609. This hymn was added in the supplement of 1889.
134 Catherine Winkworth, from the German of J. W. Meinhold, ibid., No. 402.
135 J. M. Neale, ibid., Nos. 225–8.

With jasper glow thy bulwarks, thy streets with emeralds blaze;
The sardius and the topaz, unite in thee their rays;
Thine ageless walls are bonded, with amethyst unpriced
The saints build up thy fabric, and the corner-stone is Christ.[136]

They stand those halls of Sion all jubilant with song
And bright with many an angel and all the martyr throng;
The Prince is ever in them, the daylight is serene:
The pastures of the blessed are deck'd in glorious sheen.[137]

A hymn written by Mrs Cecil Frances Alexander similarly offered vivid descriptions of the heavenly realms with 'pearly gates' and 'golden floor'. The end of the hymn, however, having presented the beautiful images of heaven, reminded the singer to live a life worthy of salvation, praying:

Oh, by Thy love and anguish, Lord,
And by Thy life laid down,
Grant that we fall not from Thy grace,
Nor cast away our crown.[138]

The devastating implication of the hymn was that the beautiful life to come could be thrown away by a sinful life – a sentiment that was echoed in a hymn by Frederick Faber (1814–63):

O Paradise! O Paradise!
I want to sin no more,
I want to be as pure on earth
as on Thy spotless shore.[139]

Hymns suggested for saints' days and festivals of holy martyrs were full of the language of light, joy, glory and rest. A life of holiness led, according to the hymns, to a world where angels, saints and martyrs lived in perpetual worship. There were holy voices 'chanting at the crystal sea', righteous ones, walking 'in golden light',[140] where the 'countless host' streamed through 'gates of pearl'.[141] The scenes were urban, it was the biblical holy city of Revelation that was described rather than a rural idyll, but the city was a beautiful place; it gleamed with precious jewels and with the brightness of the

---

[136] Ibid., No. 227.
[137] Ibid., No. 228.
[138] Mrs Alexander, ibid., No. 229.
[139] F. W. Faber, ibid., No. 234.
[140] Christopher Wordsworth, ibid., No. 436 (Hark the sound of holy voices).
[141] Bishop William Walsham How (1823–97), ibid., 437 (For all the saints).

white-robed throng. In this city there was simultaneously rest from the labour of life and yet also the endless activity of worship and praise.

In hymnody, ordinary church members were presented with images of heaven that were rooted in the Bible and yet were tremendously vivid. There was, however, no theological commentary alongside these hymns, and little in them to suggest whether the dead attained the heavenly joys immediately, or whether what was described was the life beyond the General Resurrection.

During the second half of the nineteenth century, then, Church of England teaching concerning the afterlife was more likely to warn people that actions in the earthly life had eternal consequences than to speculate on the exact nature of heaven and hell. Where there was speculation, it was couched in biblical language. In sermons, hymns and in the Prayer Book, the Church offered only two possibilities after death. One possibility was a state of eternal torment, the 'wrath of the Lamb', perishing, worm and fire; the other was a place of glory, light, angels and 'everlasting felicity', although it was unclear whether either of these were realised immediately or after a period of sleep. Running through the Church's teaching was the message that the individual's actions in the present determined which of these two states he or she inhabited for all eternity.

The possibilities for post-mortem repentance, forgiveness and spiritual progress gradually emerging in academic theology were not widely or publicly offered to ordinary churchgoers in the late nineteenth century. The theological landscape of the afterlife certainly shifted in this period, but it only really shifted within the debates taking place among theologians. When ordinary individuals encountered Church teaching they were told to expect that God would judge them on their earthly life alone, and that there was no possibility that, once judgement had been made, God would change his mind. They would either be in heaven, or in hell. Although the spiritualists' critique of orthodox 'traditional' teaching was a caricature, it was not excessively exaggerated. As an alternative, spiritualists offered a vision of the afterlife that proved attractive to many: full of possibility, where the individual determined – and continued to determine – his or her eternal state, and was surrounded by simple beauty, light and the friendship of angelic guides. The following chapter examines how the Church of England, faced with this alternative to its own 'traditional' teaching, engaged with modern spiritualism.

6

The Church of England and spiritualism

From the 1850s until the early part of the twentieth century Church of England clergy expressed concerns that spiritualism was widespread. Despite this anxiety, there was no 'official' response to spiritualism until 1920, when the Lambeth Conference briefly discussed spiritualism, along with Christian Science and Theosophy, and concluded that there were 'grave dangers' in the 'tendency to make a religion of spiritualism'.[1] It was not until 1936, however, that a small committee, gathered by the archbishop of Canterbury, began to consider spiritualism formally for the Church, presenting its report to the bishops in 1939. Seven of the ten members of the committee concluded in the report that, despite the instances of fraud associated with séances, it was 'probable' that in some cases discarnate spirits did indeed communicate with the living.[2] The majority advised the Church to maintain contact with 'intelligent' spiritualists. The three other members of the committee advised that spiritualism needed to be investigated further by scientists, rather than clergy.[3] The report was suppressed, much to the annoyance of some spiritualists, who had heard rumours that the conclusions of the majority were favourable towards spiritualism.

With the exception of the comments made at Lambeth in 1920, between 1852 and 1939 there was no official Church of England response to modern spiritualism. Despite this, there were many unofficial responses in this period, as spiritualism was discussed and analysed in sermons, pamphlets, newspapers and journals, and at the Church Congress. Historians of spiritualism have tended to assume that, apart from a few interested clergymen, the Church was 'cautious' and 'negative' about spiritualism. Janet Oppenheim sees this exemplified by an article written by Edward White Benson for the first edition

[1] Rene Kollar, *Searching for Raymond. Anglicanism, Spiritualism and Bereavement between the Two World Wars* (Maryland, 2000), Appendix, 156.
[2] *Report of the Archbishop of Canterbury's Committee on Spiritualism*, 22.
[3] Ibid., 30.

of the spiritualist newspaper *Borderland* in 1893, which condemned spiritualism as uncivilised and for people of low intellect.[4] The fact that this was the same Benson who had been a member of the Ghost Club some years earlier, however, ought to discourage the easy assumption that condemnation of spiritualist séances was the same as condemnation of *any* communication between the living and the departed.

In fact, although there were undoubtedly some clergymen who were 'negative' and 'cautious', there were others who were as curious as anyone else about spiritualism and who visited séances; a small but significant number were prepared to admit this in public. More importantly, there were still others who not only visited séances but also engaged wholeheartedly with the ideas and images that spiritualism offered.

Criticisms of spiritualism

There were three sorts of negative response to spiritualism. The first of these was articulated as a concern about members of the public who attended séances, and their mental, moral and spiritual welfare. The second was a reaction to the physical séance phenomena; and the third was a scornful criticism of the theology and ideas within spiritualism.

At the 1881 Church Congress in Newcastle, a layman, Stewart Cumberland, argued that it was the duty of the Church to expose spiritualism as fraud.[5] When Edmund McClure, honorary canon of Bristol, addressed the Congress at Leicester about spiritualism in 1919, he listed some well-known mediums who had been exposed as frauds since the 1880s.[6] The bishop of London, Arthur Foley Winnington Ingram, during a sermon preached at Fulham in the same year, cautioned his hearers that spiritualism was fraudulent, 'disappointing' and 'but a shadow' of real faith.[7] Viscount Halifax, president of the Church Union, thought that the manifestations of spiritualism were the result of 'imposture' which was 'often unconscious' as mediums did not 'necessarily desire to deceive'.[8]

No one was in any doubt that spiritualism was riddled with fraud. Even staunch supporters acknowledged that many mediums had been caught

---

4 Oppenheim, *The Other World*, 68.
5 *Church Congress at Newcastle*, 65.
6 *Church Congress at Leicester*, 103–5.
7 A. F. Winnington Ingram, ' "The Life after Death", preached on the Sunday after All Saints Day at All Saints, Fulham, 1919', in *The Spirit of Peace* (London, 1921), 156–7.
8 Halifax, *'Raymond'. Some Criticisms*, 6.

cheating. Sir Arthur Conan Doyle admitted, with sorrow, that even some 'true' mediums cheated occasionally when their psychic power temporarily deserted them.[9] It was not only clergy who claimed that spiritualism was fraudulent; as has been observed, journalists had made that same criticism since the 1850s. However, with the advent of the Great War clergymen became less concerned with the fraudulence of spiritualism *per se*, and more concerned that bereaved and vulnerable people were being 'preyed upon' by fraudulent mediums.

Thus Thomas Hardy, the Anglo-catholic warden of St Mary's House, Regent's Park Road, in a series of published lectures to the Mothers' Union, claimed that 'thousands' of bereaved people were 'snatching eagerly at any promise of the continued existence of those they mourn'.[10] Viscount Halifax was anxious that those bereaved by the Great War had turned to spiritualism out of heartache and longing.[11]

Not only was spiritualism potentially damaging to those made vulnerable by grief, it was also, thought some, more generally a danger to mental well-being. Disquiet grew as the period went on and by the beginning of the twentieth century anxieties were voiced about the mental health of mediums as well as people regularly attending séances. Words such as 'danger', 'risk' and 'mental instability' were used in order to persuade people that an interest in spiritualism would be detrimental to their health.

Canon William Newbolt of St Paul's Cathedral said that spiritualism was not a harmless pastime, but full of 'danger'.[12] George Longridge, from the Community of the Resurrection at Mirfield, claimed that while spiritualism might be a matter for scientific enquiry it was dangerous to ordinary people, and led to nervous disorders.[13] John A. V. Magee, vicar of St Mark's, St John's Wood, expressed concern for the dangers to mental health he saw

---

[9]   Conan Doyle argued that some mediums were 'jet-black' (i.e. complete frauds) and others were 'snow-white' and free from stain of fraud. There was, however, a 'large belt of grey' in between made up of those with 'undoubted psychic power' who cheated occasionally. See *Verbatim Report: A public debate on the 'Truth of Spiritualism' between Sir Arthur Conan Doyle and Joseph McCabe. Held at the Queen's Hall, Langham Place, London W., on Thursday, March 11, 1920* (London, 1920), 21.

[10] T. J. Hardy, *Spiritism in the Light of Faith. A Comparison and a Contrast* (London, 1919), 10.

[11] Halifax, *'Raymond'. Some Criticisms*, 12.

[12] Reported in *The Times*, 8 Dec. 1913, pg. 4, col. B.

[13] George Longridge CR, *Spiritualism and Christianity* (London and Oxford, 1918), 37.

inherent in spiritualism.[14] Ernest Barnes, in a lecture delivered to the Liverpool Diocesan Board of Divinity when he was a canon at Westminster in 1921, thought similarly that spiritualism was connected with insanity and mental instability or weakness.[15]

The Lambeth Conference of 1920 invited episcopal delegates to discuss spiritualism as one of its subjects. The conference made four resolutions in relation to spiritualism, Christian Science and telepathy and concluded that,

> the practice of spiritualism as a cult involves the *subordination of the intelligence* and the will to unknown forces and personalities and, to that extent, the *abdication of the self-control* to which God calls us. [my italics][16]

Spiritualists did not deny the possibility that dabbling in spiritualism could lead to mental instability. An anonymous former medium wrote in 1861 of how he had discovered mediumistic powers at a young age, but had renounced spiritualism when he found his psychic powers taking over his life and causing problems to his mental strength.[17] A doctor who became involved in séances and joined various spiritualist societies decided to end his fascination when he realised he was becoming 'neurotic'. Looking at fellow spiritualists at a gathering one day he saw signs of physical and mental deterioration that grew with increased involvement.[18] Of equal pastoral concern to the clergy, however, was the moral welfare of their congregations. Spiritualism, as well as preying on the bereaved and potentially causing mental instability, was liable to lead to moral breakdown, a loss of faith and the 'abdication of self-control' to which the Lambeth Conference resolution referred.

Some clergy, rather than criticising mediums, rounded instead on those Christians who visited mediums for being weak in their faith. Thomas Hardy, writing from an Anglo-catholic perspective, claimed that if people knew and practised their religion properly they would have no need for spiritualism. Some people tried spiritualism looking for the assurance that faith should give, but if they had learned their Creed, or learned to apply it, then spiritualism would not be needed.[19] Another Anglo-catholic, Charles Rouse, similarly

---

14 *Church Congress at Leicester*, 114.
15 E. W. Barnes, *Spiritualism and the Christian Faith* (London, 1920), 48. Barnes became bishop of Birmingham in 1924.
16 Resolutions to the 1920 Lambeth Conference (Resolution Four), in Kollar, *Searching for Raymond*, Appendix, 156.
17 Anon., *The Spiritualists at Home: The Confessions of a Medium* (London, 1861).
18 C. Williams, *Spiritualism: its True Nature and Results. With Some Personal Experiences and an Earnest Appeal to Spiritualists* (London, 1921), 42–3.
19 Hardy, *Spiritism in the Light of Faith*, 3, 10.

confronted his readers with his contention that spiritualism was 'gross selfishness'. Those who hankered after the assurances of spiritualism had forgotten that their duty was to God, not to themselves, nor even the departed. He compared bereavement with the weaning of a child – something painful to the mother but necessary for the child. He advised, 'Endure bravely the bereavement. Pray for the soul's advancement. Plead on its behalf the (memorial) sacrifice of Calvary, but do not think to have it at your constant beck and call to assist you in your frivolous and profane experiments.'[20] George Longridge claimed that spiritualism hindered the living person's true spiritual union with God.[21] John Magee was concerned for the dead, rather than the living. 'They [the dead] are moving onward and upward and you do them the worst turn in your life if you try to bring them back to satisfy your own selfish craving for their companionship.'[22]

Moreover, it was argued that the Bible expressly forbade attempts to converse with the dead. Quoted in a number of pamphlets and lectures against spiritualism were references to Leviticus xx. 6:

> And the soul that turneth after such as have familiar spirits, and after wizard, to go whoring after them, I will even set my face against that soul, and will cut him off from among his people.

Also Deuteronomy xviii. 10–12:

> There shall not be found among you any one that maketh his son or daughter to pass through the fire, or that useth divination, or an observer of the times, or an enchanter, or a witch. Or a charmer, or a consulter with familiar spirits, or a wizard, or a necromancer. For all that do these things are an abomination unto the Lord: and because of these abominations the Lord thy God doth drive them out before thee.

Witchcraft was named among the catalogue of 'works of the flesh' in Galatians v. 20, the practice of which disinherited a person from the Kingdom of God. In Revelation xxi. 8 'sorcerers' were among those due to be cast into the lake 'which burneth with fire and brimstone: which is the second death'. The connection with 'witchcraft', 'necromancy' and 'divination' ought to have been enough, according to some opponents of spiritualism, to dissuade people from dabbling. Charles Frederick Hogg, in *Spiritism in the Light of*

---

[20] C. H. Rouse, *Through Séance to Satan, or, The Lure of Spiritualism* (London, 1921), 34–6.
[21] Longridge, *Spiritualism and Christianity*, 37.
[22] *Authorized report of Church Congress held in Southend* (London, 1920), 173.

Scripture (1923) and the evangelical William Sheppard in *Messages from the Dead* (1926), certainly thought so.[23]

Some scriptural references were claimed both by opponents and advocates of spiritualism, in particular the story of the Witch of Endor in I Samuel xxvii. 7–20 and the story of Dives and Lazarus found in Luke xvi. 20–31.[24] In the first of these passages, Saul, the king of Israel, finding that the Lord does not speak to him in dreams or prophecy, visits a witch 'that hath a familiar spirit'. She conjures for him the spirit of the dead prophet Samuel. Samuel's initial words to Saul are of complaint for disturbing him, and he follows by predicting Saul's demise at the hands of the Philistines.

According to those opposed to spiritualism the witch was condemned by her involvement in Saul's enterprise. That Saul was already beyond righteous living was shown by the fact that the Lord no longer spoke to him. His visit to a witch, or medium, was evidence of his sin. Likewise, Samuel's complaint at being disturbed was further proof of Saul's wrongdoing in consulting a medium. The silence of God, the visit to the medium, the anger of Samuel and the dismal message made clear that attempting conversation with the dead was not an enterprise that met with God's approval.[25]

The story of Dives and Lazarus presents two dead men, one rich (traditionally known as Dives) and one a beggar (Lazarus). In life the poor man had sat at the rich man's gate and been ignored. In death Dives is in 'hell' and sees Lazarus carried by angels to 'Abraham's bosom' in heaven. Dives cries to Abraham and asks that Lazarus be sent to dip his finger into water to cool his tongue, 'for I am tormented in this flame'. Abraham tells him that there is a 'great gulf fixed' between them that cannot be passed either way. On hearing this Dives asks that Lazarus be sent to his father's house to warn his living brothers against the torment of hell. Abraham refuses, saying that they have the prophets and Moses to guide them and would not be persuaded even if one rose from the dead to speak to them.

For the opponents of spiritualism this story provided a clear message that the dead were not to converse with the living and that it was contrary to God's wishes to invite them to do so. Beyond death souls were allocated to one of

---

[23] C. F. Hogg, *Spiritism in the Light of Scripture* (London, 1923); W. J. L. Sheppard, *Messages from the Dead* (Stirling, 1926).

[24] For the use made of these texts by advocates of spiritualism see later in this chapter, pp. 168 and 172.

[25] See for example the comments of C. C. Dobson in *The Bible and Spiritualism* (London, 1920) and, by the same author, *Modern Spiritualism under the Biblical Searchlight* (London, 1925).

two separate waiting places and did not move from them, there being a great gulf fixed between the two states. Everything necessary to eternal salvation was provided in life and the living had no need to consult the dead. Cyril Dobson, evangelical vicar of St Peter's Paddington, went so far as to argue that the story was not a parable, but Christ's teaching about the reality of the afterlife: 'There is nothing to indicate that this is a parable. It does not begin in the customary way "the Kingdom of Heaven is like". It bears all the marks of a true story related by our Lord of his superhuman knowledge to give mankind this true unseen world information.'[26]

Such comments as these stemmed from a broad anxiety about the impact of spiritualism on mental and moral and spiritual well-being. Other critics concerned themselves more with the physical and psychical phenomena of séances, arguing either that the alleged conversations and the phenomena revealed spiritualism to be something not of God – even that they were signs that it was demonic – or else that the phenomena were a matter for scientific, rather than theological, speculation.

John Henry Elliott, speaking to a discussion class of the Chelsea branch of the Young Men's Christian Association in 1866, said that he thought it difficult to hear of what were called the 'higher manifestations' (i.e. the séance phenomena) without a flush of anger or shame that any intelligent creature would accept as truth something so 'debasing and puerile'.[27] Concluding his lecture he said that spiritualism was 'pernicious ... useless and uncalled for, not consolatory ... not supported by scripture and [is] no true antidote to materialism'. It was therefore, he thought, worthless and wicked.[28]

Cyril Dobson, offering another line of argument, envisaged a spiritual world that existed around the living; this world was organised into two forces: those of God and those of Satan. Satan's chief success, Dobson argued, lay in the way he managed to imitate and counterfeit the truth. Thus the spirits that people claimed to converse with were evil spirits. 'This is the key to modern spiritualism. Mediums are agents of Satan not God.'[29] Alfred H. Burton, in *Spiritism: Is it Real?* (1898), thought that it was real in the sense of being supernatural, but that it was also of the Devil and was satanic.[30] Even opponents who offered on the whole more sophisticated comment, such as the Anglo-catholic Charles Rouse, were content to conclude that spiritualism was

---

[26] Dobson, *The Bible and Spiritualism*, 5.
[27] John Henry Elliott, *A Refutation of Modern Spiritualism* (London, 1866), 3.
[28] Ibid., 16.
[29] Dobson, *The Bible and Spiritualism*, 4, 10.
[30] Alfred H. Burton, *Spiritism: Is it Real?* (London, 1898).

of the Devil.[31] To Viscount Halifax the alleged manifestations of the spirits seemed attributable to natural causes, or imposture; but if they were spiritual agencies then there was reason to doubt their source. 'Why,' he asked his audience, 'may they not be the utterances of agencies intending to deceive?'[32] In 1920 Thomas Leech Lomax, vicar of Ferryhill in Durham, told the Church Congress that 'evil spirits are tremendously real, very very wise, and their object above all things is that they may get us not to believe in Jesus Christ as the victor over sin and over Satan'. He was clear in his mind that spiritualism was of Satan.[33]

The Church was in a difficult position with this line of argument. On the one hand some of those opposed to spiritualism wanted to argue that it was all fraud and deception. On the other hand it was hard to deny that strange things did take place, and these could not be dismissed as mere conjuring tricks. In the face of what looked like the 'facts' of the phenomena, some churchmen, critical of spiritualism, argued that they were of diabolical provenance. Yet in arguing this they were also agreeing that the phenomena were, in some way, real.

Others were less ready to make judgements about the séance phenomena, preferring instead to suggest that such matters lay in the realm of science rather than theology. This type of response to spiritualism came from a real concern among some clergy that they were not 'qualified' to give opinions on what looked like science. And, although some clergy, as has been noted, joined the SPR and went to séances as part of their 'research' into psychic phenomena,[34] others thought such scientific enquiry ought to be left to 'professionals'.

George Longridge, for example, was convinced that spiritualism was a matter for science. Indeed, he even argued that the resurgence of spiritualism that he observed around him was due in no small part to the way that it had awakened scientific interest in human psychology: people wanted to investigate the psychic powers of mediums.[35]

The fact that scientific investigators referred to the spiritualist phenomena as 'supernormal' rather than 'supernatural' was, he argued, a reminder that the activities associated with spiritualism were not religious, but scientific. This was a matter of scientific enquiry, rather than theology. He wrote a

---

[31] Rouse, *Through Séance to Satan*.
[32] Halifax, *'Raymond'. Some criticisms*, 6.
[33] *Church Congress at Southend*, 172.
[34] Chapter three, pp. 51–53.
[35] Longridge, *Spiritualism and Christianity*, 2.

warning to those prone to dabbling in matters they could not understand. 'What has to be remembered is that, while specially trained scientific minds may investigate spiritualism as a matter of purely scientific inquiry, it is quite another thing, and in many ways a dangerous thing, for ordinary people to use it either as a new form of religion, or to meddle with it out of curiosity or the love of what is strange and occult.'[36]

The 1920 Lambeth Conference resolutions recognised the work of 'competent' psychologists. Yet the conference noted that their task was not complete and warned people against accepting as final any theory about the matter until further investigation had taken place. In other words, the conference put its trust in the scientists not only to provide the answer to the questions asked of spiritualism, but also to set the very questions.[37]

The archbishop of York, William Temple, sought an accurate account of how the phenomena of spiritualism were produced, and believed scientists would be better able to provide the answer than theologians. Writing to Archbishop Lang of Canterbury in 1936 as the committee investigating spiritualism was being gathered together, he advised him to look for scientists to be part of it. 'It seems to me that what we want is a group of scientists who will really study the alleged physical facts and try to work out the uniformities governing these. It is not till we know what are the laws in the matter that we shall be in any position to begin estimating the probable causes of any one phenomenon.' To emphasise that spiritualism was not a matter for clerical interest he added, 'Apparently it is true that under the proper conditions a table, for example, will bounce about the room: that is on any showing extremely odd, but it is not necessarily at all spiritual.'[38]

Some churchmen and women believed that the phenomena of spiritualism were effected by telepathy, and thus by human rather than supernatural power. Ernest Barnes acknowledged that some mediums possessed unusual powers, but they were powers of telepathy, rather than powers to contact the dead.[39] Viscount Halifax thought that if spiritualist messages were not from diabolical agency then they were due to 'natural causes', the mysterious power that the mind had over matter.[40] Lily Dougall, novelist and religious essayist, in a paper to the Church Congress held in the diocese of Chelmsford

---

[36] Ibid., 5.
[37] Resolutions of the Lambeth Conference, Resolution Two (56), in Kollar, *Searching for Raymond*, 155.
[38] Temple to Lang, 23 Mar. 1936. *LPL: Lang Papers*, Vol. 70, fol. 42.
[39] Barnes, *Spiritualism and the Christian Faith*, 55.
[40] Halifax, *'Raymond'. Some Criticisms*, 5.

in 1920, believed that it was possible for a range of thoughts to be 'tapped' by a medium or clairvoyant by autosuggestion or telepathy.[41]

The spiritualist newspaper *Light* criticised the Church for relying too heavily on the hope that spiritualism was mere telepathy. In 1900 *Light* referred to an article in the *Church Times* and congratulated the article for its gravity, fairness and good taste. However, the article had advised that spiritualism was simply telepathy and *Light* was unimpressed. 'Really now, is not this [telepathy] a rather desperate remedy for keeping out "discarnate spirits?" ... We prefer the much simpler, the very much simpler, explanation of spiritualism.'[42]

If these criticisms of spiritualism were concerned with the *activities* of spiritualism – the visiting of séances and the séance phenomena – then a number of arguments were also employed to counter the *theology* or ideas of spiritualism. One such argument was that the teachings of spiritualism made Jesus seem unimportant. As was seen in chapter four, spiritualists certainly struggled to maintain that Christ was divine. Dr Robinson Thornton, of St John's Church Notting Hill, thought that spiritualism had diminished the significance of Jesus, making him merely an 'adept' or medium.[43]

Spiritualism was criticised for taking no account of sin and judgement. Viscount Halifax noted,

> A common feature of all such communications (generally) is not only that they disregard the whole of the Church's teaching, but that they have no realization of sin and its consequences, and that they all deny that man's time of trial is here and not hereafter. Whatever purification may be necessary after death, we either die in God's grace or we do not.[44]

This condemnation was rebuffed by the Christian supporters of spiritualism, who, as noted earlier, said that the spirits taught quite clearly that actions of earthly life had consequences for the future life.

Another criticism was that spiritualism suggested a vision of the afterlife that made the Christian life too easy. There was no room for faith, no call to a better or holier life. Indeed, spiritualism demanded scientific evidence rather than faith, and encouraged intellectual pride rather than humility.[45] It made few demands on discipline or self-examination, but rather appealed to mortal

---

41 *Church Congress at Southend*, 168.
42 *Light*, 28 July 1900, referring to *Church Times*, 6 July 1900.
43 *Church Congress at Newcastle*, 54.
44 Halifax, *'Raymond'. Some Criticisms*, 39–40.
45 Rouse, *Through Séance to Satan*, 18.

weakness and the desire for signs, in contrast to the real way of faith offered by the Church, which was a way of prayer and self-denial.[46] Ernest Barnes, thinking through spiritualism in the light of contemporary theories of the universe, the nature of man and spiritual reality, concluded that Christians needed to be content, in the end, with faith rather than the sight that spiritualism purported to offer.[47]

Some opponents disparaged spiritualism by identifying it with earlier heresy or heterodoxy or by pointing out its internal inconsistencies. Canon Edmund McClure, speaking to the Church Congress in 1919, coupled spiritualism with Swedenborgianism.[48] Others dismissed it as the latest manifestation of age-old heterodoxy. Necromancy was mentioned in the Bible and even the 'planchette', an instrument used by mediums for automatic writing, had been used in China many years before.[49]

For some, the teaching of spiritualism was but a pale reflection of Church doctrine. It was, Viscount Halifax thought, but a 'miserable substitute' for the Church's teaching about the Communion of Saints. He advised people to read John Henry Newman's *Dream of Gerontius* instead of *Raymond* if they wanted to know of eternal life.[50] Edmund McClure believed the apostolic doctrine of the Communion of Saints offered 'infinitely more solace to the bereaved than spiritualism can give'.[51] And, as Robert Benson, an Anglican convert to Roman Catholicism, argued, 'The spirit teachings seldom surpass in intelligence of knowledge the average works of writers even still incarnate, much less do they approximate in knowledge or spirituality to the teachings of the greatest spiritual leaders of the past.'[52]

Perhaps the most subtle response to spiritualism came from William Ralph Inge at the 1919 Church Congress. Opening the debate on 'The Christian Doctrine of the Future Life' he argued that many hopes articulated – even among Christians – concerning the future life were not religious at all. Hoping for survival, wishing for a better life, hoping to be repaid for good works, none of these desires was particularly religious. People had lost the sense of heaven, and in the context of materialism and a fixation on progress modern men and women had exchanged the idea of eternal life for a concrete and intelligible picture of it. In doing so they had, he thought, brought heaven

---

[46] 'EAG' and 'PWSS', *True and False Spiritualism* (London, 1918), 26.
[47] Barnes, *Spiritualism and the Christian Faith*, 61.
[48] *Church Congress at Leicester*, 102.
[49] Longridge, *Spiritualism and Christianity*, 2.
[50] Halifax, *'Raymond'. Some Criticisms*, 12.
[51] *Church Congress at Leicester*, 106.
[52] Benson, *Spiritualism*, 15.

down to earth and created a 'trifling', 'child's-picture-book' heaven. What he termed 'the pitiable revival of necromancy' offered only spurious satisfaction, while true faith believed that 'those who live unto God live also with those whom they have loved on earth. Beyond this we know nothing, and there are good reasons why we cannot know.'[53]

Some clergy and laity in the Church of England began to question among themselves why on earth people would want to turn to the 'spurious', 'trifling' and 'false' assurances of spiritualism rather than the Christian faith. They concluded that the Church itself was partly to blame for the increasing numbers of bereaved seeking solace in spiritualism and they shared this thinking with fellow clergy and laity. It wasn't so much that the teaching about the afterlife was too harsh or judgmental, as spiritualists claimed; rather that it was too hesitant. Thus at the Church Congress of 1881 Dr Thornton expressed the opinion that spiritualism was a reminder to the Church of England that its teaching was sometimes uncertain regarding life beyond death.[54]

Forty years later, at the 1919 Church Congress, similar anxieties were voiced. The dean of Manchester, William Shuckburgh Swayne, recognised that not only had there been 'considerable development' in the practice of spiritualism, but also that the Church had been timid and hesitant in supplying the great human need with the doctrines of the Christian faith regarding immortality and the Communion of Saints. Perhaps the Church had been too silent, he thought, with regard to the relations between the Church on earth and the Church 'beyond the veil'. During the same debate Canon McClure expressed the opinion that the 'illicit efforts' made by mediums to break through the barrier of life and death had proved popular with many who sought a continuous association with the departed that was not properly taught by the Church. 'The conception of that barrier, moreover, rises from a practical ignoring of the Paraclete, the Comforter. Without the fellowship of the Holy Ghost we are shut out from the Spirit world.'[55] At the Congress held the following year Harold Anson agreed that the vogue for spiritualism was due in part to 'the craving of the ordinary man to have some external authorisation for a wider hope of the hereafter than the religion of the Sunday School or the revival meeting has given him'.[56]

Some Anglo-catholic clergy and laity used the growing anxiety about

---

[53] *Church Congress at Leicester*, 90–91.
[54] *Church Congress at Newcastle*, 52.
[55] *Church Congress at Leicester*, 96, 106.
[56] *Church Congress at Southend*, 149. Anson went on to become master of the Temple and a canon at Southwark. He wrote articles concerning prayer, health and spiritualism.

spiritualism in order to further their own ambition to see prayers for the dead reinstated into the liturgy and practice of the Church of England. The argument followed that inadequate teaching about the Communion of Saints and the inability of Anglicans to pray in public for the dead had driven many people away from the Church and into the arms of mediums who claimed to connect them with their departed. People felt the need for some sort of 'communication'. Thus Charles Rouse argued that, 'The bishops have in fact paved the way for spiritism and are now in difficulty. They have done this by banning the Catholic doctrine of the Communion of Saints. That article has been retained in the Creeds, but we have not been allowed to put it into practice. We may believe in the Communion of Saints, but must not consider ourselves to be on speaking terms with them.'[57] Viscount Halifax agreed that the real problem was that the Church had neglected prayers for the dead. Of the dead he suggested, 'Let us ask their prayers, let us pray for them, let us seek their help, let us realize the closeness of union we have with them. No such union and fellowship with them as is promised by spiritualism can come near the reality of that intimate communion vouchsafed to the members of Christ's Body one with another.'[58]

It was not only the view of a few Anglo-catholics that the Church had been found wanting regarding its concern for the dead and the needs of the bereaved. As will be seen, the suggestion was made in both the majority and minority conclusions in the 1939 *Report of the Archbishop of Canterbury's Committee on Spiritualism* that prayer for the dead needed to be taken into further consideration. The Church's reticence to pray for the dead, according to the committee members, did not satisfy the needs of bereaved people.

Embracing spiritualism

While some clergy and laity responded to spiritualism with derision, anger or concern, and others decided that decisions made about it should be undertaken only after full scientific investigation, a not insubstantial number of the clergy embraced spiritualism. These clergymen embraced it with varying degrees of enthusiasm, and as a result occasionally incurred the disapproval of their bishops. Some kept quiet about their inclinations towards spiritualism, but their interest was registered by spiritualists. *Light*, for example, noted a private meeting in 1881 at which twenty-one Church of England clergy were present.

---

[57] C. H. Rouse, *Spiritism and the Voice of the Church* (London, 1923), 111.
[58] Halifax, *'Raymond'. Some Criticisms*, 41.

The newspaper claimed that, with only one exception, 'not a word was raised against spiritualism'.[59] Other clergy joined Christian spiritualist societies where there was a certain safety in number, although not all did; clerical spiritualists were not all, straightforwardly, part of one organisation. Some, however, were apparently willing to ruffle episcopal feathers by encouraging fellow Christians to try spiritualism, writing spiritualist books, organising séances in their churches or advocating spiritualism in newspapers.

Clergy were present at séances from the earliest recordings of spiritualism in England. The *Yorkshire Spiritual Telegraph* claimed as early as 1855 that they were attending séances and even acting as mediums. Indeed, the newspaper was at pains to point out that spiritualism was not confined *only* to the Church of England.[60] Charles Dickens in the journal *All the Year Round* recorded a visit to a séance in 1860 where a clergyman was present – and keen to be involved.[61]

Given that spiritualism pervaded society in all social classes and in all geographical locations, and all sorts of people encountered it in lectures, demonstrations and debates as well as séances, it is unsurprising that clergy as well as laity heard its claims and tried the spirits for themselves. Others, as has been noted, chose to join the SPR and investigated the claims of spiritualism under the auspices of scientific enquiry.

Percy Dearmer (1867–1936) is an example of a well-known clergyman who was interested in spiritualism. Dearmer was ordained priest in 1892. After serving four curacies he became vicar of St Mary-the-Virgin, Primrose Hill, London. He was active in the Alcuin Club, a society founded in 1897 that sought to introduce an Anglo-catholic worship into the Church of England that was rooted in medieval English tradition rather than the Roman liturgy of the day. Dearmer exercised a strong influence over English Church music, editing the *English Hymnal* with Ralph Vaughan Williams in 1906. He was secretary of the London branch of the Christian Social Union from 1891–1912, professor of ecclesiastical art at King's College London from 1919 and was made a canon of Westminster Abbey in 1931.[62]

Dearmer's second wife, Nancy, whom he married in 1916, recorded that he also experimented with spiritualism:

> Among the many interests which claimed his attention was Psychic Research. He had been a member of the Society for Psychical

---

59 Letter from G. Damiani in *Light*, 17 Dec. 1881.
60 *Yorkshire Spiritual Telegraph*, May 1855.
61 'Modern Magic', *All the Year Round*, No. 66 (28 July 1860), 370.
62 See Donald Gray, *Percy Dearmer, A Parson's Pilgrimage* (Norwich, 2000).

Research (SPR) since 1910 and had given considerable study to the subject. After his first wife Mabel and his younger son Christopher died during the war in 1915 he had 'sittings' both with Mrs Gladys Osborne Leonard and Mrs Fernie with some interesting results. Later he contributed a series of articles to the *Morning Post* as the result of some special investigations, and from time to time he both wrote and spoke on the latest discoveries.[63]

Mabel and Christopher died within a short time of one another during the war. Dearmer had travelled to Serbia as chaplain to a nursing unit; Mabel went as an orderly. She became sick very soon after arriving and died in 1917. The nursing unit was the 'Stobart Serbian Unit' led by Mrs St Clair Stobart – who, as has been noted, had certainly by this date tried spiritualism at home and who later became an ardent advocate.

Dearmer's experiments with spiritualism came even closer to home when Nancy discovered her own mediumistic powers. With his wife he put his name to a book called *The Fellowship of the Picture. An Automatic Script taken down by Nancy Dearmer* (1920). He also wrote the introduction for the book. In it he told of how he and his wife were staying in their country cottage when, on 31 July 1919, Nancy felt

> impelled to sit down and allow her hand to write automatically … She had previously felt a marked dislike of all such supposed manifestations or communications as are now classed under the name of Psychics; nor had she ever imagined herself to have any psychic powers or gifts, or whatever they may be.[64]

She wrote for half an hour each day until 10 September of the same year. Each day, having written, she took the script to Percy for him to read aloud. Neither Nancy nor Percy expressed any opinion as to the merits of the book, Percy saying only that

> We find it very difficult to frame any hypothesis except that in some way it did emanate from the mind of a friend whose name, or initials, was frequently appended to the morning's chapter. From the beginning this name was signed in a different handwriting from that of my wife – in fact, with the same signature which we found on looking through his letters; and the last page was signed with his initials. All along, the script was written as from one who was urgent to give a

[63] Nancy Dearmer, *The life of Percy Dearmer* (London, 1940), 275.
[64] Percy and Nancy Dearmer, *The Fellowship of the Picture. An Automatic Script taken down by Nancy Dearmer* (London, 1920), 7.

message to the world, who was the friend we had known, and whose identity was familiar and unmistakable.[65]

The 'friend' was described as a man of academic distinction who had been killed in France in 1918. He remained anonymous throughout the book. The automatic writing was witnessed by others staying with the Dearmers and they took the work to the Society for Psychical Research – although little more was said of the SPR's involvement.

The book itself was a collection of thoughts about prayer and God. It was not especially profound, but the 'author' said from the outset that he had wanted to keep things simple.[66] He wrote of prayer, happiness, fellowship and community, but said nothing of any great magnitude about the afterlife. As a work it certainly lacked Dearmer's own scholarship and style, and Dearmer offered no analysis or comment on the contents.

Along with spiritualism, Dearmer was interested in the wider investigations into human psychical health and the bearing of faith on healing. He attended a meeting in 1904, six years before joining the SPR, to consider the formation of a society to revive the principles and practice of the ministry of healing in the Church of England. About four hundred gathered in a room at the Paddington Hotel and Dearmer shared the platform with theosophists, spiritualists and Christian Scientists. The outcome of this was the founding of the Guild of Health. He wrote a book in 1909, while at Primrose Hill, entitled, *Body and Soul. An Enquiry into the effects of religion upon health, with a description of Christian works of healing from the New Testament to the present day*. In it he examined healing in both the Old and New Testaments, concluding that wholeness and peace and inner feelings were an important part of physical health.

It was possible that others knew of his interests in spiritualism and psychical research. Conrad Noel's autobiography, for example, tells of an occasion when Dearmer stayed with him and a ten-shilling note had, unexpectedly, fluttered down out of a book 'as at a spiritualist séance through the ceiling from Heaven'.[67] The way that Noel used this imagery in connection with his friend suggests that he may have associated Dearmer with the phenomena of spiritualism.

Dearmer strongly disliked the traditional Christian teaching on hell and eternal punishment, believing that universal salvation had become a

---

[65] Ibid., 8.
[66] Ibid., 12.
[67] Gray, *Percy Dearmer*, 76. Conrad Noel (1869–1942) was the 'Red Vicar' of Thaxted and founded the Church Socialist League in 1906.

commonplace by the 1920s.[68] He connected the spiritualist idea of the after-life and the possibility of communication with another Christian idea: the Communion of Saints. He was comfortable with séance phenomena, investigating from a scientific perspective and encouraging his wife at home. Moreover, he used the knowledge gleaned from his SPR investigations to support his theological argument and found no dissonance between the psychic experiments and either spiritualism or the Christian faith. In 1906, for example, when writing about the Christian belief in the Communion of Saints, he mentioned the SPR:

> And now in recent years there has arisen a body of scientific investigators – F. W. H. Myers, and Edmund Gurney, and Professor Sidgwick, and Professor Barrett, and Sir William Crooks, and Mr Alfred R. Wallace – the scientist who shares with Darwin the honour of the discovery of the secret of evolution; these men founded a society for the free investigation of the new (and yet old) phenomena that can no longer be passed over. The investigation is still proceeding. Some of the greatest minds are convinced by the great mass of evidence already accumulated that the power of the departed, not only to know about us, but to communicate with us, has been proved ... And nothing is more likely than that the Fellowship of Souls – the Communion of Saints, living and departed – may soon everywhere be accepted as a matter which has been scientifically proved.[69]

Walter Matthews (1881–1973), dean of St Paul's, was another well-known and senior clergyman who declared a quiet interest in the teachings of spiritualism. Matthews was professor of theology at King's College London, becoming dean in 1918. He was made dean of Exeter in 1931 and then dean of St Paul's in 1934. Although, like Dearmer, he didn't expose his enthusiasm for spiritualism by writing explicitly about it, he certainly didn't hide the fact that it interested him. In his autobiography he wrote of how, even as a boy of sixteen, he was fascinated by thoughts of death and immortality which led him to spiritualism:

> Quite early in life, before I left school, I had read about psychical research and either at school or soon after I went into the Westminster Bank [he worked as a clerk] I read F. W. Myers' pioneer work *Human*

---

[68] Percy Dearmer, *The Legend of Hell. An examination of the idea of everlasting punishment* (London, 1929), 72.
[69] Percy Dearmer, *The Communion of the Saints* (London, 1906), 21–2.

Personality and its Survival of Bodily Death. It happened too that, when I went into the Bank, one of the clerks in the head office named Podmore was the brother of a man who was among the group which pushed ahead in research. Strangely, I do not remember at this time meeting anyone who had been to a séance or claimed to be a medium. My knowledge was derived from books, but the evidence impressed me.[70]

Matthews joined the SPR as soon as he had finished his studies and could afford the subscription, and over the course of many years sat with mediums and went to séances. While he was dean of Exeter he had a secretary, Miss Longridge, who was gifted in automatic writing. Although recognising that some mediums were frauds, and that it was impossible to prove the veracity of spirit messages, Matthews nevertheless found that spiritualism appeared to offer an indication that the soul survived beyond death. Like Dearmer, he hoped that it might be possible for the Church to 'consider whether the needs which are met by spiritualism cannot be met by a deeper understanding of the communion of saints':

> I fully admit that the fear of opening the way to superstition is justi-
> fied; but is it fantastic to suggest that the Feast of All Souls could be
> given a wider reference than has been customary and express a wider
> hope? I have often felt that the 'souls of the faithful' will rest in peace
> whether we pray for them or not; it is the souls of the unfaithful who
> need our prayers.[71]

Dearmer and Matthews managed, without hiding their interest in spiritu-alism, to maintain the approval of senior clergy. Other clergymen, a little more extravagant in their enthusiasm for spiritualism, were prepared to risk ridicule and jeopardise their preferment in order to be known as men who believed that spiritualists really did have the power to communicate with the dead. One such was Graeme Maurice Elliott, Church of England clergyman, writer of the book *Angels seen today* (1919), and co-founder – with Mabel St Clair Stobart[72] – of the 'Confraternity of Clergy and Spiritualists'. Elliott was vice-chairman of the Confraternity and rector of St Peter's, Cricklewood from 1934 to 1936, having been previously rector of Over Wallop (1930–4), rector of Honily, and Snitterby.[73] By 1935 he was the cause of some trouble for the

---

[70] W. R. Matthews, *Memories and Meanings* (London, 1969), 344.
[71] Ibid., 348.
[72] See chapter three, pp. 45–46.
[73] Elliott went on to become a founder member of the Christian Psychic Society in the 1950s.

bishop of Guildford, John Victor Macmillan. Macmillan wrote to the arch-bishop of Canterbury on 27 November 1935 complaining that Elliott, a priest in the diocese of London, appeared 'to be going into the dioceses round London speaking about spiritualism'.[74] He continued,

> Some weeks ago he was given out to speak at a so-called Spiritualist Church at Walton-on-Thames. Belatedly and after the meeting was announced, he asked me if I minded his coming. I had been in touch with the Vicar of Walton who is a good and capable man. I observed to Elliott that he was only asking me after everything was settled and that I did not see the necessity for him to come into another parish except at the invitation of the parish priest, which had not been given.
>
> He completely ignored this and went to Walton, where I understand he tried to produce the impression that I had tried to inhibit him. I asked the Bishop of London about it at the time. He said he was a very tiresome person, but he did not seem to know how he could be prevented doing this kind of thing.
>
> The matter has now gone further in that Mr. Elliott together with a certain Mrs St. Clair Stobart have advertised a Meeting to be held at Camberley, described as being 'In connection with the Confraternity between Clergy and Spiritualists'.
>
> He has been in the neighbourhood of Camberley and has got various people to urge the local clergy – the Vicar of Camberley itself, St. Peter's, Camberley, Frimley and Bagshot – to attend the meeting. Two of them have consulted me and I have told them to have nothing whatever to do with it.
>
> Among the papers circulated is one of the long interview which Mr Sharp purports to have had with the late Archbishop Davidson in the other world!
>
> You may say on the Archbishop's behalf that I ought to consult the Bishop of London again about this. I am quite ready to do this, but I wanted to know whether the Diocese of Guildford was the only one that was being afflicted in this way? The thing is being done with a certain amount of cleverness, as it is mixed up with literature about the opulence of bishops and the practical difficulties, financial and other, of the clergy; and appeals for homeless people. A district like Camberley is rather good hunting ground for this kind of propaganda, as there are a number of leisurely people who have not got regular occupation.

---

[74] Macmillan to Alan Don, 27 Nov. 1935. *LPL: Lang Papers*, Vol. 133, fol. 297.

The Mr Sharp referred to in the correspondence was Arthur Sharp, vicar of St Stephen's, Hampstead from 1913 and rural dean of Hampstead from 1921 to 1935. He had spent time overseas when first ordained, holding positions in Singapore Cathedral and Kuching, and being archdeacon of Sarawak from 1900 to 1911. Sharp was holding séances in the Lady Chapel of his church in early 1935 with a medium called Vivian Deacon. During the séances the late archbishop, Randall Davidson, had appeared and told the meeting that there was no truth in the doctrine of eternal punishment.[75]

On 4 December 1935 the archbishop's chaplain, Alan Don, replied:

> The Archbishop is not altogether surprised to hear of the activities of the Rev. G. M. Elliott who is evidently in league with Mr Sharp who recently, at the bishop of London's instigation, resigned his post of rural dean. The bishop of London, who has been considerably troubled by these people, has prohibited spiritualistic meetings being held in any churches or church halls within his diocese. This may account for the fact that these people are making expeditions into neighbouring dioceses.
>
> His Grace considers that you are perfectly right in warning your clergy off these people. He feels sure that it is dangerous to experiment with spiritualistic seances and the like and greatly deprecates the fantastic statements which have been made about communications with the late Archbishop. If spiritualism has anything in it the matter ought to be investigated by trained scientific enquirers and certainly not by the ordinary clergy.[76]

The bishop of Guildford responded with thanks, saying that he would take the opportunity at a Diocesan Conference to emphasise his feelings, strengthened by the archbishop's comments.

The Confraternity of Clergy and Spiritualists, however, continued to grow. Its literature described its members as 'those whose lives are dedicated to their various Ministries, and on the other hand, those who are devoted to the Cause of Survival – of spreading the Truth of Man's Survival of physical death, and the possibility of communicating with those who have survived'.[77]

By 1939 it had expanded and was called 'The Confraternity of Clergy, Ministers, Laymen and Spiritualists'. The Confraternity wrote to the archbishop of Canterbury asking to know the outcome of the investigations into

---

75 Arthur F. Sharp, *The Spirit Saith*, 2 Vols (London, 1956), 2: 9–14.

76 *LPL: Lang Papers*, Vol. 133, fol. 299.

77 *The Confraternity of Clergy and Spiritualists. Its Aims and Objects and the Reason Why* (Pamphlet produced by the Confraternity, Grotian Hall, London, n.d.).

spiritualism conducted by the Archbishop's Committee. The headed letter included the names of all the Confraternity members. This was a list of those people prepared to admit in public (and to the archbishop) that they agreed with the object of the Confraternity given above. The list included laity, nonconformists and more than twenty-five Church of England clergy.

It is possible to know a little of these clergymen's circumstances, the dioceses in which they ministered, their church tradition, and also something of their pre- and post-1930s careers. The diversity of the group is worth noting. Spiritualism, certainly by the 1930s, was attractive to Anglo-catholics, evangelicals and liberals. It was not confined to any one geograph-ical location, and was not necessarily metropolitan – there were clergy spiritu-alists in places as diverse as Paignton, London, Bromsgrove and Norwich. Some of these clergymen had served as army or navy chaplains, but not all of them. Their educational backgrounds were diverse: not many of them had spent time in Cambridge colleges. Harry Finnie, the acting curate of Barnes, for example, had studied at King's College London. Herbert Crabtree, the vicar of St Matthew, Blackburn, was at the University of Manchester and Robert Irons, the vicar of St Paul's, Gatten in Portsmouth, had studied at St Andrew's.

According to *Crockford's Clerical Directory*, some of these clergy were preferred. Richard Keble Cheeseright, for example, who in 1939 was curate at Bishop's Hatfield in the diocese of St Alban's, became rector of a Duchy of Lancaster living, Beeston Regis in Norwich diocese in 1941. Archie Webling, the rector of Risby in the diocese of St Edmundsbury and Ipswich, was made an honorary canon of the cathedral. Edwin Ernest Fitz-Hugh moved from East Stoke with Syerston in Southwark, to become the public preacher for the diocese and vicar of Stockwith. Others remained in post. Harry William Browning, the vicar of St Mildred, Lee, in the diocese of Southwark, did not lose his position as a result of his spiritualism, but was still vicar there ten years later. Walter Bowdon remained vicar of St Merryn in Truro; Walter Freeman continued as vicar of Brixworth in Peterborough; Frederick Horan stayed as vicar of Kingston, Salisbury; and Henry Paterson remained as chap-lain to the bishop of Worcester and rector of the very generous living at Hartlebury. James Cryer was vicar of St Benet, Stepney until his death in 1943 and William Geike-Cobb remained as rector of St Ethelburga, Bishopsgate until his death in 1941. His obituary in *The Times* described him as 'not only religious but good'.[78]

---

[78] *The Times*, 15 Dec. 1941, pg. 6, col. D.

It is difficult to gauge exactly how these clergymen made use of their spiritualism. Members of the Confraternity, according to their literature, travelled 'all over the country' and especially in 'country districts' in order to urge 'men and women of all grades of religious belief' of the importance of spiritualism for Christianity. Spiritualism would, they hoped, 'restore Christianity to its spiritual impetus' and to renewed 'Pentecostal Power'.[79] If this was true, then a small and diverse but committed group of people, connected with one another by their membership of the Confraternity, actively sought to use the teachings of spiritualism to renew the Christian Church.

There were other clergy who were not only prepared to have their names associated with spiritualism, but who, like the members of the Confraternity, actively tried to engage with its theology, ideas and imagery; they did so by publishing books inspired by spiritualism.

Charles Maurice Davies (1828–1910) is best known as the author of various works concerning the variety of religious life in London during the 1870s.[80] He is less well known as an advocate of spiritualism. He was made a fellow of Durham University in 1849, ordained deacon in 1851 and priest in 1852. After various curacies he was headmaster at West London Collegiate School between 1861 and 1868. Although his career lay more in journalism than ministry, he described himself as 'a Sunday Evening Lecturer at Chelsea Parish Church' in 1881.[81] And, although he abandoned holy orders after 1882, he continued to insist that spiritualism had much to offer Christianity.

In *The Great Secret and its Unfoldment in Occultism* (1895) Davies charted his involvement with spiritualism. He published the book under the pseudonym 'A Church of England Clergyman' because he believed his 'professional' title to be of more importance than his personal name. 'I am sure my name would not add any weight to my remarks, while the statement of my clerical calling warns my readers what kind of criticism they might expect.'[82]

The story of his involvement with spiritualism began in Paris in 1856. He had recently left Durham and married and, having no duty at home either clerical or lay, the couple settled for a time in Paris, where Davies taught Classics and Modern English. At the time Paris was alive with stories of séances at the Tuilleries, conducted by Daniel Dunglas Home. Davies' wife

---

[79] *The Confraternity of Clergy and Spiritualists*, 5.
[80] *Unorthodox London* and *Orthodox London* (London, 1874), in particular.
[81] Open letter: Davies to Tait, 14 April 1881. *LPL: Tait Papers*, Vol. 270, fols 8–18. Also printed in *Light*, 26 Mar. 1881.
[82] Davies, *The Great Secret*, 6. His name might not have added weight because, by that point, he had also been involved in two sexual scandals.

began experimenting with automatic writing, encouraged by the French governess who lodged with them.

When Davies' brother arrived on a visit from England he brought news of spiritualism in London, having been present himself at a séance in the home of a Dr Rymer in Ealing. It was, Davies noted, these séances in Ealing that, in 1860, formed the basis of the article, 'Stranger than fiction' in the *Cornhill Magazine*.[83]

Eventually Davies was persuaded by his wife and brother to try the spirits. The séance was a success and the table span in the air.[84] The table tilted to answer questions, three times for yes, once for no and twice if the reply was doubtful. It also tilted to the alphabet to answer in more detail. Davies tried to test the spirits and wrote questions surreptitiously:

> 'By what power is the table moved?'
> *Answer: 'To the spirits of the departed this power is given'.*
> 'What is the use of it?'
> *Answer: 'It may make men believe in God'.*
> 'What was the nickname we called R B (naming a deceased friend) at college?'
> *Answer: 'Peepy'.*[85]

No one else, he thought, would have known this. 'Then I was "converted." They tell me my face was a treat to see, so complete was my mystification.'[86]

For a period of nine years he did little with his new-found spiritualism, returning to England for teaching and some clerical duties. Then his son Johnny died of scarlet fever and his need to communicate was stronger and more focused.

He took part in a conference of spiritualists held in Gower Street, London, on 6 August 1874 at the time when his book *Unorthodox London* was being serialised in the *Daily Telegraph*. At that point he claimed that he had not come to any strong conclusions regarding spiritualism. When pressed at the conference he said that he believed there to be some truth in it initially, but had

---

[83] See chapter three, p. 70.

[84] Davies, *The Great Secret*, 33–5. Davies must have read something about spiritualism before all of this, as he was aware that Michael Faraday had claimed that tables span and moved because of involuntary muscular action on the part of sitters. This could not have been the case here, Davies claimed, as the table was 'one of those French affairs which always had something wrong in the works'. In this case, the screw was worn, so that the top would twist, but the legs stayed still.

[85] Ibid., 35.

[86] Ibid., 36.

become increasingly sceptical.[87] He was still interested enough in spiritualism to become a member of the National Association of Spiritualists the following year.[88]

A few years later he was much more open about his beliefs. By 12 March 1881 the *Spiritualist* newspaper was noting plans for a 'Church for Christian Spiritualists'. A clergyman was going to lead it and there would be an organist. The newspaper announced that, 'Public services will be at 11 and 7 and will consist of the Church of England offices slightly modified and considerably abridged; but there will also be numerous services of a more private nature during the week'.[89] The plans never quite came to fruition, and the name of the clergyman was not given, but given the open letter to the archbishop of Canterbury that appeared the following week, it is likely to have been Davies.

In his letter Davies gave as his reason for writing 'the recognised inclusion within the National Church of many persons whose orthodoxy is now unduly suspected' – he meant spiritualists.[90] He had no means, he said, of knowing how many people were spiritualists in England, but 'in America they are said to number some millions'. He claimed to speak not only for himself but also for other clergy who would append their names privately to the letter. 'But I have special means of knowing that the number of those who hold the doctrines of so-called spiritualism while remaining staunch members of the Church of England is very large and constantly increasing.'[91]

He claimed that spiritualism was important to the Church because it helped bring about belief, and offered the evidence of the distinguished editor of the *Art Journal*, Mr Samuel Carter Hall, whom he described as a 'literary man' who had been renewed in his Christian belief through spiritualism.[92] Davies' letter asked for toleration and appreciation of spiritualists within the Church, and recognition by bishops and Church authority that spiritualism might offer a means to faith for some.

---

[87] *Spiritualist*, 21 Aug. 1874.
[88] Ibid., 22 Jan. 1875. A list of members includes Davies. He had also, in 1876, published a novel, *Maud Blount, Medium* (London, 1876), a thinly disguised autobiography of a clergyman with a medium for a wife. See esp. 208–25.
[89] *Spiritualist*, 12 Mar. 1881.
[90] Ibid., 19 Mar. 1881.
[91] Unfortunately, although the letter to the archbishop appears in the Tait Papers at Lambeth Palace, the appended list of names is not included with it. See *LPL: Tait Papers*, Vol. 270, fols. 8–18. Letter is dated 14 Apr. 1881.
[92] Samuel Carter Hall (1800–1889) was a writer, and editor of the *Art Journal* from 1839 until his retirement. He championed the cause of leading modern artists and art critics and was a tireless campaigner for public art exhibitions. *ODNB*.

In the personal narrative of his spiritualism Davies argued that spiritualism had tightened rather than loosened his faith in Christianity. It was not that he simply had a fascination with séance phenomena, but he thought that the teachings of spiritualism had something to offer Christianity. In addition, he found sanction for his spiritualist beliefs in 'every creed, in every sacrament and ceremony. I lay my hand on the Bible and I say, "It is written".'[93]

His published sermons encouraged people to use their imagination in matters of faith, for 'all the beauty of our religious life, the beauty of holiness, the beauty of worship, is a direct outcome and result of this religious use of the Imagination'.[94] He encouraged them to explore beyond Church teaching. 'God writes in other books besides the Bible; writes on the broad sheet of nature, writes in our own inner consciousness, writes in every new discovery and invention, something about himself and our own immortal destinies.'[95]

Davies offered a reading of the story of Dives and Lazarus that was markedly different from that noted earlier from the opponents of spiritualism. Rather than concentrating on the separation of the two realms of heaven and hell, he saw the story as revealing that both men were active and conscious after death, and that the rich man was developing in his character, being now concerned for the well-being of others.[96] This suggested to Davies that after death there was possibility for the soul to progress and develop.

His heaven was a blend of spiritualist and biblical imagery. The spiritualist imagery of progress in the afterlife was confirmed for him by the writing of St Paul. He commented on St Paul's 'beautiful illustrations' about the spiritual body. 'There are even now,' he wrote, 'different bodies, rising one above the other in grades and tiers of sublimation, from the gross animal to the refined human form. You may ascend higher still, he says, in a passage often misunderstood.'[97] It was important to live lives as 'Good Samaritans'. 'Then, when the seed-husk of the natural body drops off and the spiritual body speeds to its place in the spirit-land, you shall realise the truth of those very last words of holy scripture which were read over your sleeping body here below ere they laid you in your narrow bed: Your labour is not in vain in the Lord.'[98] He imagined that heaven would be full of light, 'like one of our rare English summer days'.[99]

---

93 Davies, *The Great Secret*, 274–5.
94 Charles Maurice Davies, *London Sermons* (London, 1875), 87.
95 Ibid., 89.
96 Ibid., 56.
97 Ibid., 173. I assume the passage he refers to is II Corinthians xii.
98 Ibid., 179.
99 Ibid., 255.

As far as communicating with the dead was concerned, he shied away from writing directly about this spiritualist activity in his sermons, but instead affirmed the idea of an active connection between the living and the dead. He believed that the dead were aware of the earthly life of the living. 'One can see no possible reason why memory should be denied them, or why the event that cuts them off from our gaze should cut us off from theirs: though we must believe that, even if their old interest in us survives, it survives in such a shape as to exist without disturbing their peace.'[100]

In a series of six sermons preached in two London churches at Eastertide Davies took the story of the Resurrection appearances of Christ and applied them to the bereavement experienced by ordinary people. Again, although not explicitly commending spiritualist practice, his writing was suffused with its imagery and ideas. Thus, when regarding Jesus' encounter with Mary Magdalene in John xx. 17, for example, he argued that the words of Christ ('Touch me not') were a reference to a gradual ascension, the sort of slow detachment of the soul from the body that spiritualists claimed took place at death.[101] What he sought to convey most, he said, was that by his appearance to Mary, Christ was telling her 'it is not all over', and was moving her onward to a 'higher' truth.[102]

The final sermon on the Ascension of Christ fixed on the empty place or the empty chair of bereavement and the disciples' recognition, common to all who were bereaved, that their 'beloved' was not returning. After the Ascension, the disciples rejoiced because they believed that they were heading to where Jesus had gone, the reality of the Resurrection had been demonstrated and they knew that death was the gate of life. They had despaired at Calvary and doubted during the Resurrection appearances but only began to rejoice when he had gone. From that point they went out in courage.[103]

Davies was concerned to integrate the teachings of spiritualism into the doctrine of the Church, introducing séances with church services in the two rooms he rented in Great Russell Street over the offices of the British National Association of Spiritualists. For all his commitment, however, he was erratic in his ordained life, spending more time in education and journalism, and was not, it seems, so committed to parochial ministry.

---

100 Ibid., 201.
101 See chapter four, pp. 84–85.
102 Charles Maurice Davies, *The Future that Awaits Us. The appearances of Jesus during the Great Forty Days, viewed as a revelation of the Unseen World* (London, 1884), 9.
103 Ibid., 56–64.

Other clergy were more settled in parish ministry. They were actively committed to the ideas of spiritualism and commended spiritualism in their writing. They did not tend to become members of clergy spiritualist societies; they did not acknowledge one another, although they may have known of one another; they came to spiritualism in different ways and for different reasons. What was common to all of them, however, was not so much an interest in the phenomena of spiritualism, or psychic science, but a belief that the ideas and images of spiritualism were potentially important for the Christian faith.

George Vale Owen (1860–1931) was vicar of Orford in Lancashire in the 1920s. In 1919 Arthur Conan Doyle described him as not only a devoted parish priest, but also 'the greatest writing medium in England today'.[104] Owen became convinced by spiritualism over a period of twenty-five years studying it as a subject. Writing of his experiences he said that it took ten years to convince him that spirit communication was a fact and another fifteen to convince him that it was legitimate and good.[105] Once convinced, he became an advocate for the assimilation of spiritualism into Christianity and encouraged people to prove the survival of the human soul for themselves by trying spiritualism.

Owen was concerned that spiritualists and Christians should recognise the value of what each had to offer the other. A true spiritualist and a true Christian, he thought, would, even if they did not understand each other, at least be able to resist verbal assault.

> A clergyman writes to me complaining that Spiritualists, at the present time, are making an attack on Christianity. I was once asked, when addressing a meeting, how I accounted for the fact that so many Christians reviled Spiritualism. My reply was, 'The reason seems to me to be perfectly apparent; it is that they are not true Christians.' To my clerical correspondent I make the same answer, in inverted phrase, 'Any Spiritualist who decries Christianity is no true Spiritualist.[106]

Owen's support for spiritualism extended beyond theory; indeed, he was unafraid to admit that he had communicated with the departed. 'Just before Sir Arthur Conan Doyle left England for his Australian tour, in July, 1920, he was given a farewell luncheon in London. During his speech he suddenly paused and asked all those who could swear that they had spoken to their departed friends to stand up. There were 290 people there and, of this number,

---

104 Doyle, *Our Reply to the Cleric*, 7.
105 Owen, *Life beyond the Veil*, 1:8.
106 George Vale Owen, *Facts and the Future Life* (London, 1922), 167.

no fewer than 250 stood up. *I was one of them.*' Owen went on to note that when Conan Doyle told people in Melbourne about the occasion he had added that 'in that room were peers and peeresses, high officers of the army and navy, and the chairman was a Harley Street doctor'.[107]

In *The Life beyond the Veil* he offered two volumes of descriptions of what he termed the 'Lowlands' and 'Highlands' of heaven. These descriptions were transmitted through inspirational or automatic writing and were the communications from his late mother and other departed spirits. His mother's descriptions were in keeping with those offered by spirits, as outlined in chapter four. She communicated, for example: 'About our home. It is very bright and beautiful, and our companions from the higher spheres are continually coming to cheer us on our upward way ... We have hills and rivers and beautiful forests and houses too, and all the work of those who have come before us to make it ready.'[108] Elsewhere she described how the houses had baths, music and 'apparatus' to help them in their work. The atmosphere had an effect on clothing, so that the tint changed according to where people were and their spiritual quality. The whole place, she said, was pervaded by life.[109]

Owen claimed to have communicated not only with his mother but also with 'higher' spirits, called Zabdiel, Astriel and Arnel. They gave these names to him in order to make matters simple for him, although they were, they said, beyond the need of names. These spirits communicated more about the theological aspects of heaven, and the differences between what the Church taught and what was 'Truth'. Thus Astriel told him that, 'what goes by the name of orthodoxy among Christians in the Church on earth is not a fair and true presentation in many ways, of the Truth as we have come to know it here'.[110]

Owen's hope that Christianity would assimilate spiritualism meant, from his reporting of the spirits' teachings, that the Church would abandon any recourse to the 'traditional' language of hell and judgement and teach instead post-mortem progress, purgation and forgiveness. However, he was not an advocate of Universalism. The spirit teaching that he wrote down and published suggested that, although departed spirits were encouraged and assisted to climb out of the 'darker regions' of the afterlife and grow towards the light of love, faith and truth, a few 'obstinate ones' refused help and remained in the darkness of ignorance.[111]

---

107 Ibid., 21.
108 Owen, *Life beyond the Veil*, 1:17.
109 Ibid., 1:27.
110 Ibid., 1:157.
111 Ibid., 1:31.

Arthur Chambers was vicar of Brockenhurst, Hampshire, when in 1894 he published a set of sermons under the title *Our Life after Death, or The teaching of the Bible concerning the Unseen World.* He had given the sermons for Advent at St Mark's, Battersea Rise and, although he did not commend the practices of spiritualism to his readers, he offered a dynamic image of life after death that bore strong similarity to spiritualist teaching. This was, initially, unacknowledged, but in the end he admitted he was a spiritualist.

Chambers argued, as F. W. Farrar had, that the biblical words 'gehenna' and 'hades' had been confused into one English word, 'hell', to signify a place both of future punishment and the place of the departed. Hades was rather, he said, understood by the Early Church to mean an intermediate place where all of the departed travelled before judgement. Even Jesus went to Hades before heaven.[112]

From the Bible, Chambers argued that life after death involved the progress of the conscious personality, and that there were possibilities for repentance and growth. In the 'Hades life' the dead were reacquainted with those who had died before them, because love, friendship and sympathy – the development of which virtues enabled spiritual growth – were the characteristics of human nature only gained through others.[113]

He understood the story of Saul and the witch of Endor as a positive commendation of spiritualism. Just as Samuel was recognised by the witch of Endor and Saul, the powerful figures of the Old Testament – Moses and Elijah – were recognised by Jesus and the disciples at the Transfiguration in Mark ix. 4. In addition, according to the account of the crucifixion in Luke xxiii. 43, Jesus told the penitent thief that they would be together in Paradise. So, Chambers concluded, the dead are recognisable and meet one another again after death.[114]

Chambers deduced from scripture that there were different states in the next life. There were, in life, different levels of spiritual growth; some were spiritual babes and others fully grown men. The state of the soul in the next life would be gauged on character and spirit and not on professed faith alone. In the 'Hades life' there would be time and opportunity for perfecting and development; this was not 'Purgatory' but was, he argued, a time of purgation.[115]

Intriguingly, Chambers initially said that he wrote in order to *prevent*

---

[112] Chambers, *Our Life after Death*, 4–35.
[113] Ibid., 72.
[114] Ibid., 36–7.
[115] Ibid., 89.

people from turning to spiritualism. *Our Life after Death* ran to fifty editions. He received 1,700 letters from the public about it and the book was published on the Continent, in America, India and Japan. In a subsequent work, *Man and the Spiritual World* (1900), he again claimed that he wanted to 'stem the tide' of those turning to spiritualism.[116] Yet he offered a vision of the next life similar to that of the spiritualists, wrote positively about clairaudience and clairvoyance, and acknowledged that the dead were sometimes seen by the living. Although he was critical of spiritualism, he spoke about the departed state in language that was certainly very close to the language of spiritualism.

In 1907 Chambers finally wrote positively about spiritualism. In *Problems of the Spiritual* he claimed that the dead could be objectively present among the living, and that there was a large amount of testimony to that fact.[117] Although he was still anxious not to encourage people to attend séances, in case 'evil spirits' were present, he saw nothing intrinsically wrong with communicating with the dead.[118]

Chambers was, at the very least, sympathetic to the *ideas* of spiritualism and, although not an advocate of spiritualist practice like Vale Owen, he was sufficiently sympathetic to its teachings to be recognised by Arthur Conan Doyle in 1919. Although neither Chambers nor Owen was a member of a clergy spiritualist society, both were grouped by Conan Doyle together with other clergy spiritualists such as Charles Tweedale, Hugh Haweis and William Stainton Moses.[119] Chambers was also regarded by Charles Tweedale as one of a number of clergy prepared to 'avow a belief in the supernatural as well as the spiritual'.[120]

Charles Tweedale was vicar of the village of Weston, near Otley, and an advocate of spiritualism by the 1920s. In 1909 he wrote a book cautiously commending spiritualism and offering evidence for it, called *Man's Survival after Death, or, the Other Side of Life in the Light of Scripture, Human Experience and Modern Research*. He began his book by articulating a desire that his words might 'bring the joy of the resurrection to those who either do not possess it, or see it so dimly that it affords no real consolation of mind'.[121]

---

116 Arthur Chambers, *Man and the Spiritual World as disclosed by the Bible* (London, 1900), xi.

117 Arthur Chambers, *Problems of the Spiritual* (London, 1907), 1.

118 Ibid., 71, 46.

119 The list also included the late Archdeacon Thomas Colley and Archdeacon Wilberforce. Doyle, *Our Reply to the Cleric*, 7.

120 Charles Tweedale, *Man's Survival after Death, or, the Other Side of Life in the Light of Scripture, Human Experience and Modern Research* (London, 1909), 409.

121 Ibid., 11.

His reason for explaining spiritualism to Christians came, he said, from his ministry as a parish priest visiting the dying and observing the different approaches people had to death. He sought to give Christians a greater hope and confidence in everlasting life in the light of what he saw as the physical evidence provided by spiritualism.

By 1920 he had become a more ardent advocate. He published a slim volume, *Present Day Spirit Phenomena and the Churches*, which was, the front cover proclaimed, placed by the archbishop of Canterbury into the hands of every bishop attending the Lambeth Conference. The book was more critical of traditional Church teaching than his earlier work. He argued that the idea of the intermediate state as presented by the Church was vague and the notion of sleeping until the General Resurrection meant, for many people, 'simply ages of sleep'.[122] The slumber-filled intermediate state was also, he argued, according to scripture itself, untrue. If there was no resurrection until the last day, then it was difficult to explain why Christ was able to converse with Moses and Elijah at the Transfiguration.[123]

Tweedale thought the Church's claim to believe in the Communion of Saints to be disingenuous if it did not include any form of communication. In this light he criticised Viscount Halifax, who had claimed that the Church said of the Communion of Saints: 'We can speak to them and they to us'. This was, Tweedale thought, 'sentimental nonsense' and 'pious make believe' on Halifax's part, as he had never had any direct communication from the dead by clairaudience, dreams or directed writing.[124] He also criticised those who dismissed the manifestations of spiritualism as trickery, telepathy or psychological disturbance, claiming that the spiritual manifestations of the Bible might be explained in the same way.[125]

Despite his increasing frustration with the Church of England's lack of acceptance of spiritualism, Tweedale remained a parish priest. He became a contributor to the *Christian Spiritualist* newspaper and was a member of the 'Society of Communion', a small and rather obscure group of clergy, ministers and laity committed to furthering spiritualism within the Church. Literature from the Society of Communion suggested that they approached their spiritualism 'with complete acknowledgement of the Lord Jesus Christ as Master, Lord, Leader and Saviour', beginning séances with hymns and Bible

---

[122] Tweedale, *Present Day Spirit Phenomena and the Churches*, 5.
[123] Ibid., 8.
[124] Ibid., 10.
[125] Ibid., 14.

reading.[126] The society was founded in 1921, and galvanised by J. W. Potter, 'Minister of St Luke's Church of the Spiritual Evangel of Jesus Christ, Queen's Road, Forest Hill, London', and editor of the *Christian Spiritualist*. Potter, although frustratingly elusive, was a man of means, purchasing Erlestoke Park in Wiltshire for the society and publishing the *Christian Spiritualist* for fourteen years.

The other clergymen mentioned by Arthur Conan Doyle as supporters of spiritualism were William Stainton Moses and Hugh Reginald Haweis. Stainton Moses (1839–92), after his ordination in 1863, held livings in the Isle of Man and Dorset and taught at the University College School, London from 1871 to 1890. He often wrote under the pseudonym 'M. A. Oxon.' and was, as has been noted, for a time the editor of *Light* and was committed to integrating Christianity and spiritualism.[127]

Hugh Reginald Haweis (1838–1901) was perpetual curate of St James the Less, Marylebone, London from 1866 until his death, and as well as being sympathetic to spiritualism was an advocate of cremation[128] and member of the SPR. He was noted as a gifted preacher and theatrical character. He was claimed as a supporter of spiritualism not only by Arthur Conan Doyle, but also by his friend, Charles Maurice Davies, in *Orthodox London* (1874). Davies, listening to a sermon, remarked, 'On the unpopular subject of "Modern Spiritualism" (which rightly or wrongly claims Mr Haweis as at least a partial convert) he has thus delivered himself in a volume of sermons called, "Thoughts for the Times," which, unlike the general run of these compositions, went through three editions in a short space of time'.[129]

The volume mentioned by Davies, *Thoughts for the Times* (1872), was a collection of sermons, and was dedicated to the Right Hon. William Francis Cowper-Temple M.P., who was also a spiritualist.[130] Although the sermons did not concern spiritualism and did not commend it, spiritualism was mentioned in passing and Haweis' tone was decidedly sympathetic. Regarding his own opinions he wrote that

> I commit myself to no theory. I have none. I merely aspire to be honest enough to admit what I believe – that a class of phenomena are daily

---

[126] J. W. Potter, *From beyond the clouds. A year with Counsellor* (London, 1927), preface.
[127] Chapter three, p. 69.
[128] H. R. Haweis, *Ashes to Ashes. A Cremation Prelude* (London, 1875).
[129] Davies, *Orthodox London*, 18.
[130] William Cowper-Temple and his wife Georgina were responsible for introducing John Ruskin to spiritualism and were also friends of Robert Chambers, the publisher, another noted spiritualist. See Burd, *Christmas Story*.

occurring in our midst which have not been explained; and perhaps I may be allowed to indulge in the vague hope that many thousands who are so far of my opinion throughout the civilized world, are neither born fools nor confirmed lunatics, although I regret to say that some who are believers are impostors as well. But whatever the truth or untruth there may be in these opinions, one thing is tolerably evident to my mind, and it is this – that if you accept the Christian miracles, you cannot reject all others.[131]

As Arthur Conan Doyle named the members of the clergy whom he believed sympathetic to spiritualism in *Our Reply to the Cleric*, so Tweedale in *Man's Survival after Death* (1909) included such a list. His list included the bishop of Ripon, William Boyd Carpenter, who became president of the SPR when he retired as a bishop, and Harvey Goodwin, the bishop of Carlisle, another member of the SPR.

Tweedale also included Fielding Fielding-Ould, evangelical vicar of Christ Church, Albany Street. Fielding-Ould wrote *The Relation of Spiritualism to Christianity, and of Spiritualists to Christ* (1921), in which he argued that spiritualism had much to offer the Church. A vicar who conversed with the departed, he claimed, and knew what the afterlife was like, would be better able to instruct his congregation on how to live their lives.[132] Also in Tweedale's list were the above-mentioned Dearmer, Haweis, Chambers and Owen, along with the Anglo-catholic Geikie-Cobb, a member of the Confraternity of Clergy and Spiritualists.

There is a surprising addition to these clergymen: a layman who is worth noting. It was well known to the press that Gladstone attended séances and tried the spirits;[133] what was less well known was that he read and annotated spiritualist texts in private. Although exposure of his séance attendance in 1884 limited his public engagement, he corresponded with spiritualists, was a member of the SPR and kept a library of spiritualist books at St Deiniol's. Recent research by Ruth Clayton Windscheffel has revealed how Gladstone read these texts and made notes, suggesting that his interest was spiritual and serious. In particular, she observes that he read spiritualist texts on Sundays, the day which he reserved for reading religious works, suggesting that he

---

[131] H. R. Haweis, *Thoughts for the Times* (London, 1872), 86.
[132] F. Fielding-Ould, *The Relation of Spiritualism to Christianity, and of Spiritualists to Christ* (Beverley, 1921), 15. Fielding-Ould had been curate of St Barnabas, Kensington and St John, Buckhurst Hill before becoming vicar of Albany Street.
[133] H. C. G. Matthew, *Gladstone 1809–1898* (Oxford, 1997), 544–5.

thought spiritualism worthy of close attention as theology rather than simply phenomena or entertainment.[134] He was particularly keen, she notes, on passages which advocated living a godly life in the present, but appeared untroubled by what she calls the 'more dubious' aspects of spiritualist theology.[135] Here, then, was a serious Christian who, like some of the clergy above, flirted briefly with séances, engaged with the theology of spiritualism and placed it alongside other Christian works.

The uncovering of such a diverse collection of clergy, and lay, spiritualists is significant to the contention that the language and ideas of spiritualism, circulating in the common culture, helped to shape the Church's language and ideas concerning the afterlife. Some of these clergymen were, as has been noted, members of spiritualist societies, the Confraternity or the more elusive Society of Communion. These were not men who simply enjoyed séances from the safety of a self-contained organisation, however; they were actively engaging with the ideas of spiritualism and sought to integrate these ideas into Church teaching. Beyond these societies there were other parish clergy, some of whom, as we have seen, published their spiritualist-inspired teaching. Again, although their interest in spiritualism may have begun in a flirtation with séances, it similarly resulted in an engagement with ideas and imagery. All were prepared to be publicly associated with spiritualism, with séance phenomena, mediums and even fraud, in order to encourage the Church towards a different view of the afterlife. Eventually, the Church responded in a more official manner.

The 1939 Report

At the Church Congress in 1919, the archbishop of Canterbury (Davidson) declared that the 'best men and best women' were examining it in preparation for the Lambeth Conference.[136] The efforts of this committee resulted in the Lambeth Resolutions, already mentioned.

The Church of England had still failed to make an official response by 1935, however there was a sense that spiritualism was gaining ground among Church members. In a motion to the National Assembly, the dean of Rochester, Francis Underhill, proposed that,

---

[134] Ruth Clayton Windscheffel, 'Politics, Religion and Text: W. E. Gladstone and Spiritualism', *Journal of Victorian Culture*, 11, 1 (Spring 2006), 1–29.
[135] Ibid., 19.
[136] *Church Congress at Leicester*, 116.

in view of the growth of Spiritualism among the clergy and communicant laity of the Church, this Assembly respectfully requests their Graces the Archbishops to consult with the Convocations as to the appointment of a Commission to investigate the matter and report to the Assembly.[137]

The archbishop (by now Lang) appeared initially unwilling to give the matter much importance. Eventually, a meeting of the bishops decided that the best course of action was to set up another committee, under the chairmanship of Underhill.[138] This committee included Walter Robert Matthews, the dean of St Paul's, Canon Harold Anson, master of the Temple – both of whom were interested in spiritualism[139] – and Professor Laurence William Grensted, Nolloth professor at Oxford, who had an interest in the psychology of religion. Guy Mayfield; Dr William Brown, a Harley Street psychologist; Mildred Rawlinson, wife of the bishop of Derby (Alfred 'Jack' Rawlinson); Paul E. Sandlands KC; and Lady Gwendolen Stephenson were also members. Walter Somerville Wigglesworth, a lawyer, acted as secretary. In October 1936 Lang, with Underhill, invited the members of the committee to take part. The terms of reference were given as being, 'To investigate the subject of communications with discarnate spirits and the claims of Spiritualism in relation to the Christian faith'.[140] They began their investigations in November 1936, visiting séances, questioning witnesses and speaking to psychic researchers.

The report acknowledged concerns among some clergy who were 'continually finding that numbers of their congregations drift towards spiritualism' seeking consolation, guidance from the spirit world or evidence of survival after death.[141] The report highlighted how spiritualism had become part of a wider Christian experience:

> Some break away from the fellowship and worship of the Church altogether. Others, who remain loyal to their membership of the Church, supplement their religious experience through the practice of spiritualism.[142]

---

[137] Motion to National Assembly made 10 July 1935. *LPL: Lang Papers*, Vol. 70, fol. 4.

[138] The narrative of the 1939 report is well documented in Kollar, *Searching for Raymond*.

[139] Anson regularly attended séances and, at the Church Congress in Chelmsford in 1920, was cautiously supportive of a deeper Church engagement with spiritualism. *Church Congress at Chelmsford*, 147–54.

[140] *LPL: Lang Papers*, Vol. 70, fol. 57. Not all of those invited took part. Charles Raven refused, as did Cyril Bailey.

[141] Archbishop's committee on spiritualism, *Report*, 4.

[142] Ibid., 4.

The report decided that spiritualism was part belief, part practice. It had elements of a cult or religion, a 'more or less' philosophical account of the universe and an 'assemblage of facts' that fell 'outside the normal range of experience'.[143]

After presenting the 'Seven Principles of Spiritualism' as defining what spiritualists believed, the report offered its analysis of the different types of séance phenomena associated with spiritualism. Finally it gave an account of the evidence offered by nine witnesses to the committee. These witnesses were both spiritualists and non-spiritualist psychic researchers, and their identity was concealed in the report.

The first, Miss Mercy Phillimore, was the secretary to the London Spiritualist Society. She thought that both the Church and spiritualism could benefit from closer connections: spiritualism could give new vitality to the Church, and the Church could give spiritualism badly needed leadership. The second witness, Dame Edith Lyttelton, had spent many years as a member of the SPR, but had found spiritualism to be true to her experience of prayer. Kenneth Richmond of the SPR thought that spiritualism could not be reconciled with the Church, but recognised that people sought evidence of immortality.

His honour Mr Justice Atkinson had found solace in bereavement; the editor of the *Two Worlds*, Ernest Oaten, found his faith in a God of love strengthened. Two scientists, Dr William Brown and Dr Oliver Gatty, were critical of the deceptions in spiritualism; Baron Palmstierna was a medium who offered a séance for the committee. Dr Nandor Fodor, a research officer for the International Institute for Psychical Research, suggested that the Church take note of how spiritualism apparently helped some people in their faith.[144]

After visiting séances and examining the witnesses, seven members of the committee concluded that, although many alleged communications 'fell below the highest standards of Christian understanding and spiritual insight', spiritualism mostly confirmed the convictions of religious people. The spiritualists' understanding of the divinity of Christ was problematic, but the communications from the spirit world 'added richness' to the Church's teaching about the Communion of Saints.

There was, the majority concluded, no satisfactory scientific evidence for the séance phenomena, but nevertheless there was a strong case for survival

---

[143] Ibid., 5.
[144] Ibid., 13–19. The names, although concealed in the report, were given to Lang. *LPL: Lang Papers*, Vol. 70, fol. 167.

after death and the possibility of communication between the living and the dead:

> When every possible explanation of these communications has been given, and all doubtful evidence set aside, it is very generally agreed that there remains some element as yet unexplained. We think that it is probable that the hypothesis that they proceed in some cases from discarnate spirits is a true one.[145]

A minority group of three, Guy Mayfield, Mildred Rawlinson and Walter Wigglesworth, disagreed. They thought that the alleged communications were not only valueless but might also be dangerous because they were misleading and full of fraud. Instead of investigating spiritualism the Church needed, they thought, to teach more about the Communion of Saints, the Christian belief in eternal life (they did not explain how they understood 'eternal life'), the mystical nature of Christianity, and how the living and departed met in the celebration of the Eucharist.[146]

Both the majority and the minority saw the popularity of spiritualism as being, in part, due to the Church's failure to teach about the afterlife. The majority said that 'there is little real fellowship even between the living, and the full and intimate reality of the Communion of Saints is often a dead letter'.[147] Spiritualism was 'filling in the gaps' in Church teaching. Both groups suggested that the Church needed to be less hesitant about praying for the departed.

In January 1939 Lang wrote to thank Underhill for the report but confessed that he was 'disappointed' by it. He was concerned that the report might appear to encourage people towards spiritualism and he had rather hoped that it would instead have laid greater stress on the 'dangers' of spiritualism.[148] He took the report to the bishops in July, who discussed it very briefly and agreed with Lang that it should remain unpublished and private.[149] Underhill was, in response, 'disappointed' that the bishops had given so little time to the discussion.[150]

The report remained unpublished until the 1980s. In October 1939, however, one of the witnesses to the committee, Baron Palmstierna, asked to

---

[145] Archbishop's committee on spiritualism, *Report*, 22.
[146] Ibid., 25–6.
[147] Ibid., 22.
[148] Lang to Underhill, 30 Jan. 1939. *LPL: Lang Papers*, Vol. 70, fol. 187.
[149] Lang to Underhill, 26 July 1939. Ibid., Vol. 70, fol. 192.
[150] Underhill to Lang, 28 July 1939. Ibid., Vol. 70, fol. 194.

see the report.[151] He was allowed to do so, but was instructed that it was strictly confidential. Palmstierna, it appears, ignored the instruction, and by early 1940 the spiritualist press were claiming that the report had been favourable to spiritualism, and that the committee had been divided in its conclusions. The archbishop was forced in July 1940 to issue a statement:

> In 1937 the archbishop of Canterbury appointed a committee 'to investigate the subject of communications with discarnate spirits, and the claims of spiritualism in relation to the Christian faith.' The committee presented its report to him. It was marked 'Private and Confidential' and was not unanimous. He submitted it to the diocesan bishops. After consultation with them and on their advice he has come to the conclusion that it would not be advisable to publish the Report. The Report contains valuable information about the various phenomena with which spiritualism is concerned. But in respect of practical guidance to Christian people on a subject fraught with grave dangers, it did not seem to be so clear or conclusive as to make its publication desirable.[152]

The statement appeared in *The Times* and spiritualist publications.

This report concluded the Church's official response to spiritualism. Yet, as we have seen, unofficially, across the period 1852–1939, the clergy of the Church of England reacted to spiritualism, seeing it either as a threat to health, morality and theology, or else as offering something useful to the Church's teaching about life beyond death. A small but significant number of clergy, along with the majority of the archbishop's committee, found it 'probable' that the dead communicated with the living.

Clergy responses to the phenomena of spiritualism and the theology of spiritualism were decidedly mixed. Yet throughout the period many were aware, and spoke about, how spiritualism was 'gaining ground', regardless of whether they welcomed this or feared it. The language and ideas, as much as the phenomena, of spiritualism had become part of the common culture. The following chapter will suggest that, even as clergy, separately, formed their responses to the phenomenon that was modern spiritualism, the spiritualist language and ideas that had been absorbed into the common culture were helping to re-frame the Church's own teaching about the nature of the afterlife.

---

151 Baron Palmstierna to Lang, 6 Oct. 1939. Ibid., Vol. 70, fol. 196.
152 Ibid., Vol. 70, fol. 307.

7

Re-imagining the afterlife in the twentieth century

During the second half of the nineteenth century, as language and ideas of spiritualism permeated the common culture, the Church of England's theology of the afterlife had, in some quarters at least, shifted towards the possibility of post-mortem spiritual progress. At the same time, as we saw in chapter five, sermons and liturgy remained largely framed in the traditional language.

During the Great War this traditional frame was disrupted. The Church of England, confronted by the deaths of so many young men, became more inclined to speak about the state of the *dead*, as distinct from the living, and thus re-evaluated the imagery of the afterlife. Theologians moved decisively from discussing the duration of eternity, and the punishment of the wicked, to emphasising with increasing confidence the possibility of forgiveness and progress beyond death. Prayers and liturgies written during and immediately after the First World War employed language that was markedly different from the memorial sermons of the nineteenth century, and was instead strikingly similar to that offered in spiritualism. The preachers spoke with confidence, rather than caution, about the afterlife, and offered vivid images which suggested that the dead soldiers enjoyed a new life beyond the grave – thus presenting a fresh vision of a dynamic afterlife and a certainty of heaven.

Once again, this is not a straightforward narrative of a movement away from traditional theology and language towards more liberal expressions of faith. The Church's development of ideas about the afterlife was more complex, and indeed, when the war was over, the Church lost some of the vivid images and returned to a more cautious theology when the Prayer Book was revised. What was offered in 1928, however, was a liturgical expression of a twentieth-century theology that was born out of late-nineteenth-century debates and the beliefs circulating within the common culture. The Church rejected both the traditional theology of the seventeenth century and the more radical language of the war period in a new presentation of the afterlife.

Redefining the afterlife in doctrine

In twentieth-century academic discussions about the future life, theologians moved away from the considerations of God's punishment of the wicked and the definition of eternity that had exercised them a few years earlier. Instead they began to think about the future life in relation to the nature of God, forgiveness and the possibility of progress. A more critical approach to scripture was, generally, no longer considered to present a threat to belief; it was rather embraced as a means of offering new possibilities in theological debate. Meanwhile, new considerations, such as the importance of emotions and psychology, were also taken into account.[1] A series of lectures on 'Immortality' presented at King's College London included a lecture by Alfred Caldecott that emphasised the importance of 'feelings' in consideration of the future life.[2]

In another lecture, James Bethune-Baker (1861–1951), Lady Margaret Professor of Divinity at Cambridge and distinguished patristic scholar, considered the teachings of Jesus on the future life in the light of recent developments in biblical criticism. He concluded that Jesus had used the 'low level' conceptual framework of first-century Hebrew eschatology in order to speak about the future life.[3] Jesus had, he argued, generally concerned himself more with the issues of the present world than the future but, when it came to the future, 'eschatological conceptions which were current at the time are freely used, unamended, to support the new valuation of human life. That is to say, the Christian valuation is set in an old unchristianised frame.'[4] His argument implied that Jesus' own teachings were not helpful to a Christian idea of the afterlife. Vernon Storr agreed that recent biblical study, and in particular the study of Jewish eschatology and apocalyptic literature from the time of Christ, had enabled new doctrinal developments. By seeing more clearly the background against which Christianity had risen, scholars were now able to recognise that Jesus was apparently reluctant to speak of the future life precisely because he did not want to give authority to a 'primitive' view.[5]

---

1 Not without criticism: Ralph Inge, dean of St Paul's, lamenting the rising importance of psychology, commented that, 'the centre of gravity in religion has shifted from authority and tradition to experience'. Inge, *Lay Thoughts of a Dean* (London, 1926), 323.
2 W. R. Matthews (ed.), *King's College Lectures on Immortality* (London, 1920), 43.
3 Ibid., 34.
4 Ibid., 35. The 'new wine' of Christianity was, he said, put in the 'old skins' of an older conceptual framework, and didn't always burst them. Reference can be found in Mark ii. 22; Matthew ix. 17; Luke v. 37.
5 *Church Congress at Leicester*, 93.

In a 1916 article tracing the history of the debate concerning the word 'αἰώνιος' (eternity) in the nineteenth century, the editor of the Modern Churchman and vice-principal of Ripon Clergy College, Henry Major (1871–1961), likewise acknowledged that biblical criticism had opened up theological debate. Much of the confusion surrounding 'αἰώνιος' lay in nineteenth-century unwillingness to abandon both a belief in the verbal inspiration of scripture and the pervading impression that the Bible was one book made up of two volumes, he argued. New scholarship had enabled theologians to study a single word not only in its textual context, but also in its historical context.[6] Although all serious theologians still needed to root their thinking in the words of scripture, new biblical scholarship enabled them to abandon the use of 'proof texts' and discern more generally what they understood as the sense of the Gospel and its meaning for twentieth-century life.

For Hastings Rashdall, Bampton lecturer at Oxford in 1915, this was crucial. In the preface to the Bampton lectures he stated that, 'One of the most crying needs of the Church at the present moment is a serious attempt at re-thinking its traditional theology.'[7] Rashdall re-assessed the doctrine of the atonement, which had at its heart the question of how it was that human beings 'fell' from grace but were reconciled to God through the actions of Christ on the cross. The doctrine of atonement had, Rashdall pointed out, never been defined by any creed or council of the Church and, in his lectures, he examined the many interpretations of the doctrine over the centuries. Bound into the central question were issues concerning the nature of God, his judgement and punishment of sinners, the nature of forgiveness and the nature of eternal life.

Rashdall cast aside much of the traditional language and ideas about the afterlife, although he was aware that they still carried much weight. He argued that, looking closely at scripture, 'The clear, unmistakable, invariable teaching of Jesus was that men were judged according to their works, including in the conception of works the state of the heart and intentions as scrutinized by an all-seeing God.' The ideas of punishments and rewards in the afterlife were not to be understood literally; rather they were 'vague and clothed in the language of metaphor'. There was 'little reason for supposing that Jesus thought of the punishment of the wicked as of everlasting duration'.[8] Indeed, he said,

---

[6] H. D. A. Major, 'ΑΙΩΝΙΟΣ. Its use and meaning especially in the New Testament', *Journal of Theological Studies*, XVIII (Oct. 1916), 7–23.
[7] Rashdall, *The Idea of Atonement*, preface. Rashdall (1858–1924) was a fellow of New College, Oxford and became dean of Carlisle in 1917.
[8] Ibid., 12.

If God be the sort of Being whose nature is best expressed by a self-sacrificing life and death, He could not have designed everlasting, meaningless, useless torments as the sole destiny in store for the great bulk of his creatures. That doctrine is dead, though much of the language which really implies it is still repeated in the church, the school, and the theological classroom.[9]

It was right actions and right intentions rather than right beliefs alone that were commended by Jesus as ways of entering the Kingdom of Heaven. The idea that the inheritance of the Kingdom came from belief in Christ was, he argued, something added on by later Christian teachers. Entry into the Kingdom was, according to Rashdall, rooted in a universal morality; meaning that it was not exclusive to Protestant Christians. No longer was the Kingdom of Heaven only for those who kept the letter of the Law; it was open to everyone. Goodness, rather than intellectual belief, descent from Abraham or the outward performance of a rite, was required.[10]

Rejecting ideas of the atonement that were rooted in transaction or punishment, he championed the more subjective, experiential theology of the twelfth-century thinker Peter Abelard, mixed with the biblical verse that was heard at almost every memorial service during and after the war:

> The death of Christ is looked upon as completing that revelation of the nature and character of God which it was the object of Christ's whole mission to set forth. If the heart of that revelation is to be found pre-eminently in the self-sacrificing death of Christ it is because the character of God as revealed by Christ may be summed up in the statement that God is love. 'Greater love hath no man than this, that a man lay down his life for his friends.'[11]

As a consequence, Jesus' teaching carried with it, Rashdall admitted, a 'latent Universalism'.[12] He was hesitant here, perhaps because, in time of war, it was not expedient to assume the ultimate salvation of all human beings (including enemies), but he presented the *eschaton* in a positive light. The afterlife might include some purgation, but it was open to those beyond the limits of the Christian faith:

> [Eschatology] will hope that in the end there is some kind and some

---

9 Ibid., 458.
10 He doesn't say what sort of 'rite' he means here. Possibly he is thinking of baptism, given later comments regarding the possibility of other religions sharing in the Kingdom. In other words, baptism is not the only means of entry into the Kingdom. Ibid., 19.
11 Ibid., 437.
12 Ibid., 19.

measure of good reserved for each individual human soul which God has brought into the world – enough good to make it well on the whole for that soul to have lived. It will certainly not be ashamed or afraid of the doctrine that in the life for which it hopes, as in this earthly life, much painful purgatorial discipline may form part of the remedy for sin both for those who have not known Christ at all in this life and for those who have imperfectly responded to His call. But it will not deny that some measure of salvation from sin has resulted from many religions and teachings besides those which come from the lips or in the name of Christ.[13]

He also envisaged salvation as progressive, dynamic and beginning in this world. His words suggested progress, more than purgatory: it was individuals who would 'become' better, rather than be made so:

We must not, indeed, allow ourselves to treat salvation as wholly belonging to the world beyond the grave. Salvation means primarily being saved from sin and becoming better: and goodness is an end in itself whether it is to last for a few years or for all eternity.[14]

The mortal life was a training ground for a better and richer life of infinite possibilities beyond the grave. Training and education in this world continued after it and led 'to higher achievement'[15] in happiness and holiness. And potentially, if salvation was a gradual process, beginning in the present and completed hereafter, there might also be 'degrees' of salvation.[16]

Rashdall did not offer simplistic 'images' of the afterlife. In his re-assessment of the doctrine of atonement, however, he offered a vision of a dynamic, progressive, universal salvation, rooted in the nature of God's self-sacrificing love and entered into as a result of a combination of human goodness and God's forgiveness.

There was a clear desire among other thinkers to communicate such recent theological developments with fresh images. Canon Burnett Streeter of Hereford, writing an essay in 1917 on 'The life of the world to come', suggested that contemporary religion needed to find new ways of presenting what he termed 'the Christian hope of immortality' in a clear and definite way. The traditional images, for all they were 'morally revolting',[17] had at least been

---

13 Ibid., 458.
14 Ibid., 460.
15 Ibid., 460.
16 Ibid., 461.
17 Burnett H. Streeter et al., *Immortality. An essay in discovery, co-ordinating scientific, psychical and biblical research* (London, 1917), 135.

clear. For Streeter, the crucial expression was 'progress'. 'There is no need why we should not make progress one of the most fundamental and characteristic elements in our conception of the future.'[18] Progress was not the same as the Roman Catholic doctrine of purgatory, which he argued was penal and was there to remove the undesirable elements of sin. Instead, 'what is wanted is a conception of progress in the next life in which the leading idea shall be that of addition, rather than subtraction'.[19]

He was concerned that the traditional images of heaven were as unhelpful as the images of hell. They suggested an 'unbroken monotony'.[20] Instead he thought that heaven should be envisaged as a quality of life, rather than a place, expressed in terms of love, work, thought and beauty. 'The highest and most complete activity of the aesthetic instinct demands for its satisfaction not merely the grandeur of an Alpine vista, of an Indian sunset, or of a great cathedral, but the quiet homely appeal of the violet, the mossy nook, the village church.' In heaven there would be humour, as well as the vision of God.[21] In the same volume the essayist and journalist Arthur Clutton-Brock described his dream of heaven in similarly flowery terms:

> Whatever we have really loved here will be there to be loved again, to be recognised like the sound of bells from an old city church, like the swinging open of gates, like the sunrise over the mountains, like all those things that are eternal to us, that seem to call us into that place when no more time shall be 'but steadfast rest of all things firmly stayed upon the pillars of eternity'.[22]

Ten years later, Percy Dearmer, in a consideration of traditional teaching about hell, claimed that a strain of universal salvation throughout Christian teaching had been for too long ignored or considered heterodox. Yet Universalism was, he said, true to Jesus' teaching. Born out of questions put to him during the war about the nature of the future life, Dearmer gave a full account of the traditional images and ideas about hell, where the imagery came from and how it was developed over the centuries. Although the traditional afterlife was still taught, among 'intelligent people' the idea of eternal torment had disappeared and the 'battle' for Universalism had been won in the nineteenth century.[23] Dearmer approved: from the Gospel of John he argued

---

18 Ibid., 139.
19 Ibid., 140.
20 Ibid., 152.
21 Ibid., 154–9.
22 Ibid., 234–5.
23 Dearmer, *The Legend of Hell*, 72.

that judgement was a process begun in the present life, rather than an event after death. What continued beyond death, he thought, was life and forgiveness, rather than the vengeance of God.[24]

Although such progressive ideas and images of the afterlife became the prevailing ones in theological debate, some theologians expressed misgivings. These misgivings were not reactionary; they were made within the context of a debate that had embraced biblical criticism and contemporary ideas like psychology. Thus Charles Gore, bishop of Oxford and editor of *Lux Mundi*, could claim that 'eternal does not mean everlasting' and that the temporal images of the Book of Revelation should be understood as non-temporal ideas. Yet he also cautioned that the 'awful warnings' of Christ concerning the possibility of 'self-chosen ruin' must be heeded.[25] Inge acknowledged that the prevailing notion of hell had been modified in recent times, but was anxious not to let go of the 'tragic reality' of what being cast away from God's presence might mean, even when stripped of the cruder imagery of the bodily torments of a traditional hell.[26] Conscious of the colourful images of the afterlife presented by spiritualism, and, indeed, by some in the Church, he sought to encourage a sense of awe, mystery and reticence regarding the afterlife.[27] Many images of heaven and many ideas held about the afterlife were, he cautioned, not religious at all, but merely longings after personal survival, or empty wishes. Contrary to those who looked to describe the afterlife in words, he warned that, 'we cannot translate eternity into any pictures drawn from mundane experience'.[28]

For all the misgivings of thinkers such as Gore and Inge, in the theological debate about the afterlife the tide had turned towards the idea that progress towards salvation could be made both in the present and beyond the grave. God's forgiveness was emphasised more than his judgement, as was the importance of human moral goodness over right belief.

In 1922 a commission was set up by the archbishops in order to 'survey the whole field of theology and produce a systematic treatise'.[29] It was appointed because tensions between different 'schools of thought' in the Church were

---

[24] Ibid., 277. Elsewhere he used the parable of the foolish bridesmaids. Although the bridesmaids were cast out of the wedding, there might have been the chance of another wedding to attend at a later point. 257.

[25] Charles Gore, *The Holy Spirit and the Church* (London, 1924), 308.

[26] Dean Inge et al., *What is the Real Hell?* (London, 1930), 8.

[27] W. R. Inge, 'Risen with Christ', in Basil Matthews, *Christ: and the World at War. Sermons preached in war-time* (London, 1917), 92.

[28] *Church Congress at Leicester*, 91.

[29] *Doctrine in the Church of England*, 4.

believed to be 'imperilling its unity and impairing its effectiveness'.[30] The commission was asked to discuss those subjects which were thought to be causing the most controversy and problem, one of which was the idea of judgement and the future life.

Archbishop Randall Davidson initially invited the bishop of Oxford, Hubert Burge, to chair the commission. Burge died in 1925 and William Temple, who had moved from Manchester to become archbishop of York, took over. Between 1922 and 1938 a number of the original commission died, but over the course of sixteen years it contained around twenty-two men, of whom several were bishops, or were made bishops in that time, as well as deans, canons and theologians. Two members of the commission were also sitting on the committee investigating spiritualism, as was the wife of a third member.[31]

When, in 1938, the commission issued its report, it contained an affirmation of much of the prevailing mood for spiritual progress and universal salvation, while simultaneously trying to uphold a more traditional teaching. Thus it noted that there were a variety of opinions regarding what happened after death. The more evangelical position had been to 'think of the faithful departed as being immediately in joy and felicity', whereas other theologians, although rejecting the medieval idea of purgatory, nevertheless affirmed a state of progressive growth and purification beyond death. The report concluded that, in the contemporary Church of England, there was room for both views.[32]

The commission was concerned to uphold some notion of judgement as integral to the traditional teachings of scripture:

> There is great peril in the easy-going sentimentality of some modern Christianity, which supposes all who have departed this life to be forthwith 'in joy and everlasting felicity' – a perversion of the evangelical view mentioned above. Such a view is inconsistent with the solemn warnings of scripture and especially the Gospels themselves, and converts the hope of immortality from a moral stimulus to a moral narcotic.[33]

---

30 Ibid.
31 The commission included, for example, Alfred 'Jack' Rawlinson, the bishop of Derby, Walter Matthews of St Paul's, and Laurence Grensted, Nolloth Professor at Oxford. Grensted and Matthews were both also sitting on the committee for spiritualism at the time, as was Jack Rawlinson's wife Mildred. Matthews was very familiar with spiritualism. See previous chapter, p. 160.
32 *Doctrine in the Church of England*, 211–13.
33 Ibid., 217.

However, the commission also argued that there was a possibility of salvation for all beyond death:

> It would not be easy to find in the New Testament a basis for definitely and rigorously excluding all hope of further opportunity; indeed there are passages which taken by themselves are Universalist in tendency.[34]

This hope of salvation for all was extended, according to the report, not on grounds of scripture, but rather from an inference from the Christian doctrine of God as a whole. God was love and could not deny himself the possibility of offering forgiveness.

The report was clear that every action in life, whether good or evil, had eternal consequence; there was no mention made of right belief being important. Ultimately, although the commission attempted to hold on to the inherited and traditional teaching about judgement and salvation, it acknowledged that many in the Church had moved away from that perspective. The essence of heaven, it concluded, was the adoration of God and union with him. Some sort of judgement was included in the afterlife, but so also was the possibility of repentance because God's nature was to love and forgive.

Re-framing the new doctrine

According to commentators of the time, it was the war that did the most to encourage the Church to re-examine its teaching concerning the afterlife or, more importantly, how the afterlife was best communicated to churchgoers. Thus Alfred Earnest Garvie (1861–1945), Congregationalist and principal of New College, Hampstead, thought that the future life was one of four 'key questions' being asked, as rarely they had been asked before.[35] Percy Dearmer similarly claimed that it was one of the most frequently asked questions during the war.[36] William Worsley, an army chaplain, agreed that certain theological issues had become more 'in the foreground' as a result of the war, the future life being one.[37]

---

[34] Ibid., 217. The report did not reveal which passages of scripture it saw as 'Universalist' in tendency.

[35] The other three he identified as Original Sin, the nature of evil and the relationship between Just War and Pacifism. See A. E. Garvie, 'The Theological Outlook in Time of War', in Matthews, *Christ: and the World at War*, 53.

[36] Percy Dearmer claimed in the preface to his book, *The Legend of Hell*, that it had been written in answer to this frequently asked question.

[37] F. William Worsley, 'Beliefs emphasised by the War', in F. B. Macnutt, *The Church in the*

Vernon Storr noted in 1919 at the Church Congress that the Church had been confronted with the fact of 'millions of young lives cut off in their prime, immature, untrained in spiritual things, many of them never having had a decent chance of living'.[38] He added, '[And] it is here that the influence of the war is most marked. What has the war done? It has helped to revive interest in the problem of the future.'[39] The concern, articulated by, among others, Viscount Halifax, was that increasing numbers of people were turning to mediums in their bereavement in search of answers to theological questions, rather than the clergy.[40] This added to the Church's closer focus on the nature of the afterlife.

The general public's renewed interest in the afterlife was, perhaps, understandable. Denied the opportunity of being present at the death of a family member who was serving overseas, and unlikely ever to see the place where the loved one had died, the question for many bereaved families was, 'is it well with those who have fallen?'[41] The answer to this question, given in the sermons of the time, was a resounding 'yes'.

Whereas in the nineteenth century preachers had been cautious with regard to the state of the departed, or else had maintained a traditional framework of language, by the time of the war preachers were more certain that they knew the fate of the departed, or at least of departed soldiers. John Primat Maud, the Anglo-catholic bishop of Kensington, for example, considered that, although fellowship with Christ for all eternity was the preserve of 'the *blessed* dead' [my italics], the numbers of those who could be called 'the blessed dead' had increased in the war. In a series of addresses given at a weekly service of intercessions at St Martin-in-the-Fields he spoke of how the self-sacrifice of the soldiers was enough to number them among the blessed:

> We need not surely hesitate to count among the 'blessed dead' all those to whom death came in answer to the offer of the best which they could give, in a supreme endeavour to fulfil life's highest purpose … [We] can surely number them among the blessed dead,

---

Furnace. Essays by seventeen temporary Church of England chaplains on active service in France and Flanders (London, 1917), 89.
38 *Church Congress at Leicester*, 92.
39 Ibid.
40 This was noted, for instance, by Viscount Halifax in his address to St Martin-in-the-Fields in 1917, '*Raymond*'. *Some Criticisms*, and appears to be confirmed by the statistics of the Spiritualists' National Union, claiming that the number of local societies becoming affiliated to the National Union doubled over the course of the war.
41 Garvie, in Matthews, *Christ: and the World at War*, 55.

who laid down their lives in obedience to a clear call of duty which
they instinctively owned

He went further, suggesting that even those who had shown no evidence of
a Christian faith in life were, by death in battle, made blessed. The sacrifice
they made was for a righteous cause, and was, therefore, enough to make
reparation for past sin:

> Whatever their past life may have seemed to us; however its oppor-
> tunities may have been missed or its promise have been unfulfilled;
> at least we know that at a supreme moment of call to give their life
> for its highest ends, they did not falter. They gave all that they had;
> they rose to the level of those who have laid down their lives for their
> brethren, – a level to which only love at its best can rise. By offering
> themselves to risk death in the fulfilment of a high and noble end
> they entered into the secret of life's purpose. *That act, it may be, was
> done in reparation of many past failures and neglects of duty.* We
> can see in it the energy of penitence throwing itself upon God. It was
> love, when once it had come to itself, forcing its way back along the
> road homeward. The Father, who had long waited for that first sign
> of return hailed it afar off, and went forth with joy to meet it. He took
> His child at his word. *The sacrifice which he offered was accepted*,
> and the seal of its acceptance was that kiss which fell on his brow
> with death. [my italics].[42]

Maud counted the fallen among the 'blessed' in the afterlife. He then
suggested what the afterlife might hold for them, many of them still young
men: they progressed. One by one, he said, God 'takes from the earth's school
the scholars who are ready to enter on the next stage of learning and discipline. He appoints a new course of studies and a new round of duties, fitted to
bring out the powers which are to be developed by use in the sphere best
adapted for their employ.'[43]

The suggestion, offered in a sermon to people gathered to pray for serving
soldiers and mourn those who had already died, was that the afterlife was a
place where young men progressed, completed an education and a life unful-
filled on earth. It was a place of employment and usefulness, and a place
where each found their niche, or 'sphere'. The language Maud employed was
similar to that offered by spiritualists regarding the progression of an
individual from one life to another. Death was 'but a passing into another

---

[42] John P. Maud, *Our comradeship with the Blessed Dead* (London, 1915), 27.
[43] Ibid., 40.

stage for perfecting God's servants'.[44] And beyond death the dead were actively engaged still in 'helping' with the war. Perhaps drawing on stories that had captured the public imagination, such as the 'Angels of Mons',[45] he claimed,

> They have not ceased to be comrades, fighting with us and working with us ... Established in those advance posts, out of sight of their comrades and masked from the enemy, watched and directed by the Great Commander, they make it possible for their brethren to win their way onward ... Because He is there, and they who are our comrades still are with Him, victory is sure.[46]

It is possible that Maud was referring, metaphorically, to the 'battle' of life, but his language is ambiguous enough that anyone hearing his sermon might reasonably have assumed that he was telling them that the dead soldiers were, with Christ, assisting the British forces.

Paul Bull, from the Community of the Resurrection at Mirfield, was equally ready to preach that those who died in battle were counted immediately among the blessed of the afterlife. In one sermon he told the story of a sailor who chose to save the life of another and lose his own, as he had no parents to grieve for him. The story concluded, '[Nay] a soul like that can never die. He leaps triumphant into the arms of God, to find what he has never known on earth, a Father's love.'[47]

In another address, made to the English Church Union at Taunton, he counted the departed soldiers and sailors as Christian martyrs:

> Some think that our sons must not be ranked among the noble army of martyrs because they do not die directly to witness to the formulated articles of the Christian faith, and because a soldier often inflicts death as well as enduring it ... We can rest content with the knowledge that our sons are staking their lives on the great spiritual issues which are the background of the Christian faith, the foundation of the throne of God, and the only bond of the brotherhood of man, those foundation principles of righteousness and justice, faith and freedom, without which the Kingdom of God cannot be established among men.[48]

---

44 Ibid., 53.
45 The story was a fictional one of angelic bowmen assisting British soldiers at Mons. It first appeared, written by Arthur Machen, in the *Evening News* of 29 September 1914. Although fictional, the story became circulated as fact. 29 September is the feast of St Michael and All Angels.
46 Maud, *Our Comradeship with the Blessed Dead*, 72.
47 Paul B. Bull CR, *Peace and War. Notes of Sermons and Addresses* (London, 1917), 56.
48 Ibid., 91.

Bull also referred to the trenches as the soldiers' own 'purgatory', which again suggested that, having already passed through their time of ordeal, they were now in heaven.

In a collection of sermons from preachers of various denominations called *Our boys beyond the shadows* (1917), Ernest Barnes, the bishop of Birmingham, argued that the Church needed to 'readjust' its teaching in the light of the 'sacrifice' of the soldiers.[49] The Church could not ask every able bodied man in England, he said, to give up his life thinking that he may be going to eternal punishment. He thought that after death there would be some sort of refinement, or 'training'. 'Whatever the process may be whereby those who enter the Paradise of God are refined and purified, we none of us can say, but I have no place in my heart's belief for harsh judgement upon any who die nobly, though their lives may have been very imperfect.'[50]

Eternal life would be won for soldiers by their sacrifice, which was 'Christ-like'. 'Even if he had blemishes upon his character and went over the parapet with a swear word, he may well be received by Christ with the words, well done thou good and faithful servant.'[51]

The bishop of London, Arthur Foley Winnington Ingram, took this further and employed striking and vivid language to support his teaching. He was an energetic and fervent preacher in the war, and proud to acknowledge that his sermons had stirred many to enlist. He was vehemently opposed to spiritualism, seeing it as a waste of time and a mistake,[52] yet when he preached about the afterlife, and the state of the dead soldiers, his language was remarkably similar to the language of the spiritualists.

Thus, in a sermon called 'The Bridal Procession' preached to a clergy quiet day, he offered his hearers reasons to rejoice, even in time of bereavement, comfortably using common spiritualist expressions for death: 'I do not die;

---

[49] Fred Hastings (ed.), *Our boys beyond the shadows* (London, 1917), 65. This collection included in its cover an advertisement for a new edition of a book called *The Gate's Ajar*. Written by an American, Elizabeth Stuart Phelps, in 1868, this novel, although not explicitly spiritualist, shared much of spiritualism's imagery for the afterlife. Following the death of her brother, the heroine, Mary, is taught by her aunt that heaven is a place of reunion, potential and growth. The landscape of the afterlife is vivid, yet domestic. The book sold 80,000 copies in America and 100,000 in England before 1900. E. S. Phelps, *The Gate's Ajar*, Harvard edn by Helen Sootin Smith (Cambridge, 1964. 1st pubd 1868). It was commended by spiritualists; see, for example, *Medium and Daybreak*, 18 Aug. 1871. The new edition advertised in *Our boys beyond the shadows* was the work of Fred Hastings.
[50] Hastings, *Our boys beyond the shadows*, 75.
[51] Ibid., 65.
[52] Winnington Ingram, 'Life after Death', 156–7.

my brother, my son, my wife, do not die. They *pass from life here to a life of glorious happiness*. Do I believe this? If I do it takes away all sorrow and mourning; it takes away the sting of death.'[53] 'We are for a short time here in this school of trial and training, and then *pass into the eternal tabernacle, the eternal mansions*, for ever.'[54] Again he said that, 'Every single day *thousands pass into the other world* ... All these young lives that *pass by hundreds into the other world* do not cease, they do not come to an end because of death' [my italics].[55] Although 'passing over', 'passing into', 'passing on' had been used since the Middle Ages to signify death, they became, according to the *Oxford English Dictionary*, expressions that were particularly associated with spiritualism. 'Passing into', or 'over', certainly suggested that death was more of a transition in a journey, rather than an end to life. It was startling that a bishop who was outspoken in his criticism of spiritualism chose to use such phrases.

To a congregation in Poplar in the East End he went further, suggesting that,

> Five minutes after death every child of God is the same as five minutes before. He is born into the other world as quietly and peace-fully as he is born into this, even if he dies a violent death ... death is only passing from life here to life there, to still greater happiness, and still greater fullness of the life of the world to come.[56]

Occasionally he offered a more guarded and traditional opinion about the afterlife, suggesting that there would be, one day, a Day of Judgement, when wrongs would be righted and unseen good would come into the light.[57] Those who died in battle would be forgiven of their sins only if they had repented and were at peace with God.[58] However, more characteristic of his preaching style were the vivid passages claiming that those who died at war were imme-diately in a state of happiness:

> [And] the life promised is one that young men can enjoy, for our Lord knew perfectly well what was in a man. 'Jesus, beholding the young man, loved him'; and He loved all those young men passing in the prime of life into the other world, and they live today, redeemed,

---

53 A. F. Winnington Ingram, *The Church in Time of War* (London, 1916), 133.
54 Ibid., 165.
55 Ibid., 159.
56 Ibid., 186.
57 Sermon preached at All Hallows, Barking, ibid., 189.
58 Sermon preached at St Martin-in-the-Fields, ibid., 212.

restored, forgiven, a *life they can enjoy*, purified in character, spiritualised in vision. [my italics][59]

Do not tell me that when God finished making this world, with all its interests and activities, and brightness and glorious service, that His imagination became bankrupt, and that he had none left to make another world with. In that ghost like unattractive world which our imaginations have conjured up a young man would not be at home. But Jesus Christ loved young men. 'Jesus, beholding him, loved him.' He knows how to make young men happy. He knows your boy. He knows what he can enjoy and the sort of life he can live, and the *company in which he will be happy*; and *he has got it all ready for him*.[60] [my italics]

The life to come was, for the soldiers, a life of growth and development. In language strikingly similar to the sunshine language of spiritualism, in 1919 he told the congregation at All Saints, Fulham that

Souls, like flowers, grow best in sunshine, and it must comfort thousands of mourners today to think that the husband or brother or son who was so manifestly growing in character here, is carrying on his education in the *sunny land of Paradise* ... He must be growing as he grew at school, at college, in business. [my italics][61]

Winnington Ingram did not differentiate too carefully between paradise, eternal life, heaven and a more general afterlife in his sermons. Thus the 'eternal mansions' of heaven were interchangeable with paradise, 'heavenly Jerusalem',[62] and even the 'spirit world'. This last expression for the afterlife, frequently used by spiritualists, was used by the bishop more than once. In the memorial service at St Paul's Cathedral in 1915 for Canadian servicemen, he mis-quoted the final line from Robert Louis Stevenson's essay on death, *Aes Triplex*, claiming that, 'the happy-starred, full-blooded spirit of the young shoots into the spiritual world'.[63] He used the quotation (incorrectly) again

---

[59] Ibid., 160.
[60] Ibid., 299.
[61] Winnington Ingram, 'Life after Death', 159.
[62] Winnington Ingram, *The Church in Time of War*, 236.
[63] Ibid., 286. The final line of the essay reads: 'The noise of the mallet and chisel is scarcely quenched, the trumpets are hardly done blowing, when, trailing with him clouds of glory, this happy-starred, full-blooded spirit shoots into the spiritual land.' There is no reference to youth in the quotation, although the essay offers, in part, a homage to those who die young or in violent circumstances. Robert Louis Stevenson, *Aes Triplex and other essays* (Portland, 1902), 23.

when he preached to the London Rifle Brigade in June 1915, a brigade to which he was chaplain, exchanging 'spiritual world' for the even more spiritualist-sounding 'spirit world' on this occasion.[64]

In the 'spirit world' the dead were connected with the living, not by common faith in Christ, but by their memory of loved ones, and in the next life they still took an interest in the mortal world.[65] They were not far off and appeared, from Winnington Ingram's words, to be hovering around the mourners like spirits at a séance:

> In that long life, you who are the mourners today will have a share; they are yours today, and you are theirs; the bond is unbroken; the family circle is still complete. Were you seven before? You are seven still. Unseen hands uphold you; unseen spirits speak to yours, close by, though hidden by a veil, the real, lasting activities of the other world proceed apace. Death has been for them a great promotion and they long for you to share their honours.[66]

However blessed the afterlife was, however full of God and Christ, it was not a complete life, the bishop told his hearers, without the presence of those left on earth:

> He will be waiting for the mother, the sister, the wife to come over too … And best of all, you will see him again. It is not for ever, the parting; you will see him again with your own eyes. Every day brings that day of meeting nearer. You will see him again, purified in character, in the sunshine of his Lord's presence, but the same person, the same son you love, and with the same love for you.[67]

The soldiers were, according to Winnington Ingram, immediately after death, in a place of happiness. He was prepared to admit that he referred to them as 'saints', because they had died 'so gloriously' and were a lesson to all of 'purity and devotion'.[68] They were, in other words, sanctified by death in battle.

Men like Maud, Bull and Winnington Ingram were not seeking to share subtle theological opinion with the people who filled churches for memorial services. They were, as representatives of the national Church, offering comfort. The ideas they embraced and the images they presented, of young

---

[64] Winnington Ingram, *The Church in Time of War*, 299.
[65] Ibid., 235.
[66] Ibid., 288.
[67] Ibid., 299.
[68] Winnington Ingram to Upper House of Convocation (Canterbury), 7 Feb. 1918.

men leaping cheerfully into a new, sunnier and happier life, or born in another land quietly, hovering around the bereaved, were not so far removed from the language of the mediums they criticised for leading people to disappointment and injury.[69]

A further, and significant, way in which the Church of England responded to bereavement during the war was through prayer and liturgy. At a national and a local level the Church played a prominent role in helping the bereaved articulate their faith in time of grief; in particular through the liturgy. The language of the prayers that were issued during the war, and the discussions that lay behind their drafting, suggest that this was the period when the Church revised its language about the afterlife. Some of the prayers for dead soldiers moved a significant distance from the language and theology of the Prayer Book, and when considering the soldiers killed by war, the language of the Church's liturgy, as with the sermons, erred on the radical rather than the traditional.

The Church of England had only one official way of conveying teaching about the afterlife in prayer beyond the Prayer Book, namely the issuing of 'Forms of Prayer'. By law, clergy were allowed to use only the Prayer Book for public worship, with the exception of Forms of Prayer issued by the special authority of the Privy Council.[70] Since the issuing of the 1662 Prayer Book over ninety Forms of Prayer had been published to respond to national crisis or war. In February 1900 a Form of Service was issued entitled 'A Form of Intercession with Almighty God on behalf of His Majesty's Naval and Military forces now in South Africa to be used in all churches and chapels in England and Wales and in the town of Berwick-upon-Tweed. On such occasions as each bishop shall appoint for his own diocese.'[71] Controversially, the Form of Prayer included a petition that read:

> For all those who have fallen in the true faith of Thy Holy Name – that they with us may enter into the rest which Thou hast prepared for them that believe in Thee.

The inclusion of the petition, an optional prayer in only one of five different Forms provided, resulted in a number of letters of complaint. The reason for the complaint lay in the words 'they with us'. This phrasing placed the emphasis upon the departed, and made them the subject of the prayer, rather

---

[69] Winnington Ingram, 'Life after Death', 156.
[70] This is not to say that clergy kept to the law, as witnesses to the *Royal Commission on Ecclesiastical Discipline* (1906), for example, bore testimony.
[71] *LPL: F. Temple Papers*, Vol. 42, fol. 97.

than the living, whereas the Prayer Book, when it made reference to the dead, placed the emphasis on the living ('we with them'). This was, therefore, according to some of the complainants, a prayer for the dead. Prayers for the dead, although not forbidden in the Church of England (according to Breeks v. Woolfrey), were discouraged in public and this was a prayer authorised for public use. The bishop of Worcester, John James Perowne, for example, saw the petition as a move away from the Prayer Book. He wrote to his diocesan clergy that, 'I cannot help regretting the introduction of such a petition in a Form of Service for public use ... It is a distinct departure from the language of our Prayer Book.'[72]

Randall Davidson faced similar letters of concern regarding his intentions to include a prayer for those killed in the Great War. He began preparing prayers appropriate to a time of war as soon as war was declared and called upon noted liturgical experts to draft Forms of Prayer.[73] By mid November 1914 a 'Day of Humble Prayer and Intercession' was scheduled for 3 January 1915, allowing time for suitable liturgy to be drafted and approved by both archbishops. These Forms of Prayer were reissued in May 1915. A subsequent Form of Service was issued for use on 4 and 5 August 1917 and three others were issued after the end of the war.

Davidson was aware that any mention of the dead might be controversial and was anxious to avoid unnecessary complaints. He was also clear that the Forms of Prayer were the Church of England's unique opportunity to offer the nation the words and phrases of faith in a time of crisis. In his private journal he wrote on 13 December 1914,

> We are now preparing the Forms of Service for use on Sunday January 3rd, the day appointed for special prayer. The task is very difficult and the endeavour to discharge it makes one think about these questions, for we want to put into the minds and mouths of our people the right thoughts and the right words ... We have thought it

---

[72] *LPL: F. Temple Papers*, Vol. 42, fol. 298. Temple's response to complaints was two-fold: that he didn't believe the petition implied a doctrine of purgatory, and that, anyway, clergy had a choice of five Forms of Prayer and did not need to use the offending petition if they didn't want to. See also *LPL: F. Temple Papers*, Vol. 42, fol. 339.

[73] Davidson to Lang, 5 Aug. 1914. Davidson noted the involvement of the bishop of Ely (Frederick Henry Chase, 1853–1925, formerly Norrison Professor of Divinity at Cambridge, principal of the Cambridge Clergy Training School and president of Queen's College); the dean of Wells (Joseph Armitage Robinson, 1858–1933, formerly dean of Westminster); and Canon George Russell Bullock Webster (1858–1934, canon of Ely). *LPL: Davidson Papers*, Vol. 367, fol. 37.

best on the whole to avoid the sort of prayers for the dead which would certainly, as my correspondence shows, evoke an acrid controversy.[74]

The task facing the liturgical scholars was to find ways of putting into the 'right words' a theology of the afterlife that offered comfort and assurance to the bereaved and yet remained faithful to the traditions of the Prayer Book. The Prayer Book, as we have seen, suggested that divine judgement took place at death, and that the eternal state was fixed and irrevocable. Apart from the burial service, the dead were not considered as distinct from the living.

The war, and the particular consideration of departed soldiers, presented the Church with the possibility of moving away from the language and the theology of the Prayer Book, but it could do so officially only under the (still traditional) Forms of Prayer. The prayers proposed for January 1915 were circulated among the bishops as early as August 1914. Immediately the evangelical bishops of Liverpool, Chelmsford and Manchester expressed concern that one phrase of petition in the prayers, 'Have mercy on the fallen', was troubling 'not a few of our people'.[75] The trouble with the petition was both that it identified the dead separately from the living and that it appeared to seek to persuade God in his judgement of specific human souls. Judgement was God's prerogative and dependent upon the spiritual condition of the departed individual, and not alterable by the petitions of the living.

The archbishop's response was that there was a distinction between the prayers of the Prayer Book and prayers to be used in a time of emergency – such as during war, when people's hearts were 'deeply moved'. People had, he noted, already begun to focus their attentions on the dead and sought comfort in the prayers of the Church. 'I know what was felt at the time of the South African War when people went to the Roman Catholic churches because they failed to find in ours any prayer for the dead.'[76]

Davidson was aware that any official sanction of prayers for the dead was going to be difficult, even in a time of emergency. Initially, he thought that the Day of Humble Prayer and Intercession might include some of the unofficial prayers that were already being used by some clergy, but changed his mind when the archbishop of York pointed out that if a decision about prayers was left in the hands of the clergy, then the day would be a disaster.[77] In the end,

---

[74] *LPL: Davidson Papers*, Vol. 13, fol. 26.
[75] Letter from the bishop of Liverpool (Francis James Chavasse) to Davidson, 9 August 1914. Ibid., Vol. 367, fol. 73. The bishop of Manchester was Edmund Arbuthnott Knox.
[76] Davidson to the bishop of Chelmsford (John Watts-Ditchfield), 18 Aug. 1914. Ibid., Vol. 367, fol. 88.
[77] Archbishop of York to Davidson, 16 Nov. 1914. Ibid., Vol. 367, fol. 227. The 'unofficial'

Davidson decided on prayers to fit around the usual Sunday services: collects, readings and propers[78] for Holy Communion, and extended prayers for use with matins and evensong. These included prayers for deliverance from sin, for pardon and spiritual renewal, for the king, country and allies, for the navy and army, for enemies, for the speedy triumph of Britain's cause, and thanksgivings for mercies already received. In the end, there was no prayer solely for the dead; in fact the only mention of the dead came in the phrase, 'For the devotion of those who have laid down their lives for their country', within the prayers of thanksgiving for mercies already received.

Evangelical clergy around the country were keen to make sure that the public prayers did not include an explicit prayer for the dead. Davidson received, along with letters from the bishops of Manchester, Liverpool, Newcastle and Chelmsford, a letter from the evangelical dean of Canterbury, Henry Wace, which included an article from the *Record* arguing that the Prayer Book collects for the dead were 'enough' and the Church need not write new prayers.[79] He also received in December 1914 a petition from a conference of evangelical clergy in London claiming that they would have difficulties offering any prayers for the dead beyond those of the Prayer Book.[80]

Davidson was frustrated by such letters and petitions and vented his feelings to Lang. 'I am slightly indignant with the sort of way in which some bishops and some laymen write about the prayers for the dead. They speak from a sort of superior standpoint as though you and I were incapable of weighing these things, and they talk about the holy beauty of uniformity which means that others must all give way to them. It is the tone I object to rather than the proposals themselves.'[81] In spite of his strong feelings, however, there was no explicit prayer for the dead included in the Day of Humble Prayer and Intercession, when the prayers were published in 1915. As far as the official and public prayers of the Church were concerned,

---

prayers referred to by Davidson were most likely prayers offered by clergy in their own churches, prayers used by chaplains at the front and communicated home, or prayers contained in small pamphlets. The Society of St Peter and St Paul, an Anglo-catholic anti-authority publishing group founded under the inspiration of Ronald Knox in 1910 (before his conversion to Rome in 1917), published a pocket-sized *Red Cross Prayer Book*, which ran, so it claimed, into at least 25,000 copies. The Society of SS Peter and Paul, *The Red Cross Prayer Book* (London, 1915).

[78] Sentences relating to the liturgical seasons inserted into the prayer of consecration.
[79] Wace to Davidson, 21 Nov. 1914. *LPL: Davidson Papers*, Vol. 367, fol. 238.
[80] Ibid., Vol. 367, fol. 331.
[81] Davidson to Lang, 14 Dec. 1914. Ibid., Vol. 367, fol. 335.

therefore, in January 1915, the nature of the departed state was as it had been in 1662. The Forms of Service were reissued in May 1915 with only minor alterations and no alteration to the mention of the dead.

In June of the same year Davidson received a letter from the dean of Wells, Joseph Armitage Robinson:

> I have just received from my brother Arthur the enclosed prayer which appears to be worthy of appendation and sanction. If you have suggestions to make, you will kindly let me know. The prayer referred to begins:
> *Omnipotens sempiterne deus, cui nunquam sine spe misericordiae supplicatur.* I find it [sic] in our old Westminster Missal ...
> ...P.S. Perhaps it might be headed 'A Memorial to the Fallen' – or otherwise as you think best.

The appended prayer read:

> Almighty and everlasting God,
> unto whom no prayer is ever made without hope of Thy compassion
> [handwriting unclear at this point and words crossed out],
> we remember before Thee our brethren who have laid down their lives
> in the cause wherein their King and Country sent them;
> grant that they who have readily obeyed the call of them
> to whom Thou hast committed authority upon earth
> may be accounted worthy of a place among Thy faithful servants
> in the Kingdom of Heaven,
> and give both to them and to us forgiveness of our sins,
> and an ever clearer understanding of Thy will,
> for His sake, who loved us and gave Himself for us,
> Thy Son our Saviour, Jesus Christ. Amen.[82]

The prayer suggested the possibility of post-mortem spiritual development, with the words 'ever clearer understanding'. Davidson was pleased with the prayer and authorised it immediately for use within the diocese of Canterbury, either in private prayers or special services, changing only the words 'an ever clearer understanding' to the slightly stronger 'an ever increasing understanding'.[83]

---

[82] Robinson to Davidson, 14 June 1915. Ibid., Vol. 368, fol. 127.
[83] Ibid., Vol. 368, fol. 170. It should be noted that although the number of the bereaved was already great at this point in the war, it was not as great as beyond 1916. In other words it cannot be assumed that it was the level of bereavement that made Davidson decide to authorise this prayer.

This was a significant step beyond the Prayer Book consideration of the dead and their state. Within the limited boundaries of authorised prayer the theology of the Prayer Book was abandoned. The prayer identified those who had died in the war as exclusively worthy of petition; in other words, they were not prayed for, as in earlier prayers, only in conjunction with the living. It suggested also that their state was not fixed at point of death, but open to change and development ('an ever increasing understanding of Thy will'). It prayed an imperative to God, suggesting how he might deal with them ('Grant that they ... may be accounted worthy of a place among Thy faithful servants'; 'Give ... to them ...forgiveness of [their] sins').

The prayer was commended to the nation two years later when new Forms of Prayer were issued in August 1917. Davidson received only two letters of complaint, from the bishops of Liverpool (Chavasse) and Manchester (Knox), before the prayer was published. Chavasse and Knox claimed that it would cause 'strong feeling, distress and resentment' among many Church people. In reply to the bishop of Liverpool Davidson wrote,

> It must be remembered that there are thousands who are eagerly anxious for some prayer which can to them as they use it convey the idea of intercession with our heavenly Father on behalf of those whose life is now going on beyond our sight. I have passionate appeals to that effect, and it goes to my heart not to be able to meet their needs more fully, believing as I do that such prayers are not forbidden by any doctrine of the Church of England, although their use liturgically was for many obvious reasons practically abolished.[84]

When the bishop of Jerusalem wrote in the same year seeking advice for army chaplains about praying for fallen soldiers, Davidson was encouraging. He noted that the number of people objecting to the practice of praying for the dead was diminishing.[85]

By sanctioning the prayer of 1917 for inclusion in the authorised Forms of Prayer Davidson implicitly sanctioned prayers for the dead and the clear movement away from the Prayer Book theology of the departed. This bold step was a brief one. At the end of the war three further Forms of Prayer were

---

[84] Davidson to bishop of Liverpool, 18 July 1917. Ibid., Vol. 369, fol. 78. In a private letter, a relative, Archibald Thomas Davidson, vicar of Scorton and honorary canon of Manchester, wrote that Bishop Knox of Manchester was 'temporarily deprived of his reason' because his son, Ronald, had become a Roman Catholic. As a consequence the bishop was 'pouring out the vials of his wrath upon an astonished diocese'. Ibid., Vol. 369, fol. 87.

[85] Ibid., Vol. 196, fols. 120–22.

issued, but these moved back from the theological developments of 1917 and were more measured in tone. The prayers praised God for the victory, but made scant mention of the servicemen who had died to secure it. Once again, in the official public prayers of the Church, no petitions for the dead were offered.

Such prayers may not, by that point, have been necessary. The end of the war meant that the prayers of the Church were heard in a different way, as memorials were erected across the country in honour of those who had died in service. The building of war memorials was not without precedent. Within recent memory over two hundred memorial plaques, statues and windows had been erected to remember the wars in South Africa.[86] The majority of these were regimental monuments, or else private memorials to one or two men; some even offered thanks for the safe return of sons.

The memorialisation of the Great War was, however, much more widespread. After 1918 over 7,600 memorials of various types were erected in villages, towns and cities across the country.[87] These had sometimes begun as simple shrines to the serving and departed soldiers, but became more permanent memorials when the war ended.[88]

Each monument or memorial was unveiled with a ceremony that included a service, prayers and usually hymns. In subsequent years remembrance ceremonies took place focused around these memorials. Despite the profusion of ceremonies for the blessing and unveiling of memorials and monuments, and the possibilities for liturgical experimentation, there was not much variety in the choice of hymns, readings and prayers leading up to the moment of unveiling. The hymns, 'O God, our help in ages past', 'O valiant hearts' and 'For all the saints' recurred with regularity in the service texts. The most frequently used Bible readings were Psalm xxiii ('The Lord is my shepherd'), Revelation xxi ('He shall wipe every tear from their eyes') and, most commonly, John xv ('Greater love hath no man than this, that a man lay down his life for his friends').

Away from the home front, army chaplains had, during the war, begun to experiment with burial liturgy. Eric Milner-White (1884–1963), who became

---

[86] The Imperial War Museum National Inventory of War Memorials records 223 memorials of various styles erected between 1892 and 1914.

[87] The National Inventory at the Imperial War Museum counts 7,602.

[88] For some extensive work on this see Mark Connelly, *The Great War, Memory and Ritual. Commemoration in the City and East London, 1916–1939* (London and Woodbridge, 2002). Connelly writes a lot about the memorials themselves and the people involved at public unveilings, but includes little about the services that took place at the 'unveilings'.

dean of King's College, Cambridge in 1918 and dean of York in 1941, was an army chaplain for three years in the war. In the book, *The Church in the Furnace* (1919), written with sixteen other former chaplains, Milner-White said that the chaplains had been discontented with the Prayer Book in the field. The burial service, he claimed, had 'failed badly in the days of death'. The Prayer Book was 'semi-used and semi-usable'.[89]

Frustrated by the traditional liturgy, chaplains often simply made up new forms of service from pieces of the Prayer Book and other prayers they knew or shared with one another. As far as burial services were concerned, not one was the same as another; and not one, thought Milner-White, had been entirely that of the Prayer Book. The structure remained the same, but new opening sentences were added that bore a greater resemblance to the tone of the post-war memorial services than did those of the burial service: 'Though I walk through the valley of the shadow of death', 'Greater love hath no man than this'.

The prayers, unlike those of the burial service, were more explicitly for the departed and for mourners at home. Popular prayers stressed the sacrifice made by the dead soldier, the mercy of God and the petition that God grant rest and salvation to the dead. For example:

> Almighty God,
> we commend to thy loving-kindness the soul of Thy servant,
> who has given his life to defend us.
> Accept, O Lord, the offering of his self-sacrifice;
> and *grant to him*, with all Thy faithful servants,
> *a place of refreshment and peace,*
> *where the light of Thy countenance shines for ever,*
> and where all tears are wiped away.[90] [my italics]

Some chaplains used a prayer from the Roman Office, or a prayer abbreviated from the Roman Litany of St James:

> Remember O Lord, we beseech thee,
> the souls of them that have kept the faith,
> both those whom we remember and those whom we remember not,
> and *grant them rest in the land of the living, in the joy of Paradise,*
> whence all pain and grief have fled away,
> where the light of thy countenance ever shines;

---

89 Macnutt, *The Church in the Furnace*, 177.
90 Ibid., 180.

and guide in peace the end of our lives,
O Lord, when thou wilt and as thou wilt, only without shame or sin.[91]
[my italics]

By contrast, the Forms of Prayer issued by authority, given above, were, Milner-White continued, beautiful, but cold and severe, lacking emotion and intimacy. He concluded, 'We beg you and beg you again, Church of the homeland, consecrate to perpetual English use the variations that by great instinct have committed the bodies of your sons, ten thousand times over, to their victorious bed of earth.'[92]

The prayers of the post-war memorial services contained the same emotional and intimate language of the chaplains – suggesting a possible connection between the Church of the homeland and the Church of the Front.[93] Parish clergy offered these services, as did bishops. Although it might be assumed that bishops stuck rigidly to authorised Forms of Prayer and left the emotional language to the parish clergy, this is not the case. The orders of service were read at small services and at large gatherings alike, by bishops as well as lower clergy.

Some historians, recently re-examining the role of the Church in post-war memorialisation, have concluded that, by its contribution, the Church maintained traditional values and traditional language; tradition provided greater comfort than modernism and irony.[94] Mark Connelly, for example, argues that, 'The memorials and dedication services answered all doubts, not by providing new theories but by reaffirming wartime and pre-war values – which were, quite literally, set in stone.'[95] Such a conclusion misses the radical content of the prayers. Despite the 'thee and thou' phraseology, in the

---

[91] Ibid., 180.
[92] Ibid., 181.
[93] Not everyone was happy about this. Inge complained about the chaplains in 1926 that, 'We have listened with respect to the reports of the chaplains who served with the forces ... the chaplains have been very ready to give their opinions, sometimes in very dogmatic language ... it has plainly been biased by their preconceptions about religious truth and the offices of the Church'. Inge, *Lay Thoughts of a Dean*, 303.
[94] See, for example, Connelly, *The Great War, Memory and Ritual*; Adrian Gregory, *The Silence of Memory. Armistice Day 1919–1946* (Oxford, 1994); Jay Winter, *Sites of Memory, Sites of Mourning. The Great War in European Cultural History* (Cambridge, 1995); Laurinda Stryker, 'Languages of Sacrifice and Suffering in England in the First World War' (Unpublished PhD thesis, Cambridge University, 1992). These historians explicitly set themselves against the work of earlier historians of the First World War, such as Alan Clark and Paul Fussell, who argued that the war undermined the old order of Edwardian society and created the conditions for modernism.
[95] Connelly, *The Great War, Memory and Ritual*, 73.

scripted prayers the traditional Prayer Book language of judgement, sin, faith and the Kingdom of God was abandoned in favour of either a hope that the departed soldiers would be received into heaven or else, and more commonly, an articulated certainty that they were already there.

So, for example, the service for the officers and men of the Norfolk Territorial Force at Norwich Cathedral on 28 February 1918 included a prayer that moved away from the Prayer Book in two ways. It offered an opinion on what eternal life was like, namely free from sorrow and pain and full of light; and it presumed to address God with an imperative ('Give them'), asking him to offer salvation to the soldiers:

> Remember O Lord, Thou Lover of Men,
> all those, the brave and the true, who have died the death of honour …
> Give them rest in Thy presence,
> whence sorrow and pain are for ever banished
> and let perpetual light shine upon them, for Thy mercy's sake.[96]

The borough of Greenwich memorial unveiling on 11 November 1922 contained a prayer, read by the bishop of Woolwich, William Woodcock Hough, suggesting that the sacrifice of death in battle led to a place in heaven:

> Almighty God, we commend to thy loving kingdom the souls of thy
> servants, who have given their lives to defend us.
> Accept, O Lord, the *offering of their self-sacrifice* and grant to them,
> with all thy faithful servants, a place of refreshment and peace,
> where the light of thy countenance shines for ever and all tears are
> wiped away. [my italics][97]

The prayer offered by Revd Stanley Astbury M.C. at the unveiling of a memorial at Smethwick Recreational Grounds on 26 June 1924 counted death in battle as the moment of judgement from which the dead emerged righteous. The following prayer is taken, in part, from the Prayer Book office for the Visitation of the Sick, but the first two lines are an addition:

> Mercifully grant that all those who *in the service of their country*
> *have been called to their account* may find peace with thee …
> wash their souls, we pray thee, in the blood of the immaculate Lamb
> that was slain to take away the sins of the world,

---

[96] Norwich Cathedral memorial service for officers and men of Norfolk territorial force, *Imperial War Museum Ephemeral collection*: K83/2096.
[97] Borough of Greenwich memorial unveiling and dedication, *IWM Eph*: K3867.

that whatever defilements they may have contracted in the midst
of the world through the lusts of the flesh or the wiles of Satan,
being purged and done away they may be presented pure and without
spot before thee.[98] [my italics]

At one unveiling, it was the liturgical choreography that revealed some of
the theological assumptions underlying the service. The service for the
unveiling of the memorial to the Brigade of Guards at the Royal Military
Chapel, Wellington Barracks on 14 December 1924, unusually for unveiling
services, offered rubrics. The service contained the popular hymn 'For all the
saints'. The third verse of the hymn offered the prayer:

O may Thy soldiers, faithful, true and bold,
fight as the Saints who nobly fought of old,
and win with them the victors' crown of gold. Alleluia.

During this verse the procession was directed to move towards the monument. The hymn was then interrupted as the monument was unveiled by the
Prince of Wales and dedicated by the Chaplain-General 'To the glory of God
and in grateful and affectionate memory of those who gave their lives for King
and Country and a Righteous Cause'. Once the memorial had been dedicated,
the hymn continued to sing of the saints.[99]

The soldiers of the Great War were thus set within the inheritance of the
saints – 'soldiers' who 'nobly fought of old'. Their cause was righteous; they
were faithful, true and bold. They too, it was heavily implied, and as the
bishop of London had suggested, were saints.

The theology that underlay these memorial services marked a clear departure from that of the Prayer Book. Yet interestingly it did not exactly reflect
the newer theology of spiritual progress that had been emerging in the late-
nineteenth and early-twentieth centuries. The memorial services offered
something different. In the vast majority of services the prayers suggested
strongly that the departed soldiers were honoured by God for their
self-sacrifice and given a place among the saints. They were to be found,
alongside God's faithful servants, in a place of light, refreshment, peace and
glory. Their personal faith – of concern to Prayer Book theology – was either
unimportant when compared with their sacrifice, or else death in battle –

---

[98] Unveiling and dedication of war memorial, Smethwick Recreational Grounds, *IWM Eph*:
Local K3760.
[99] Royal Military Chapel, Wellington Barracks. Service of matins with unveiling of memorial,
IWM Eph: 17664.

being for the cause of righteousness – was counted as an indication of their Christian faith, almost as martyrdom.

In the language of sacrifice and saints the Church pushed to a radical point what it was prepared to say about the departed soldiers. This was the limit: those who shaped the words of official church prayers, which were to be used in ordinary, non-memorial, church services, opted for phrases that hinted at the possibility of post-mortem progress and the opportunity for repentance and forgiveness – which theologians had embraced some years before – rather than instant sanctification. The chance for conveying this theological shift within a new framework came with the revision of the Prayer Book in the early twentieth century.

The decision to revise the Prayer Book had been taken before the war began. The 1906 *Report of the Royal Commission on Ecclesiastical Discipline* judged that nineteenth-century attempts to enforce the law regarding liturgical practice had failed and that such failure had allowed for liturgical diversity that was bordering chaos.[100] In addition, the report recognised that the law concerning public worship, as it stood, was too narrow to accommodate the religious life of the present generation, and that the newer emerging liturgical sensibilities needed to be taken into account.[101]

The Royal Commission had investigated various liturgical practices, one of which was praying for the departed.[102] The Commission acknowledged that, 'the Church of England has never formally condemned prayers for the dead, as distinguished from their public use in her services',[103] and prayers for rest and refreshment for the souls of the dead were, it noted, found in the most ancient liturgies. However, belief in purgatory as an intermediate state and place of purgation and pain, and belief that the prayers of the living could alleviate the sufferings of the departed in purgatory, were condemned by the Church of England's Articles XXII and XXXI. The Feast of All Souls (2 November), when the dead were remembered, had first been observed in AD 1024, but had become associated with a belief in purgatory, so much so that All Souls Day had been omitted from both Edwardian Prayer Books and the

---

[100] For example, the 1874 Public Worship Regulation Act. See Nigel Yates, *Anglican Ritualism in Victorian Britain, 1830–1910* (Oxford, 1999).

[101] Conclusions of the *Report of the Royal Commission on Ecclesiastical Discipline* (1906).

[102] Other practices that were considered inconsistent with the teaching of the Church of England were, for example, the adoration of the sacrament, benediction with the sacrament, the observation of the Feast of the Assumption of the Blessed Virgin Mary and Corpus Christi processions.

[103] *Report of the Royal Commission*, Vol. VI, 45.

Book of 1662. In its final form the Prayer Book excluded all prayers that prayed explicitly for the departed (separately from the living).

The Royal Commission noted the Guild of All Souls, founded in 1873, whose members were committed to pray for the dead, and to attend special services for that purpose on All Souls Day. It observed that in 1904 there were 234 affiliated churches and around 6,500 members, of whom 1,000 to 1,200 were clergymen.

Members of the Royal Commission attended a variety of services, one of which, on 2 November 1903 at St Alban's, Holborn, was so elaborate in its ritual that the bishop of London demanded that it was modified for 1904.[104] Prayers in the course of the service included the following:

> O God the creator and redeemer of all them that believe, grant unto the souls of all the faithful departed remission of all their sins, that through our devout supplications they may obtain the pardon they have always desired ...
> Deliver the souls of all the faithful departed from the pains of hell and from the bottomless pit: deliver them from the lion's mouth, that hell swallow them not up, that they fall not into thick darkness.[105]

The service included prayers taken from the Mass for the Dead from the Sarum Missal, translated into English and used alongside the Prayer Book. The prayers suggested that the petitions of the living could have an influence on the eternal destiny of the departed.

Walter Plimpton, honorary secretary to the Guild of All Souls, and a witness to the Royal Commission, offered in his book *The Waiting Church* (1876) an explanation of the Guild's assumptions about the afterlife:

> After death the soul, in a state of perfect consciousness, in the place of departed spirits, awaits the day of Judgement. The Intermediate State is one of rest, of expectation, of longing for the presence of God, of perfecting, of penitence and of purification from the sins of this life. In this state the souls of the departed may be assisted by the living in three ways: first and chiefly, by the offering of the Holy Eucharist; secondly by the giving of alms; and thirdly, by prayer. The use of

---

[104] It was modified, but returned to the elaborate style in 1905 without the bishop's permission. Ibid., Vol. VI, 46. The report also notes that another London church, St John's Holland Road, held a Mass 'for the dead', at which no living member of the congregation received communion.
[105] Ibid., Vol. VI, 47–8.

these methods is not only permissible, but a duty, which has been indicated and practised by the Church in all ages.[106]

In assuming the souls of the dead to be in a place of waiting and expectation before the Day of Judgement, Plimpton's theology was akin to traditional Protestant theology. Where he departed from Protestant, and Anglican, teaching, was in suggesting that the living could alter the outcome of that judgement. The Royal Commission therefore condemned the prayers and services of the Guild of All Souls as being 'entirely inconsistent with the teaching of the Church of England'.[107]

The 1906 report was greeted with seriousness and, in the same year, the archbishop of Canterbury wrote to the Convocations and the House of Laymen asking for support in altering the sixteenth- and seventeenth-century rubrics to fit twentieth-century needs. The rubrics were, he hoped, to be 'clear in principle yet elastic in detail'.[108] His words were met with initial enthusiasm and resolutions were passed asking the archbishop to form a committee to consider the Royal Commission's report.[109]

Davidson slowly gathered together a group of liturgical experts to draft some alterations to the Prayer Book.[110] The revision of the Prayer Book was a lengthy process, marked by occasional meetings of the experts and discussions of their results at Convocation or, after 1919, at the newly created National Assembly of the Church of England.[111] Davidson, who was unenthusiastic about the process of revision, grew increasingly frustrated by it, making a list in 1920 of the bishops who had died or retired since 1907.[112]

The war, inevitably, interrupted the revision process. When the war ended

---

[106] Walter Plimpton, *The Waiting Church* (London, 1902 edn. 1st pubd 1876), 7.
[107] *Report of the Royal Commission*, Vol. VI, 48.
[108] *LPL: Davidson Papers*, Vol. 444, fol. 7.
[109] The Upper and Lower Houses of the Convocation of Canterbury, for example, voted on 22 February 1907 to ask this of the archbishop. Ibid., Vol. 444, fol. 130.
[110] The group changed as time went on, but over the years included, for example, Walter Howard Frere, bishop of Truro; Henry B. Swete, regius professor of divinity at Cambridge; Henry Wilson, liturgical scholar; Arthur Benson, son of the former archbishop of Canterbury and master of Magdalene College, Cambridge; and Percy Dearmer.
[111] The Enabling Act of 1919 gave the Church its Church Assembly. This provided the opportunity for the experts to discuss the proposals with bishops, clergy and laity together.
[112] *LPL: Davidson Papers*, Vol. 447, fol. 325. In January 1926 he wrote that his 'instinct' had been to leave the Prayer Book alone and keep to what had satisfied the English people for more than three centuries. However, he thought it was important to allow those who had been working on the changes to have their way. Ibid., Vol. 15, fol. 58–9. Henson thought that this apparent indifference was a contributing factor to the defeat of the Prayer Book Measure in Parliament. H. Hensley Henson, *Retrospect of an Unimportant Life*, 2 Vols (Oxford, 1943), 2: 162.

it became clear that some of the returning army chaplains sought to bring their experiences and thoughts to the revision. Davidson noted that many of them had, of necessity, adapted Prayer Book services and that this had led to a natural 'elasticity' in liturgical practices when they had returned home.[113] Herbert Hensley Henson (1863–1947), bishop of Durham, agreed that the war had brought changes. It had 'affected the process of revision very potently, for not only did it discredit every kind of authority in Church and State and create a new vehement passion for "self-expression", but it stirred in serious minds a great hunger for religious agreement, and a corresponding dislike of ecclesiastical partisanship'.[114]

Prayers for the dead were not the major sticking point in the revision process; the reservation of the Sacrament caused far more debate. It was acknowledged, though, that prayers for the dead needed addressing. Henson noted that, 'The fearful experience of the Great War effected a revolution in public opinion with respect to the Church's duty towards the dead. In approving the introduction of prayers for the departed into public services the bishops did but register and endorse the fact.'[115]

The House of Bishops introduced the *Revised Prayer Book (Permissive Use) Measure* to the Church Assembly in October 1922. The proposals were broadly welcomed and the further process of revision began.[116] Finally, the Church Assembly debated the use of the revised Prayer Book, called the 'Deposited Book', on 5 and 6 July 1927, passing the measure.[117] In the Deposited Book there were four places where changes had been made in

---

[113] *LPL: Davidson Papers*, Vol. 448, fol. 5. In March 1919 the archbishop of York suggested that some of the younger chaplains, such as Edward Talbot (Community of the Resurrection, Mirfield), Eric Milner-White (chaplain of King's College, Cambridge) and Thomas Pym (chaplain of Trinity College, Cambridge) might assist with the liturgical reforms. Ibid., Vol. 447, fol. 36.

[114] H. Hensley Henson, *The Book and the Vote* (London, 1928), 47.

[115] Ibid., 71.

[116] From this point rival sets of proposals for revision appeared, by custom the three principal sets are known by the colours of their pamphlet covers: the Green Book (produced by the English Church Union), the Grey Book (produced by liberal-minded clergy led by William Temple and including Percy Dearmer) and the Orange Book (which was produced by the Alcuin Club, a group committed to scholarly endeavour and an English form of Catholic worship). See G. K. A. Bell, *Randall Davidson. Archbishop of Canterbury* (London, 1935), 1327.

[117] The 'Deposited Book' did not supersede the 1662 Prayer Book, but simply added the proposed additions and deviations. The Church Assembly debate was marked by the strength of opposition from diverse minorities. For a thorough overview of the final stages of the process and what happened to the so-called 'Deposited Book' in Parliament, see John Maiden, *National Religion and the Prayer Book Controversy, 1927–28* (Woodbridge, 2009).

relation to the departed: in the order for Holy Communion, in the burial service, in the occasional prayers and in the Athanasian Creed.

In the order for Holy Communion the prayer offered 'for the whole state of Christ's Church militant here in earth' lost the words 'here in earth', suggesting now that the Church existed in heavenly as well as earthly dimensions. The end of the same prayer moved from blessing God's holy name for 'all thy servants departed this life in thy faith and fear', to commending God's servants 'to thy gracious keeping'. In other words, rather than simply thanking God for the lives of those who had died, the prayer commended the dead to God's care, suggesting an acknowledgement of their continued existence. These were minor changes but significant moves away from the Prayer Book theology.

In the burial service there were additional psalms and the possibility of a choice of Bible readings. There were also optional verses and responses, including:

V. Grant unto him eternal rest
R. And let perpetual light shine upon him.

Two additional prayers were added to the existing service, the first of which was explicitly for the departed:

O Father of all, we pray thee for those we love but see no longer,
grant them thy peace, let light perpetual shine upon them;
and in thy loving wisdom and almighty power
work in them the good purpose of thy perfect will;
through Jesus Christ our Lord. [my italics]

The second prayer invited God to 'deal graciously' with those who mourned. A third prayer was added in 1928 asking for a strengthening of faith for all Christians in the communion of saints, the forgiveness of sins and the resurrection to life everlasting.

These prayers were not simply for the individual being buried, but for all of the departed. They suggested a dynamic state beyond death and the possibility of repentance ('work in them'). They connected the living mourners with the unseen departed by prayer and acknowledged the continuance and importance of human love.

In the occasional prayers,[118] two prayers for the departed were added, both

---

[118] These followed the orders for morning prayer and evening prayer and the Litany, and included prayers for rain, fine weather, plague and Parliament.

of which suggested fellowship between the living and the dead. The second of them read:

> O eternal Lord God, who holdest all souls in life,
> we beseech thee to shed forth upon thy whole Church
> in Paradise and on earth
> the bright beams of thy light and heavenly comfort;
> and grant that we, following the good example of those who have
> loved and served thee and are now at rest
> may with them at length enter into the fullness of thine unending joy,
> through Jesus Christ our Lord.

This was strongly suggestive of an intermediate state, but one in which the faithful departed were at rest, awaiting the final resurrection. It did not petition for forgiveness or suggest repentance. The language was, however, warm. The afterlife was suffused with 'light', 'comfort', 'rest' and 'bright beams'. It had been composed originally by the bishop of Salisbury, John Wordsworth (1843–1911).[119]

Finally, the Athanasian Creed was altered and, compared with the debates in the 1870s, there was now little disagreement about the pressing need for change. Canon John Neale Dalton (1839–1931) of Windsor was given the task of creating a new translation of the creed, and changed the significant word of the damnatory clauses from 'everlasting' to 'eternal', in the light of recent theological explanations of the word 'αἰώνιος'.

In 1914, when the proposed alterations were discussed at the Canterbury Convocation, the majority of the Lower House wanted to be permitted to omit the offending clauses altogether.[120] When the creed was discussed again in 1927 in the Church Assembly, the principal of Pusey House, Dr Darwell Stone (1859–1941), argued against any change. The new translation, he argued, marked a move away from traditional doctrine, to which Hensley Henson responded that it was impossible to revise a sixteenth- or seventeenth-century book without some change in doctrine. Although the doctrinal truths in the creed itself remained, the whole thing had become 'disfigured by an obsolete attitude of mind towards dissentient believers'.[121] In the end, Dalton's translation of the creed with the damnatory clauses held, but the accompanying rubric suggested that the use of the creed was optional.

---

[119] According to Eric Milner-White. Eric Milner-White, *Memorials upon several occasions. Prayers and thanksgivings for use in public worship* (London, 1933), 63, 110 (note 51a).
[120] Canon Dalton to Davidson, 12 Nov. 1914. *LPL: Davidson Papers*, Vol. 446, fol. 48.
[121] Church of England (Church Assembly), *Report of Proceedings*, 6 July 1927.

The Deposited Book marked a movement in the Church's *public* expression of what was understood about the afterlife. In four small but significant places the prayer of the Church now suggested spiritual progress beyond death was possible, and that the living could do more than merely remember their dead: they could now petition God for their spiritual well-being in the hope of post-mortem repentance and forgiveness. The Athanasian Creed retained the belief that the wicked were separated from God, but the change from 'everlasting' to 'eternal' represented the belief that this separation was not to be understood in simplistic terms of duration.

What the Church of England did by this new liturgy was retain the traditional belief that after death there was a period of waiting before the final Resurrection, but it now suggested that spiritual progress, and even forgiveness, was possible in that intervening time. The Church did not commend the underlying theology of some war memorial services: that the dead were immediately in everlasting joy and felicity. Instead the liturgy, drawing on twentieth-century theology and the beliefs circulating in the common culture, fostered the idea that the living could be in prayerful communion with the departed, and that, after death, each soul would progress towards God.

Such evocative language in the Church's prayers, liturgies and sermons blurred several theological boundaries: the late-nineteenth- and early-twentieth-century theology of spiritual progress, the popular conviction that the dead soldiers were immediately in heaven, modern spiritualism, and perhaps an even an older preternatural discourse: all of which were circulating in the common culture. Thus, for example, John Neville Figgis, a member of the Community of Resurrection at Mirfield and critic of spiritualism, suggested in 1917 that, in order to combat spiritualism, the Church needed to recover what he called its 'Prayer Book' belief in 'unseen presences', or angels.[122] He did not offer any explanation as to what exactly 'angels' were, but his sermon was given during the war and made great mention of the departed soldiers, the 'splendour of youth' and the desire of some of the bereaved to pray for them. One, perfectly plausible, inference from his sermon was that the same dead youths were the 'unseen presences', or angels in their midst.

Viscount Halifax, in a lecture at St Martin-in-the-Fields criticising Oliver Lodge's book *Raymond*, called for a rekindling of faith in the Communion of Saints.[123] He argued that spiritualism was a 'miserable substitute' for the 'real' communion. Any conversation that took place was in Christ alone. 'Let

---

[122] J. N. Figgis, *Hopes for English Religion* (London, 1919), 182.
[123] Halifax, *'Raymond'. Some Criticisms*, 12.

us ask their prayers, let us pray for them, let us seek their help, let us realise the closeness of the union we have in them. No such union and fellowship with them as is promised by spiritualism can come near to the reality of that intimate communion vouchsafed to members of Christ's Body one with the other.'[124]

His public comments, calling for a return to an orthodox, if somewhat neglected, doctrine of the Communion of Saints, need to be held against the knowledge of his private interest in ghosts. Halifax was, according to his son, a keen collector, and writer, of ghost stories. He kept a book of stories and added to it from time to time.[125] Earl Halifax wrote of his father's interest: 'I cannot doubt that the true secret of the appeal made to his thought by the mysterious, or so-called uncanny, was the glimpse that such narratives of events might seem to afford of the hidden realities of the unseen world.'[126] The book contained fiction, but also accounts of alleged 'experiences' of ghosts, such as an account from the duke of Devonshire about a ghost he had 'seen' in 1912.[127] Halifax was not insensitive to the possibility of the 'hidden realities' around the living, even as he criticised the spiritualists.

Even Ralph Inge, who suggested to the Church Congress in 1919 that immortality ought to be conceived of in a spiritual rather than a 'picture-book' manner, being a mystery of which human beings could form 'no clear conception',[128] allowed a combination of his own imagination along with traditional heavenly imagery to provide comfort when he confronted personal grief. When his daughter Paula died in 1923 aged eleven, Inge wrote a vivid Latin elegy in her honour, suggesting that she was both already in God's presence and surrounded by angels and stars. The final part, translated, describing how a friend of Paula's painted her portrait, reads:

> In the picture my Paula is depicted as already received in heaven,
> blushing as she offers narcissuses to God.
> The little Christ, with his virgin mother, smiles at her as
> he holds out his hands to the little children, his votive offerings.
> Around him flies a throng of tender Cupids;
> a multitude of stars shines out in the azure vault.
> The ground beneath is verdant; white lilies mixed with
> golden narcissuses cover the whole plain.

---

124 Ibid., 41.
125 Halifax, *Lord Halifax's Ghost Book*, 5.
126 Ibid., 6.
127 Ibid., 131.
128 *Church Congress at Leicester*, 89.

It pleased me to imagine my daughter taken up
into heaven in this way, to whose heart had belonged
whatever is resplendent with beauty.
Look down on us, if it is permitted, there, to be mindful of your dear
ones,
where, being nearer to God, you are blessed with the sight of him.[129]
[my italics]

The poem was first included without comment in *Personal Religion and the Life of Devotion* (1924). In *The Story of Paula* (1933), however, he confessed that 'Far less has been revealed to us than we should like to know about the lot of those who have left us; and we are obliged to allow the imagination to fill in pictures of those things which it hath not entered into the heart of man to conceive.'[130] His own imagination, and his grief, allowed him to hope for the possibility that his daughter looked 'down' on him.

In books designed for ordinary Christians, some churchmen who were sympathetic to spiritualism went further in drawing on the language available in common culture in order to present the newer theology of the afterlife. Percy Dearmer, in a book to aid Sunday School teachers and offering advice for the young, claimed that fellowship with the dead was possible by means of meditation and prayer, but added that 'the scientific name for this is telepathy'. It was also the case, he told his readers, that sometimes, when a person lay dying, they would 'show themselves' to friends far away.[131]

Walter Matthews, when he was dean of St Paul's, gave a radio broadcast about the nature of the afterlife, and received around 1,900 letters in response. This prompted him to follow up with a book on the nature of immortality, in which he drew on the work of psychic science. He was careful to distance himself from spiritualists, and yet there was, he claimed, the possibility that communication with the departed could happen:

> When we have eliminated conscious fraud and hysteria we still have the formidable problem of demonstrating that there are phenomena which cannot be explained by any other theory than that of the activity of persons who have died.[132]

He assured his readers that beyond death there was spiritual progress:

---

[129] Stanzas 41–52, 'In Memoriam Filiolae Dilectissimae', W. R. Inge, *Personal Religion and the Life of Devotion* (London, 1924). Translation by Dr David and Dr Maggie Crease.
[130] W. R. Inge, *The Story of Paula* (London, 1933), 17.
[131] Percy Dearmer, *Lessons on the Way. Vol. 3. The Resurrection, the Spirit and the Church* (Cambridge, 1928), 149–50.
[132] W. R. Matthews, *The Hope of Immortality* (London, 1936), 36.

> The departed spirit must go on more or less where it left off here. Most people, when they die, are imperfect; they have started perhaps on the way to God but they have not gone very far ... I believe that the next life is an opportunity for further progress towards the ultimate good, which is perfect communion with God.[133]

Offering assurances to anxious mothers of 'wicked' sons, he said:

> It is not unreasonable to hope that, in another state of existence, the individual who seemed 'wicked' may have the opportunity of purging himself of the stain of this life and bringing to a flame the spark of goodness which has never quite been extinguished.[134]

Harold Anson, master of the Temple, entitled his memoir *Looking Forward* (1938), claiming, 'I am not without hope that it will encourage those who may read it, to believe, as I believe, that life is abundantly worth living, not only for its own sake, but as a real preparation for the next exciting stage which awaits us, when our work here is done. I am so glad to have lived, and not sorry to be awaiting the new adventures of another world.'[135]

Although he made no mention of his fascination with spiritualism in the memoir, he did add that, 'psychical research does seem to me to have proved that at least some people survive death for some time ... Yet *any* sort of survival is not a desirable thing. The only kind of survival which a Christian can desire is continuous possession of that eternal quality of life of which we already have some glimpses and flashes here, and which we trust will make time and death alike irrelevant hereafter.'[136]

The theologian and canon of St Paul's, Henry Scott Holland (1847–1918), was a close friend of both Dearmer and Anson – although not noted as a spiritualist. In a sermon that was to become famous for one paragraph, he contrasted two conflicting emotions of bereavement: on the one hand the overwhelming sense of despair and separation that resulted from the death of a friend, and on the other hand the sense that nothing had changed and that death seemed to be 'nothing at all'. There was a need in time of grief, he suggested, to reconcile the seriousness of death with the faith that life continues beyond the grave in a manner that will be familiar to the departed soul. He claimed that they were combined through the idea of 'growth'. 'We are in a condition of process, of growth, of which our state on earth is but the

---

133 Ibid., 80.
134 Ibid., 84.
135 Harold Anson, *Looking Forward* (London, 1938), vii.
136 Ibid., 293.

preliminary condition. And this means that in one sense we know all that lies before us; and in another that we know nothing of it.'[137] It is the 'not knowing' that produces the fear or terror of death. His sermon, although acknowledging the terror of death, placed great weight on the life beyond the grave being a continuity of life on earth. His words almost pre-figured the message of Raymond Lodge to his father concerning whisky and cigars.

> It is no novel world, then, into which we shall enter when we pass away, but our own familiar world in which we shall have had our conversation and fellowship. Therefore, from this point of view, death is but an accident. Nothing is broken in our vital continuity. What we shall be there will be the inevitable continuation and development of what we are now and here. We shall simply go on being what we already are, only without disguise, without qualification. We shall use the same forces, live according to the same methods, be governed by the same motives, realize the same intention. We are what we shall be. That is why, standing by the dead, we know nothing for them is changed.

Being already 'sons of God' and 'in Jesus' meant, said Scott Holland, that we could face the unknown landscape of the afterlife with confidence, even in our foreboding: 'Ah! Why do we need to know more? Why should we be afraid of the great venture?'[138]

Any analysis of the Church of England's teaching about the afterlife in the first part of the twentieth century reveals its complexity. Theologically, the Church continued where the nineteenth century had ended, developing the idea of post-mortem spiritual progress and the possibility that, ultimately, God would save all people; even if, as the 1938 report on Christian doctrine argued, the traditional doctrine of immediate judgement and the ultimate separation of the wicked from the love of God could be upheld alongside this newer understanding.

In public teaching, however, in books, sermons and liturgy, the Church began to find ways of expressing post-mortem spiritual progress. The war forced preachers to abandon traditional language about the afterlife and to find ways of making real for their hearers the new, dynamic afterlife of the theologians, making use of the language of development, education and progress. Young men killed in their prime would, surely, preachers said, be

---

137 Henry Scott Holland, 'The King of Terrors', in *Facts of the Faith. A collection of sermons not hitherto published in book form* (London, 1919), 129.
138 Ibid., 131.

developing elsewhere. In order to communicate the newer theology, the Church's preachers borrowed the vivid language that had, for more than sixty years, been part of the common culture – and which was inherent in spiritualism. Sermons and prayers suggested a continuing relationship between the living and the dead: drawing on the language of the communion of saints and angels, but also of 'unseen presences' at the table. Some churchmen, like Inge, drew on ancient images of the beatific vision for comfort; but others, like Streeter, Clutton-Brock and Winnington Ingram, offered the bereaved spiritualist-sounding sunny landscapes and pleasant rural or domestic settings. Or else, like Matthews or Scott Holland, they spoke of growth and of the similarity between this world and the next.

The war also saw an increasing level of certainty, most evident in the memorial liturgies, that the dead were immediately in a place of joy and peace. This was the resurrection of an old common belief: that at death a soul went either straight to heaven or to hell. The war dead, by virtue of their self-sacrifice, were in heaven, even as martyrs, and, although they may have found progress and development in their afterlife, they were progressing *in* heaven, and not in some intermediate state. The Church of England, in its local liturgies, appeared to bless this belief. In its national liturgy, however, the Church was more cautious, suggesting in the Forms of Prayer that if there was progress beyond death, then it was a progress *towards* heaven. This was still a marked departure from the Prayer Book and, however 'traditional' the language of memorialisation sounds to twenty-first-century ears, it should not cause us to miss the real difference between the Prayer Book theology and the prayers of the war period.

Both the 1928 Prayer Book revisions and the 1938 report on Christian doctrine, although shying away from the more radical language and theology of post-war memorialisation, revealed nevertheless that the Church was prepared to relinquish much of its 'traditional' teaching about the afterlife. The new teaching was shaped in part by the debates of the late nineteenth century, but also by the beliefs that had become part of the common culture. Thus, according to the Church of England at the end of the period, heaven was, it was to be hoped, for everyone. Post-mortem spiritual progress was not only possible, but seemed to fit with the character of God, who longed to forgive; and the judgement of each individual was based in righteous living, rather than right belief. The living and the dead could be connected, although not by the communication of a medium; they were joined together by prayer. This was what the Church was proclaiming in public, as well as in private theological debate, by the 1930s. The Church's presentation of the afterlife at this point sounded very different from the afterlife of the 1870s.

8

The negotiation of belief

When modern spiritualism arrived in England with Maria Hayden in 1852, it quickly became popular among people from all levels of society. So much so that by 1857 *The Times* noted that its 'forms, nomenclature and rules' had been absorbed into the common culture and it was 'all around'.[1] It provided fascination for society ladies, servants and Yorkshire radicals alike. In 1919 George Bernard Shaw wrote of the second half of the nineteenth century as being a time when the leisured classes were

> addicted to table-rapping, materialization séances, clairvoyance, palmistry, crystal-gazing and the like to such an extent that it may be doubted whether ever before in the history of the world did sooth-sayers, astrologers, and unregistered therapeutic specialists of all sorts flourish as they did during this half century of the drift to the abyss.[2]

Through séances and spiritualist lectures, the ideas and images of spiritualism were absorbed into the common culture and a new landscape of the afterlife was imagined. The 'spirits' and spiritualists told people that the afterlife was a place where spiritual progress was not only possible but expected; where individuals were assisted in their progress by helpful higher spirits; and where there was no hell or eternal torment. These communications were wrapped in a language of sunshine, flowers and play, and they appealed to many.

One year after Maria Hayden's arrival, in 1853, F. D. Maurice published his *Theological Essays*. Maurice's theology of post-mortem progress and his denial of everlasting torment for the wicked met with criticism from the Church hierarchy and widespread public disapproval. Maurice's *Theological*

---

[1] *The Times*, 5 May 1857, pg. 6, col. C.
[2] George Bernard Shaw, *Heartbreak House* (London, 1919), xiv.

221

Essays were welcomed by others, however, and fostered a development in Church of England teaching about the afterlife that would lead in 1915 to Hastings Rashdall comfortably describing Jesus' own teaching as 'latent Universalism'.[3] The 1938 report *Doctrine in the Church of England* suggested that post-mortem development was possible, and even that there were hints of universal salvation in the Bible.[4] The official nature of this report, and the fact that its production represented a deliberate attempt to find theological coherence among diverse theological opinions in the Church, suggest that such ideas about the afterlife were, by 1938, part of the mainstream of Church teaching.

As it endeavoured to find ways to express these theological developments, the Church made use of the language and imagery of spiritualism. In some cases this was explicit: churchmen like Davies, Moses, Owen and Tweedale openly used the teaching of the 'spirits' and the ideas and images of spiritualism to embellish their sermons and spiritual writing. In most cases, however, it was implicit, and is therefore more difficult to discern. It cannot be said that the clergy of the Church of England simply 'borrowed' the teachings of spiritualism to refresh their own teaching about the afterlife. Nevertheless, when Winnington Ingram, a avowed critic of spiritualism, used phrases such as 'sunny land' and 'passed over' in sermons to bereaved families during the war, he drew on a discourse with which his hearers were familiar – but one which was unconventional for Church teaching. When Burnett Streeter decided that the Church's imagery of the afterlife needed re-framing, he chose 'progress' as his model, and his visions of heaven bore more of the hallmarks of spiritualist domesticity than the biblical splendour of Revelation, or Christian hymnody. Mossy nooks and small flowers took the place of the azure-clad heavenly city in his imagination.[5] The next world, in the hopes of many churchmen, bore strong similarities to the world they already knew – and in sermons, broadcasts and books they shared the fruits of their imaginings with people who already expected that this would be the case.

From the mid nineteenth century onwards there was an ever-widening gap between the theological developments led by Maurice, Wilson, Birks and Farrar, and the 'traditional' language of the Prayer Book and the sermons of the time. To the general public, the Church still taught that at death an individual was judged and either condemned to hell or allowed into heaven. After

---

[3] Rashdall, *The Idea of Atonement in Christian Theology*, 19.
[4] *Doctrine in the Church of England*, 213, 217.
[5] Streeter et al., *Immortality*, 154.

a time of sleep, or conscious rest, where repentance and spiritual change were impossible, the individual was translated to the appropriate landscape for eternity. Eternity meant, straightforwardly, for ever. This traditional framework, increasingly, did not fit the emerging theology; some clergy clearly felt this dissonance and shied away from saying anything much about heaven and hell. Thus Dr Thornton of Notting Hill, addressing the Church Congress in 1881, thought that the Church was 'afraid' of speaking about the afterlife: 'the trumpet has an uncertain sound'.[6]

This dissonance grew more pronounced at the time of the Great War. Faced with the sheer numbers of young men killed in the war, the preachers in the Church were compelled not just to accept the new theology, but to frame it in a language that was already understood by the thousands of grieving people. The language of progress, certainty, domesticity, sunshine and rewards for good actions was already available in the common culture. The Church simply made use of it to clothe its own new theology.

Intriguingly, clergymen did so in two ways. Some maintained a 'traditional' or commonly held theology: that at death an individual was either immediately in heaven or hell, and they clothed this in the language of the 'sunny land'. The dead soldiers were understood to be immediately among the saints, and surrounded by joy and light. Others embraced the new theology of post-mortem forgiveness and the possibility of universal salvation, and added to this the language of progress and light. Thus the official Forms of Prayer, rather than suggesting an instant recompense for soldiers at the point of death, conveyed instead a sense of hope and growth and an ever-clearer understanding of God.

After the war the official doctrine of the Church, while allowing that 'traditional' teaching could be maintained, moved decisively towards the vision of post-mortem progress and away from the language of judgement, sin and eternal torment. In the liturgy of the revised Prayer Book not only was the afterlife presented now as a dynamic realm; it was also possible for the living to consider the departed – and even to pray for them. Exactly why the living were to pray, and what the dead would gain from it, however, was not spelled out. Nevertheless, communication of a prayerful sort was gently supported and, given that this period saw the rising influence of Anglo-catholicism, in some quarters it was actively encouraged as a revival of the Church's teaching on the communion of the saints.

Church of England clergy appeared to prefer the language of progress to

6 *Church Congress at Newcastle*, 52.

that of purgatory. Some were at pains to point out that the post-mortem progress they envisaged was definitely *not* purgatory. Ernest Barnes, for example, was keen to stress this fact even as he described the likelihood of some sort of purgation beyond death.[7] This is interesting, but not altogether surprising. There was, in the Church of England, a deep suspicion of Roman Catholicism, and of the Roman doctrine of purgatory that had been so decisively expunged from the Church of England at the time of the Reformation (Article XXII). Thus groups holding requiem masses, such as those detailed by the Royal Commission on Ecclesiastical Discipline, were frowned upon, borrowing heavily as they did from the language of the Roman Church, and speaking openly of purgatory. The cultural stigma associated with Roman Catholicism was such that, even in 1927, it was possible for a charge of 'papism' made in the House of Commons to derail what were, after all, fairly minor liturgical changes to the Prayer Book.[8]

The Roman Catholic Church itself was deeply opposed to spiritualism, condemning spiritualist practices in 1898, having reaffirmed the existence of the Devil and a literal hell by a pronouncement from Leo XIII in 1879.[9] It is also fair to argue that the Roman Catholic Church of the late nineteenth century was troubled by ideas of 'progress' more generally, as the Syllabus of Errors issued in 1864 by Pius IX so aptly demonstrated. Jenny Hazelgrove has argued that spiritualism was influenced by the ideas and spirituality within Catholicism, emphasising the sentimentality and sensuous nature of the spiritualist experience.[10] Yet the images and ideas of spiritualism were too far couched in progress and individualistic growth for this to be true. The Roman Catholic Church certainly could not see much convergence. The Church of England, by contrast, sat a little more comfortably with the ideas within spiritualism precisely because they offered a way of speaking about post-mortem progress that did not sound Roman.

The Anglican clergy who became committed to spiritualism did not come from any one Church background, and none of them made connections between spiritualism and a particular tradition. However, it is easy to see how the language of self-determination and the possibility of progress would appeal to liberal-minded clergy. The repentance for sins and consequent ascent through the spheres could be thought to sound enough like an ascent

---

[7] Barnes, *Spiritualism and the Christian Faith*, 3.
[8] Adrian Hastings, *A History of English Christianity, 1920–1985*, 3rd edn. (London, 1991), 205–6. See also Maiden, *National Religion and the Prayer Book Controversy*, 173–85.
[9] Alice K. Turner, *The History of Hell* (London, 1996), 235.
[10] Hazelgrove, *Spiritualism and British Society*, 53.

through purgatory to appeal to Anglo-catholic sensibilities. The appeal to morality of life, the seriousness of each action and the responsibility of the individual to lead a righteousness life were there for evangelicals in spiritualism. There was, however, no 'Anglican' spiritualism, as such, and no one tradition alone that embraced it. Conrad Noel claimed instead that spiritualism appealed most to those who had been brought up in a 'narrow' faith – regardless of their tradition. For many, although it did not offer profound teaching, it had proved a 'generous and liberating gospel'.[11]

Spiritualism certainly had a broad appeal, and as the ideas and images of spiritualism became embedded in the common culture, they connected, as we have seen, with pre-existing tropes. The discourses of health, science, magic, folk-lore and preternaturalism were already a part of the common culture when spiritualism arrived in England, not confined to particular social groups but pervading all areas of society. Over the course of the period spiritualism engaged with common culture, mixing further with familiar late-Victorian tropes. For example, although highly individualistic in some respects, spiritualism also made much of the importance of family ties, friendships and the possibility of maintaining connections with loved ones beyond the grave. The 'appearance' of departed family members in séance was, according to spiritualists, intended to give comfort to the bereaved and maintain the family connections. Oliver Lodge, for example, was assured that Raymond, along with other departed soldiers, wanted to make contact with living family members.[12] Such concerns were a reflection of the importance of family life and resonate with images of family and domesticity in the Victorian period. By contrast, the organic growth and progress of the individual inherent in spiritualism fitted with ideas from across the political spectrum, ranging from competitive individualism of the 'God helps those who help themselves' variety, to the sort of progressive community life envisaged by Robert Owen. Spiritualism also managed to maintain a degree of class distinction. There were, as has been noted, essentially three 'realms', subdivided, through which an individual could progress. It is telling that the most communicative spirits were those in the middle rank, or 'class'.

By the twentieth century, and certainly during the period of post-war memorialisation, the gentle landscapes of the sunny land, like the possibilities of education and growth beyond death, also connected with what some have seen as the reaction against harsh modernism, as, in need of consolation, the

11 Noel, *Byways of Belief*, 151.
12 Lodge, *Raymond Revised*, 194.

bereaved turned to tradition for comfort.[13] In the war cemeteries, for example, it was suggested to the Imperial War Graves Commission that English trees 'from English soil' be planted, and monuments reflect designs from the 'country church yard'.[14] The domestic ordinariness of Raymond's whisky sodas and cigars, and the vivid imagery of flowers and the 'English summer days'[15] resonated with the widespread yearning for images of home and comfort in time of national grief. Such imagery was perhaps more nostalgic than explicitly 'traditional', but it was clearly present within spiritualism, as well as in the wider common culture.

The relationship between spiritualism as a *movement* and the Church of England can, on the one hand, be easily discerned and described. The responses of clergy and Church members towards modern spiritualism ranged, as has been seen, from negative criticism to positive commendation. The relationship between the Church's teaching and the teaching of spiritualism is harder to define. The direct influence of the imagery and ideas of spiritualism on the teaching of some clergy has been noted. It has also been recognised that many Church members, as well as some clergy, felt able to maintain their churchgoing alongside visits to mediums, membership of the SPR and engagement with spiritualist writings.[16] The subtle influence of spiritualism, the way in which its images became mixed into the common culture and helped to shape the teaching of the Church, is more difficult to discern, but is certainly apparent in the language and imagery employed by clergymen who sought to clothe their teaching in words familiar to their hearers. In order to notice it, though, we need to be prepared to look carefully at how churchmen spoke to the general public through the means of sermons, hymns, memorial services and popular writings, as well as how they engaged with one another in academic theological circles.

The chief benefit of exploring one aspect of the Church's doctrine next to the teaching of an alternative theological system is that it does become possible to notice how the Church adapted its own ideas by engaging with, and drawing on, ideas and images beyond itself. In the elusive interface between the Church and the common culture, religious belief was negotiated

---

[13] See, for example, Winter, *Sites of Memory, Sites of Mourning*, 115.

[14] F. Kenyon, *War Graves. How the cemeteries abroad will be designed. Report to the Imperial War Graves Commission* (London, 1918), 11, 13.

[15] Davies, *London Sermons*, 225.

[16] Gladstone did not see any conflict and, as has been noted, Georgiana Houghton and Mabel St Clair Stobart continued to attend church, at least for a time. The archbishop's report on spiritualism also noted how Church members used spiritualism to 'supplement' their religious experience. *Report on Spiritualism*, 4.

and redefined: meaning that, for example, over the course of the period observed in this study, ideas such as universal salvation and post-mortem progress at some point ceased to cause controversy and instead became mainstream religious belief. Observing and describing the importance of common culture to religious belief is not as straightforward as monitoring church attendance, or even assessing the value of contributions made by churches to the social life of local communities. However, although untidy and imprecise, this approach allows us to take religious belief seriously, and to take seriously the shared ideas within common culture, their importance for the development of Church teaching and the shaping of religious belief within the Church and beyond it.

There are intriguing possibilities available to those willing to adopt this untidy approach: placing Church teaching alongside ideas circulating in the common culture and observing how they interact. This study has placed the Church's teaching on the afterlife over and against modern spiritualism. It might also be possible to note, for example, how changing attitudes to the punishment of criminals coloured the language used in relation to God's punishment of the wicked, or how the development of democracy and the widening of the franchise played a part in the slow acceptance of the universal salvation of all people as a legitimate doctrine.

Even further, it might be observed that significant cultural developments, such as the advances in communication and broadcasting, played a significant role in shaping the Church's presentation of itself. It might be interesting to place the widespread reaction to the horrors of the Second World War alongside the emerging theology of the suffering of God, or the language of the women's movement in the second half of the twentieth century next to the development of feminist theology. By engaging with common culture the Church refreshes its own teaching, and religious belief is redefined.

The implication of this approach for historians is a significant one. Religious belief emerges as something more elusive than measurable; dynamic and fluid, located within the ongoing process of negotiation between Church teaching and common culture. Belief within the institutional Church, as well as outside it, therefore changes and fluctuates. Church members move from confidently articulated belief to crisis of faith, and back again. Belief cannot be measured; it can only be observed and described. It becomes difficult, therefore, to say that religious belief has 'declined' in any period; only that it has changed as a result of the interaction of Church and common culture, albeit that, although we can't measure it, this change might include a sense of loss or decline.

Something of the negotiation of religious belief has been observed in this study. Spiritualism arrived in England at a time when the Church was, internally, rethinking its theology of the afterlife, but when its public teaching was still held within a 'traditional' frame. Spiritualism offered an alternative teaching that was appealing: rooted in post-mortem progress, an attractive, vivid, afterlife and, most importantly, the possibility of continued communication between the living and the dead. By the late 1920s, the Church, although in less flowery language, was also teaching that the afterlife was dynamic, that progress was not unbiblical, and that it was permissible for the living to communicate their love and affection for the departed through the appropriate medium of prayer.

Thus, far from being a static, monolithic institution, unable to comprehend a vibrant working-class belief or the popularity of spiritualism among alienated 'fringe' groups, the Church is revealed as susceptible to ideas within the much broader arena of what we have called the 'common culture' – even when these ideas originated in an alternative system of belief. As we have seen, the Church did not embrace spiritualism *per se* but, seeking fresh ways to express new theological developments, found that appropriate tropes had already become embedded in the common culture. In order to communicate the new teaching about the afterlife, the Church of England, over time and sometimes unconsciously, made use of the language and ideas of spiritualism, which, because they were circulating in this common culture, were already very familiar to most people. Religious belief, elusive, hovering on the borderland between Church teaching and common culture, within Church but not bounded by it, did not decline: it was simply redefined.

Bibliography

Archival Collections

Cambridge University Library, Society for Psychical Research, library and archives

Imperial War Museum, London, Ephemeral Collection

Lambeth Palace Library, London:

  A. C. Tait Papers, Vols. 167, 172, 175, 188, 193, 276

  Cosmo Gordon Lang Papers, Vols. 70, 123, 133

  E. W. Benson Papers, Vols. 15, 116

  Frederick Temple Papers, Vols. 16, 28, 42

  Thomas Randall Davidson Papers, Vols. 6, 7, 13, 15, 79, 97, 195–6, 205, 367–9, 444–50

University of Sussex, Brighton, Mass Observation Archive: Religion 1937–49, boxes 1–3

Journals, newspapers and periodicals

All the Year Round
Blackwood's Edinburgh Magazine
Borderland
Christian Spiritualist
Church Assembly, reports of proceedings
Church Congress reports (esp. 1881, 1919, 1920)
Church Times
Cornhill Magazine
Daily Express
Daily Herald
Daily News
Daily Mirror
Evening News
Express and Star (Wolverhampton)
Folk-lore
Journal for the Society of Psychical Research
Lancet
Light

Lyceum Banner
Manchester Evening Chronicle
Manchester Guardian
Medium and Daybreak
New Spiritualist
Scottish Review
Spiritual Magazine
Spiritual Truth
Spiritualist
The Nineteenth Century
The Times (Digital Archive)
Two Worlds
Yorkshire Spiritual Telegraph
Zoist

Primary Sources

'A Dean', *'The Gates Ajar' Critically Examined* (London, 1871)
'A. M. B.', *Spiritualism. What is its origin?* (London, 1892)
'A. P.', *Spiritualism: What is it, and whence does it come?* (London, 1874)
Abbott, Edwin, *The Kernel and the Husk. Letters on Spiritual Christianity* (London, 1886)
Alford, Henry, *The Great Multitude which No Man can Number: A Sermon preached in the Cathedral Church of Christ, Canterbury on All Saints Day, Sunday Nov. 1, 1857* (London, 1857)
'Anon.', *The Spiritualists at Home: The Confessions of a Medium* (London, 1861)
Anson, Harold, *The Truth about Spiritualism* (London, 1941)
———, *Looking Forward* (London, 1938)
Archbishop's committee on spiritualism. *Report of the committee to the Archbishop of Canterbury* (n.p., 1939)
The Army and Religion. An enquiry and its bearing upon the religious life of the nation (London, 1919)
Ashcroft, T., *Spiritualism and Why I object to it* (London, 1892)
Ashley, John Marks [as 'J. M. A.'], *The treatise of S. Catherine of Genoa on Purgatory newly translated by J. M. A. Edited with an introductory essay on hell and the intermediate state by a priest associate of the Guild of All Souls* (London, 1878)
Ashmead, Edward, *The Athanasian Creed. A plea for its discontinuance in public worship* (printed for the writer and issued by him, 1904)
Baggs, Thomas, *Back from the Front. An eye witness's narrative of the beginnings of the Great War, 1914* (London, 1914)

Ballou, Adin, *An Exposition of views respecting the principal facts, causes and peculiarities involved in Spirit Manifestations, together with interesting phenomenal statements and communications* (London, 1852)

Baring-Gould, Sabine, *The restitution of all things, or, The hope that is set before us* (London, 1907)

Barnes, E. W., *Spiritualism and the Christian Faith* (London, 1920)

Barnes, J. B. M., *The last flame of hell* (Manchester, 1901)

Battersby, W., *A sermon on the death of his Royal Highness the Prince Consort. Sunday 22 December 1861* (London, 1861)

Beloe, R. S., *Be ye Ready. A sermon preached in the parish church of Holton on the occasion of the death of his Royal Highness the Prince Consort (22 Dec 1861)* (London, 1861)

Bell, G. K. A., *Randall Davidson. Archbishop of Canterbury* (London, 1935)

Bennetts, H. J. T., *Prayers for the Sick, the Dying and the Departed. From sources ancient and modern* (London, 1928)

Benson, R. H., *Spiritualism* (London, 1911)

Bickersteth, Edward, *The Shadowed Home and the Light Beyond* (London, 1875)

Birks, T. R., *The Victory of Divine Goodness* (London, 1870. 1st pubd 1867)

Blake, J. M., *The making of heaven and hell. An essay towards the understanding of the Divine method of Judgement* (London, 1910)

Bland, Joseph, *The Keys of Hell: Who holds them, and why, and when will they be used?* (Birmingham, 1884)

Boyd, James, *The New Spiritism: Is it from heaven or hell? A sober examination of the New Revelation by Sir Arthur Conan Doyle* (London, 1920)

The British Spiritualists' Lyceum Manual (The British Spiritualists' Lyceum Union, 1922)

Britten, Emma Hardinge, *Modern American spiritualism*, 3rd edn. (New York, 1870)

———, *Nineteenth Century Miracles, or, spirits and their work in every country of the earth. A complete historical compendium of the great movement known as 'Modern Spiritualism'* (Manchester, 1883)

———, *Autobiography* (London, 1900)

Browne, R .W., *Justification by Faith in the Atonement. A Sermon preached in Wells Cathedral, on Trinity Sunday, 1856, at the Ordination of the Lord Bishop of Bath and Wells* (London, 1856)

Bull, Paul B., *Peace and War. Notes of Sermons and Addresses* (London, 1917)

Burge, H. M., *The doctrine of the resurrection of the body. Documents relating to the question of heresy raised against the Rev H. D. A. Major, Ripon Hall, Oxford* (London and Oxford, 1922)

Burton, Alfred H., *Spiritism: Is it Real?* (London, 1898)

'C. O. R. B.', *A few remarks on Spiritualism* (London, 1920)

Carpenter, William Boyd, *Two sermons preached at Tetsworth, Oxon, being the day after the funeral of Rev. John Witherington Peers, M.A.* (London, 1876)
———, *Life's Tangled Thread* (London, 1912)
———, *Further pages of my life* (London, 1916)
Chambers, Arthur, *Our Life after Death, or, The teaching of the Bible concerning the Unseen World* (London, 1894)
———, *Man and the Spiritual World as disclosed by the Bible* (London, 1900)
———, *Problems of the Spiritual* (London, 1907)
———, *Our Self after Death (Can we, in the light of Christ and His Teaching, know more on this subject than is commonly expressed in Christian Belief?)* (London, 1916)
Childe, C. F., *The Unsafe Anchor, or 'Eternal Hope' a false hope. Being strictures on Canon Farrar's West Minster Abbey Sermons* (London, 1879)
Chronicle of Convocation. Being a record of the proceedings of the Convocation of Canterbury (London, 1858–)
Church, R. W., *Village Sermons* (London, 1892)
Churchill, L. A., *The Truth about our dead, told by those who know* (London, 1916)
Clarke, Richard (SJ), *Spiritualism: its Character and Results* (London, 1892)
Clemance, Clement, *Future Punishment: Some current theories concerning it stated and estimated. To which is added a view that is something more than a theory* (London, 1877)
Colley, Thomas, *Sermons on Spiritualism at Stockton* (London, 1907)
The Confraternity of Clergy and Spiritualists. Its Aims and Objects and the Reason Why (pamphlet produced by the Confraternity, Grotian Hall, London, n.d.)
Constable, Henry, *The Duration and Nature of Future Punishment* (London, 1868)
Conybeare, C. R., *Those things which God prepared for them that love Him. A Sermon preached at St Mary's, Itchen-Stoke, Aug. 21, 1881* (Oxford, 1881)
Cotton, R. L., *A sermon preached in Worcester College Chapel on the occasion of the lamented death of John Hayward Southby Esq.* (Oxford, 1861)
Coward, Noel, *Blithe Spirit. An Improbable Farce in Three Acts* (London, 1976. 1st pubd 1941)
Cox, Samuel, *Salvator Mundi: or Is Christ the Saviour of all men?* (London, 1879)
A Critique of Canon Farrar's 'Eternal Hope' (London, 1878)
Croft, J. B., *Requiem. The Service for the faithful departed set to the ancient plainsong of the Lyons and Rouen use in modern notation* (London, 1901)
Crookes, William, *Researches in the Phenomena of Spiritualism* (London, 1874. Reprinted from the *Quarterly Journal of Science*)

Cundy, Henry G., '*Eschatology'. A Paper read at a Clerical Meeting* (London, 1878)

Davies, Charles Maurice, *London Sermons* (London, 1875)

———, *The Future that Awaits Us. The appearances of Jesus during the Great Forty Days, viewed as a revelation of the Unseen World* (London, 1884)

———, *Unorthodox London, or, phases of religious life in the Metropolis*. 2nd edn (London, 1874. 1st edn. 1873)

———, *Orthodox London* (London, 1874)

———, *Maud Blount, Medium* (London, 1876)

———, [As 'A Church of England clergyman'] *The Great Secret and its unfoldment in Occultism* (London, 1895)

Dearmer, Percy, *The Communion of the Saints* (London, 1906)

———, *Body and Soul. An Enquiry into the effects of religion upon health, with a description of Christian works of healing from the New Testament to the present day* (London, 1909)

———, *False Gods* (London, 1914)

———, *The Parson's Handbook*, 11th edn (London, 1928)

———, *Lessons on the Way. Vol. 3. The Resurrection, the Spirit and the Church* (Cambridge, 1928)

———, *The Legend of Hell. An examination of the idea of everlasting punishment* (London, 1929)

Dearmer, Percy and Nancy, *The Fellowship of the Picture. An Automatic Script taken down by Nancy Dearmer* (London, 1920)

Denison, Edward, *Sorrow and Consolation: A sermon preached in the cathedral of Salisbury. Easter Day 1850* (London, 1850)

Dennis, G. R., *The Quest of the Unseen. Spiritualism in the Light of Christianity* (London, 1920)

Dickens, Charles, *The Pickwick Papers* (Oxford World Classics edn, Oxford and New York, 1998)

Dobson, C. C., *Modern Spiritualism under the Biblical Searchlight* (London, 1925)

———, *The Bible and Spiritualism* (London, 1920)

Doctrine in the Church of England. The report of the commission on Christian doctrine appointed by the archbishops of Canterbury and York in 1922 (London, 1938)

Douglas, Lily ['The Author of Pro Christo et Ecclesia'], *Concerning Prayer. Its nature, its difficulties and its value* (London, 1916)

Doyle, Arthur Conan, *A Full Report of a Lecture on Spiritualism delivered by Sir Arthur Conan Doyle at the Connaught Hall, Worthing on Friday, July 11th, 1919, the Mayor of Worthing (J. Farquharson Whyte, Esq., J.P.) in the Chair.* Facsimile edition with an afterword by Richard Lancelyn Green (London, 1997. 1st pubd 1919)

————, *Verbatim Report: A public debate on the 'Truth of Spiritualism' between Sir Arthur Conan Doyle and Joseph McCabe. Held at the Queen's Hall, Langham Place, London, W., on Thursday, March 11, 1920* (London, 1920)

————, *Our Reply to the Cleric: Sir Arthur Conan Doyle's Lecture in Leicester, October 19th, 1919, following the Church Congress* (Halifax, 1920)

————, *The New Revelation* (London, 1981. 1st pubd 1918)

————, *The Vital Message* (London, 1981. 1st pubd 1919)

Dunraven, earl of, *Experiences in Spiritualism with D. D. Home* (Glasgow, 1924)

Dunston, B., *Ghost stories and presentiments* (London, 1888)

Dykes, John B., *Natural and Supernatural Life. A sermon preached in the Cathedral Church of Durham on Ash Wednesday, March 9, 1859* (London, 1859)

'EAG and PWSS', *True and False Spiritualism* (London, 1918)

Easthope, Fred, *Is Spiritualism True?, or, A step heavenward* (Newcastle and London, 1905)

Elliott, Charles J., *A sermon preached at St Peter's, Cranbourne, on Sunday, May 11, 1851, on the occasion of the death of Mrs Conyngham Ellis* (London, 1851)

Elliott, G. Maurice, *Angels seen today* (London, 1919)

Elliott, John Henry, *A Refutation of Modern Spiritualism* (London, 1866)

Ellis, Percy Ansley, *The Life of the world to come* (London, 1909)

Evans, W. H., *Spiritualism. A Philosophy of Life* (Manchester, 1926)

Farrar, F. W., *Eternal Hope. Five Sermons preached in Westminster Abbey, November and December 1877* (London, 1892. 1st pubd 1878)

Fielding-Ould, F., *Is spiritualism of the Devil?* (London, 1920)

————, *The Relation of Spiritualism to Christianity, and of Spiritualists to Christ* (Beverley, 1921)

Figgis, J. N., *Hopes for English Religion* (London, 1919)

Fletcher, C. J. H., *Divine Punishment in This Life and the Next. A Sermon preached at St Martin's, Oxford, Sunday December 8th, 1872* (Oxford, 1872)

Forms of Prayer for Public Use on the Fourth and Fifth of August, 1917. Issued by Authority, for use where the Ordinary Permits (London, 1917)

Fowle, T. W., *Our Lord's Silence as to the Future Life. A Sermon preached in the Church of St Martin (Carfax), Oxford, on November 19th, 1876* (Oxford, 1876)

Fox, Henry, *The funeral sermons preached at St Ebbe's Church, Oxford on Sunday, Sept. 8, 1872, on the occasion of the death of Catharine Louisa, the beloved wife of the Rev. Edward Penrose Hathaway, Rector of St Ebbe's* (Oxford, 1872)

Furniss, J., *The Sight of Hell* (London, 1861)

Garrick, A. W., *Spiritualism True and False and the Expansion of Consciousness* (London, 1922)

Garvie, A. E. (et al.), *Our Dead, where are they?* (London, 1934)

Gibbs, Philip, *Realities of War*. New and revised edn. (London, 1929)

Giraud, S. Louis, *Ghosts in the Great War and True Tales of Haunted Houses. Thrilling Experiences of 'Daily News' Readers* (London, 1926)

Goode, W., *A sermon on the lamented death of His Royal Highness, the late Prince Consort preached in Ripon Cathedral. 23 December 1861 – day of funeral* (London, 1861)

Gore, Charles (ed.), *Lux Mundi. A Series of Studies in the Religion of the Incarnation* (London, 1890)

———, *The Holy Spirit and the Church* (London, 1924)

Goulburn, Edward M., *Two Discourses by the Dean of Norwich on the Athanasian Creed* (London, 1872)

Gray, George, *What is it that dies? A few words to the Spiritualists* (London, 1867)

Green, Mabel Corelli, *Life in the Summerland. Given from the Spirit World through inspirational writing to her mother, Corelli Green* (London, 1922)

Green, Peter, *Old Age and the Life to Come* (Oxford, 1950)

The Grey Book and the future life. Pamphlet No. 5 (London, 1923)

Guild of All Souls, *The Manual of the Guild of All Souls* (London, 1886)

Gurney, Edmund; Myers, Frederic W. H.; Podmore, Frank, *Phantasms of the Living*, 2 vols (London, 1886)

Halifax, Viscount, *'Raymond'. Some Criticisms. A lecture given at St Martin-in-the-Fields, February 14, 1917, with the addition of a preface* (London, 1917)

———, *Lord Halifax's Ghost Book. A collection of stories made by Charles Lindley, Viscount Halifax* (London, 1936)

Hardy, T. J., *Spiritism in the Light of Faith. A Comparison and a Contrast* (London, 1919)

Hastings, Fred (ed.), *Our boys beyond the shadows* (London, 1917)

Haweis, H. R., *Thoughts for the Times* (London, 1872)

———, *Ashes to Ashes. A Cremation Prelude* (London, 1875)

Headlam, A. C., *The New Prayerbook. Being a Charge delivered to the Clergy and Church Wardens of the Diocese of Gloucester on the Occasion of his Second Visitation* (London, 1927)

Hensley Henson, H., *The Book and the Vote* (London, 1928).

———, *Retrospect of an Unimportant Life*, 2 Vols (London, 1943)

Hermitage-Day, E., *Monuments and Memorials. The Arts of the Church* (Oxford, 1915)

Hessey, James, *A sermon on the occasion of the death of Rev. William Henry Hart MA, Demy of Magdalen College Oxford and Chaplain of Grey's Inn: preached October 13, 1861 in Grey's Inn Chapel* (London, 1861)

Hoffman, 'Professor', *Magic at Home. A book of amusing science* (London, 1890)

Hogg, C. F., *Spiritism in the Light of Scripture* (London, 1923)

Holland, Henry S., *The Optimism of Butler's 'Analogy'* (Oxford, 1908)

———, *Facts of the Faith. A collection of sermons not hitherto published in book form* (London, 1919)

Home, D. D., *Incidents in my Life* (London, 1863)

———, *Lights and Shadows of Spiritualism* (London, 1877)

Hook, Walter F., *Discourses bearing on the Controversies of the Day* (London, 1853)

Houghton, Georgiana, *Evenings at Home in Spiritual Séance. Prefaced and welded together by species of autobiography* (London, 1881)

Howes, J. G., *Sermon preached in the parish church of S. Mary the Less, before the Corporation of the Borough of Cambridge on Monday, December 23, 1861* (London, 1861)

Howitt, William, *The History of the Supernatural. In all ages and nations, and in all Churches, Christian and Pagan: demonstrating a universal faith*, 2 Vols (London, 1863)

Hughes, Thomas, [As 'R. T. H.'] *Spiritualism and Common Sense* (London, 1868)

Inge, Dean (et al.), *What is the Real Hell?* (London, 1930)

Inge, W. R., *Personal Religion and the Life of Devotion* (London, 1924)

———, *Lay Thoughts of a Dean* (London, 1926)

———, *The Story of Paula* (London, 1933) [Reprint of final chapter of Inge 1924, along with 'metrical dedication']

James, John, *A sermon on the lamented death of his Royal Highness the Prince Consort preached in the cathedral Church of Peterborough (22 Dec 1861)* (London, 1861)

James, M. R., *Ghost Stories of an Antiquary* (London, 1904)

———, *More Ghost Stories of an Antiquary* (London, 1911)

James, M. R. (ed.), *Madam Crowl's Ghost and other tales of mystery by Joseph Sheridan Le Fanu* (London, 1923)

James, William, *Varieties of Religious Experience* (New York and London, 1985. 1st pubd 1902)

Jukes, Andrew, *The Second Death and the Restitution of All Things* (London, 1869)

Keith, Sir Arthur (et al.), *Where are the dead?* (London, 1928)

Kenyon, Frederic, *War Graves. How the cemeteries abroad will be designed. Report to the Imperial War Graves Commission* (London, 1918)

Kitson, Alfred, *Helps to the study of the Lyceum Manual of difficult words and phrases (arranged in alphabetical order)* (Keighley, 1927)

Knox, Wilfred L., *The Church Expectant* (London, 1919)

Lake, J. W., *The Athanasian Creed: A plea for its disuse in the public worship of the national church* (London, 1875)

Lake, W. C., *The Inspiration of Scripture and Eternal Punishment. Two sermons preached in the Chapel Royal, Whitehall with a preface on the 'Oxford Declaration' and on Mr. Maurice's Letter to the Bishop of London* (Oxford and London, 1864)

Law, Henry, *The Smitten Nation. A sermon preached in the parish church of Weston-super-Mare on Sunday, December 15, 1861, immediately after the announcement of the lamented death of his Royal Highness the Prince Consort* (London, 1861)

Lee, G. F., *Death, Judgement, Heaven and Hell. Four Advent Sermons* (London, 1853)

———, *The abolition and rejection of the Athanasian Creed. A letter to his grace, Archibald Campbell, Lord Archbishop of Canterbury* (London, 1872)

Lewis, H. Carvill, *The alleged psychical phenomena of spiritualism. An account of two séances* (From the Proceedings of the SPR) (London, 1887)

Livius, T., *Father Furniss and his Works for Children* (London, 1896)

Lodge, Oliver, *Raymond: or life and death. With examples of the evidence for survival of memory and affection after death.* 4th edn. (London, 1916)

———, *Raymond Revised* (London, 1922)

London Dialectical Society, *Report on Spiritualism, of the Committee of the London Dialectical Society* (London, 1871)

Longridge, George, *Spiritualism and Christianity* (London and Oxford, 1918)

Lovett, Edward, *Magic in Modern London* (Croydon, 1925)

MacCabe, Joseph, *The Passing of Heaven and Hell. A Criticism of the Church of England Report on Doctrine* (London, 1938)

MacDonagh, M., *In London during the Great War. The Diary of a Journalist* (London, 1935)

Macfie, M. P., *From Heaven to Earth. Messages Automatically Written* (London, 1921)

MacKintosh, H. R., *The Christian Experience of Forgiveness* (London, 1927)

Macnutt, F. B., *The Church in the Furnace. Essays by seventeen temporary Church of England chaplains on active service in France and Flanders* (London, 1917)

Major, H. D. A., 'ΑΙΩΝΙΟΣ. Its use and meaning especially in the New Testament', *Journal of Theological Studies*, XVIII (October 1916), 7–23.

Mass Observation, *Puzzled People. A study in popular attitudes to religion, ethics progress and politics in a London Borough* (London, 1947)

Matthews, Basil, *Christ: and the World at War. Sermons preached in war-time* (London, 1917)

Matthews, W. R. (ed.), *King's College Lectures on Immortality* (London, 1920)

———, *The Hope of Immortality* (London, 1936)

———, *Memories and Meanings* (London, 1969)

Maud, John P., *Our comradeship with the Blessed Dead* (London, 1915)

Maurice, F. D., *The Word 'Eternal' and the Punishment of the Wicked: A Letter to the Rev. Dr. Jelf, Canon of Christ Church and Principal of King's College* (Cambridge, London printed, 1853)

———, *Theological Essays* (London, 1957. 1st pubd 1853)

———, *Death and Life: A Sermon preached in Lincoln's Inn Chapel on 25th March, 1855* (Cambridge, 1855)

Maurice, Frederick, *The life of Frederick Denison Maurice chiefly told in his own letters. In two volumes*, 2nd edn (London, 1884)

McClure, Edmund, *Spiritualism. A Historical and Critical Sketch* (London, 1916)

Miller, A. V., *Sermons on Modern Spiritualism* (London, 1908)

Milner-White, Eric, *Memorials upon several occasions. Prayers and thanksgivings for use in public worship* (London, 1933)

Moberly, George, *A sermon preached in the chapel of Winchester College on Sunday February 17, 1861, after the funeral of the Rev. the Warden of Winchester College* (London, 1861)

Moses, William Stainton, *Higher Aspects of Spiritualism* (London, 1880)

———, *Spirit Teachings* (London, 1883)

———, [As 'M. A. Oxon.'] *Spiritualism at the Church Congress* (London, n.d.)

Noel, Conrad, *Byways of Belief* (London, 1912)

Owen, G. Vale, *The Life beyond the Veil*, 2 Vols (London, 1926. 1st pubd 1922)

———, *Facts and the Future Life* (London, 1922)

Owen, Robert Dale, *Footfalls on the boundary of another world* (London, 1860)

———, *The Debatable Land between This World and the Next* (London, 1871)

Paget, Francis, *The Virtue of Simplicity. A sermon preached in the Cathedral Church of Christ Church, Oxford on Sunday, January 23, 1898* (Oxford, 1898)

Paige Cox, W. L., *Life after Death and the Commemoration of the Saints. Church of England Handbooks No.4* (Liverpool, 1924)

Paterson, Robert, *Canon Farrar's 'Eternal Hope'. A Review of his Five Sermons preached at Westminster Abbey, November and December 1877* (London, 1878)

Phelps, Elizabeth Stuart, *The Gate's Ajar*, Harvard edn. by Helen Sootin Smith (Cambridge, 1964. 1st pubd 1868)

Philpotts, W. J., *Reply to Canon Farrar's Eternal Hope, in a Charge to the Clergy* (London, 1878)

Pitts, Herbert, *Séance or Altar. Chapters on Modern Spiritualism and the Catholic Religion* (London, 1920)

Plimpton, Walter, *The Waiting Church* (London, 1902. 1st pubd 1876)

Potter, J. W., *The 'Counsellor' Circle of the Society of Communion* (London, 1926)

————, *From beyond the clouds. A year with Counsellor* (London, 1927)

Potter, J. W. (ed.), *The Christian Spiritualist Hymn Book* (London, 1928)

Powell, J. H., *Spiritualism. Its facts and phases* (London, 1864)

Presland, John, *Heaven and Hell. A Lecture* (London, 1889)

Pridham, Arthur, *The spirits tried; or spiritualism self-convicted, self condemned and proved to be of Satan* (London, 1874)

Pusey, E. B., *The Responsibility of the Intellect in Matters of Faith. A Sermon preached before the University of Oxford* (Oxford, 1873)

————, *What is of faith as to everlasting punishment?* (London, 1880)

Pym, T. W.; Gordon, G., *Papers from Picardy, by two chaplains* (London, 1917)

Rashdall, Hastings, *The Idea of Atonement in Christian Theology. Being the Bampton Lectures for 1915* (London, 1920)

Raupert, J. G., *Spiritistic Phenomena and Their Interpretation* (London, 1913)

Re Parish of South Creake, All England Law Reports [1959], Vol 1, 197–208.

Robertson, James, *The Rise and Progress of Modern Spiritualism in England* (Manchester, 1893)

Rogers, Charles, *Our Eternal Destiny. Heaven and Hell* (London, 1868)

Rogers, Clement, *The Fear of Hell as an instrument of conversion* (London, 1939)

Rouse, C. H., *Through Séance to Satan, or The Lure of Spiritualism* (London, 1921)

————, *Spiritism and the Voice of the Church* (London, 1923)

Royal Commission on Ecclesiastical Discipline. Report of the Royal Commission on Ecclesiastical discipline and Minutes of evidence taken before the Royal Commission on Ecclesiastical discipline. In 5 Vols (London, 1906)

Rutherford, J. F., *Hell. What is it? Who are there? Can they get out?* (London and New York, 1924)

Ryle, J. C., *Heaven. Valuable Counsel on our Eternal Home* (1991)

Sharp, Arthur F., *The Spirit Saith*, 2 Vols. (London, 1956)

Shaw, G. B., *Heartbreak House* (London, 1919)

Sheppard, W. J. L., *Messages from the Dead* (Stirling, 1926)

Shorter, Thomas, *Confessions of a Truth Seeker. A Narrative of Personal Investigations into the Facts and Philosophy of Spirit-Intercourse* (London, 1859)

Sinclair, John, *A sermon on the death of the Right Hon and Right Rev. Charles James Blomfield, Late Lord Bishop of London* (London, 1857)

Skene, William, *The Descent into Hell. An Essay with copious references to the teaching of the Church and eminent Divines* (London, 1869)

Smith, D., *A brief and simple exposition of the Athanasian Creed; two sermons preached in Bramshall Church, Staffordshire, on Sunday mornings, May 26th and June 2nd, 1872* (London, 1872)

Soames, W. A., *Funeral Discourses preached at Greenwich on Sunday,*

November the 21ˢᵗ, 1852 upon the public funeral of Field-Marshal the Duke of Wellington (London, 1852)

Society of SS Peter and Paul, *The Red Cross Prayer Book* (London, 1915)

Spencer, J. W., *Christian Sorrow for the Pious Dead. A sermon preached in Wilton Church on Monday, December 23ʳᵈ, 1861* (Taunton, 1861)

Spicer, Henry, *Sights and Sounds: The Mystery of the Day: comprising an entire history of the American 'spirit' manifestations* (London, 1853)

Spiritualism in 1866 (London, 1866)

Stead, W. T., *After death. A personal narrative. 'Letters from Julia'.* 9th edn. (London, 1914. 1st pubd 1897)

Stevenson, Robert Louis, *Aes Triplex and other essays* (Portland, 1902)

Stobart, M. St Clair, *Torchbearers of Spiritualism* (London, 1925)

———, *War and Women* (London, 1913)

———, *Miracles and Adventures. An Autobiography* (London, 1935)

———, *The Either–Or of Spiritualism* (London, 1928)

———, *The Open Secret* (London, 1947)

Strang, Robert K., *Is Man a Spirit? An examination of the Bible Teaching on 'Spirit,' contrasted with the pretensions of Spiritualism* (London, 1920)

Streeter, Burnett H. (et al.), *Immortality. An essay in discovery, co-ordinating scientific, psychical and biblical research* (London, 1917)

Swedenborg, Emannuel, *Heaven and its wonders, and hell from things we have seen* (London, 1937. 1st pubd 1758)

———, *The New Jerusalem*, transl. John Chadwick (London, 1990)

Taylor, A. E., *The Christian hope of Immortality* (London, 1938)

Taylor, Joseph, *Apparitions; or, the mystery of ghosts, hobgoblins and haunted houses, developed. Being a collection of entertaining stories, founded on fact; and selected for the purpose of eradicating those ridiculous fears, which the ignorant, the weak and the superstitious, are but too apt to encourage, for want of properly examining into the causes of such absurd impositions* (London, 1814)

Theobald, F. J., *Heaven opened, or, messages for the bereaved from our little ones in glory* (London, 1870)

———, *Spirit Messages relating to the nature of Christ's person* (London, 1884)

———, *Homes and Work in the Future Life,* 3 Vols (London, 1885, 1886, 1887)

Thomas, C. D., *Life beyond death with evidence* (London, 1928)

Thompson, W. S., *The Recognition of Friends in Heaven* (London, 1866)

Trench, Richard C., *Alienation from God. A Sermon Preached in the Church of St Mary-the-Virgin, Oxford, on Wednesday, March 11, 1857* (Oxford, 1857)

Tweedale, Charles L., *Present Day Spirit Phenomena and the Churches* (Chicago, 1920)

————, *Man's Survival after Death, or, the Other Side of Life in the Light of Scripture, Human Experience and Modern Research* (London, 1909)

Underhill, Francis, *The Art of Intercession* (London, 1933)

'Victor Morton' (pseudo.), *Thoughts on Hell. A Study in Eschatology* (London, 1899)

Ward, J. S. M., *Gone West. Three narratives of after-death experiences* (London, 1917)

Watts, Charles, *Spiritualism a Delusion: Its Fallacies Exposed. A Criticism from the Standpoint of Science and Impartial Observation* (London, 1900)

Wedgwood, J. I., *Spiritualism and the Great War* (London, 1919)

White, Edward, *Modern Spiritualism judged in the light of Divine Revelation* (London, 1893)

Wilberforce, Samuel, *Commemorations of the Departed. A sermon preached at the consecration of the chapel at Wellington College, July 16, 1863* (Oxford and London, 1863)

Wilberforce-Bell, H., *War Vignettes. Being the Experiences of an Officer on France and England during the Great War* (Bombay, 1916)

Wilkinson, D. H. D., *A Christian Searchlight on Spiritualism* (London, 1937)

Williams, C., *The Truth about Spiritualism, by one who has investigated it* (London, 1916)

————, *Spiritualism: its True Nature and Results. With Some Personal Experiences and an Earnest Appeal to Spiritualists* (London, 1921)

Wilson, Edward, *Prayer for the Dead and the Mater Dei. A letter respectfully addressed to his Grace, the Archbishop of Canterbury* (London, 1870)

Wilson, H. B. (ed.), *Essays and Reviews* (London, 1860)

Winnington Ingram, A. F., *Life a Training for the Life Beyond. Addresses to Working Lads, No. 6* (London, 1893)

————, 'The Life after Death', preached on the Sunday after All Saints Day at All Saints, Fulham, 1919', in *The Spirit of Peace* (London, 1921)

————, *The Church in Time of War* (London, 1916)

The worship of the Church. Being the report of the archbishops' second committee of inquiry (London, 1918)

Secondary Sources

Almond, Philip, *Heaven and Hell in Enlightenment England* (Cambridge, 1994)

Ariès, Phillippe, *The Hour of our Death* (transl. Helen Weaver) (New York, 1981)

Auerbach, J., *The Great Exhibition of 1851. A nation on display* (New Haven and London, 1999)

Barrow, Logie, *Independent Spirits. Spiritualism and English Plebeians, 1850–1910* (London, 1986)

Benham, W. M., *Catharine and Craufurd Tait. A memoir* (London, 1881)

Benson, A. C., *The Life of Edward White Benson, sometime archbishop of Canterbury* (London, 1899)

Benz, Ernst, *Emanuel Swedenborg. Visionary Savant in the Age of Reason. New translation* (West Chester, PA, 2002. 1st pubd 1948)

Berger, Peter, *The Sacred Canopy. Elements of a sociological theory of religion* (New York, 1969)

Berger, Peter (ed.), *The desecularization of the world. Resurgent religion and world politics* (Washington DC, 1999)

Besterman, T., *A Bibliography of Sir Oliver Lodge* (Oxford and London, 1935)

Bevir, Mark, 'Annie Besant's Quest for Truth: Christianity, Secularism and New Age Thought', *Journal of Ecclesiastical History*, 50 (January 1999), 62–93.

Bogacz, Ted, ' "A Tyranny of Words": Language, Poetry and Antimodernism in England in the First World War', *Journal of Modern History*, 58 (September 1986), 643–68.

Bourke, Joanna, *Working Class Cultures in Britain 1890–1960* (London, 1994)

———, *Dismembering the Male. Men's bodies, Britain and the Great War* (London, 1996)

Brandon, Ruth, *The Spiritualists. The Passion for the Occult in the Nineteenth and Twentieth Centuries* (London, 1983)

———, *The life and many deaths of Harry Houdini* (London, 2001)

Braley, Evelyn F., *Letters of Herbert Hensley Henson* (London, 1950)

Brock, E. J. (ed.), *Swedenborg and his influence* (Bryn Athyn, Pa, 1988)

Brown, Callum, *The Death of Christian Britain* (London, 2001)

———, *Religion and Society in Twentieth-century Britain* (Harlow, 2006)

Bruce, Steve (ed.), *Religion and Modernization. Sociologists and Historians debate the Secularization Thesis* (Oxford, 1992)

Burd, Van Akin, *Christmas Story. John Ruskin's Venetian Letters of 1876–1877* (Newark, 1990)

Burns, Arthur; Innes, Joanna (eds), *Rethinking the Age of Reform. Britain 1780–1850* (Cambridge and New York, 2003)

Chadwick, Owen, *The Victorian Church*, 2 Vols (London, 1972)

———, *The Secularization of the European Mind* (Cambridge, 1975)

———, *Hensley Henson. A study in the friction between Church and State* (Oxford, 1983)

Charlesworth, M. (ed.), *The Gothic Revival 1720–1870. Literary Sources and Documents*, 3 Vols (Mountfield nr. Robertsbridge, 2002)

Cocksworth, C., *Prayer and the Departed* (Cambridge, 1997)

Collins, V. H., *Ghosts and Marvels. A Selection of Uncanny Tales from Daniel Defoe to Algernon Blackwood* (London, 1924)

Connelly, Mark, *The Great War, Memory and Ritual. Commemoration in the City and East London, 1916–1939* (London and Woodbridge, 2002)

Cooter, Roger (ed.), *Studies in the History of Alternative Medicine* (Basingstoke, 1988)

Cox, Jeffrey, *The English Churches in a Secular Society. Lambeth, 1870–1930* (Oxford, 1982)

Crabtree, Harriet, *The Christian Life: Traditional Metaphors and Contemporary Theologies* (Minneapolis, 1991)

Curl, J. S., *The Victorian Celebration of Death* (Newton Abbot, 1972)

Currie, Robert; Gilbert, Alan; Horsley, Lee, *Churches and Churchgoers. Patterns of Church growth in the British Isles since 1700* (Oxford, 1977)

Davenport, Anna; Salisse, John, *St George's Hall. Behind the scenes at England's home of mystery* (Pasadena, 2001)

Davie, Grace, *Religion in Britain since 1945: believing without belonging* (Oxford, 1994)

Dearmer, Nancy, *The Life of Percy Dearmer* (London, 1940)

Duffy, Eamon, *The Stripping of the Altars* (New Haven and London, 1992)

Engel, A. J., *From clergyman to don. The rise of the academic profession in nineteenth-century Oxford* (Oxford, 1983)

Finucane, R. C., *Appearances of the Dead. A Cultural History of Ghosts* (New York, 1984)

Fox, Adam, *Dean Inge* (London, 1960)

Fussell, Paul, *The Great War and Modern Memory* (Oxford, 1975)

Gauld, Alan, *The Founders of Psychical Research* (London, 1968)

Gibson, John Michael; Green, Richard Lancelyn (eds), *The Unknown Conan Doyle. Letters to the Press* (London, 1986)

Gilbert, A. D., *Religion and society in industrial England. Church, chapel and social change 1740–1914* (London, 1976)

Gill, Robin, *The myth of the empty church* (London, 1993)

Gray, Donald, *Percy Dearmer. A Parson's Pilgrimage* (Norwich, 2000)

Green, S. J. D., *Religion in the age of decline. Organisation and experience in industrial Yorkshire, 1870–1920* (Cambridge, 1996)

Gregory, Adrian, *The Silence of Memory. Armistice Day 1919–1946* (Oxford, 1994)

Hamilton, James, *Faraday. The Life* (London, 2002)

Handley, Sasha, *Visions of an unseen world: ghost beliefs and ghost stories in eighteenth-century England* (London, 2007)

Harris, Jose, *Private Lives, Public Spirit. A Social History of Britain 1870–1914* (Oxford, 1993)

———, 'Political thought and the State', in S. J. D. Green and R. C. Whiting, *The Boundaries of the state in modern Britain* (Cambridge, 1996), 15–28

Harrison, J. F. C., *The Second Coming. Popular Millenarianism 1780–1850* (London, 1979)

Hastings, Adrian, *A History of English Christianity 1920–1985*, 3rd edn. (London, 1991)

Hazelgrove, Jenny, *Spiritualism and British Society between the Wars* (Manchester, 2000)

Helmstadter, R. J.; Lightman, B. (eds), *Victorian Faith in Crisis. Essays on Continuity and Change in Nineteenth-Century Religious Belief* (London, 1990)

Hill, J. Arthur, *Letter from Sir Oliver Lodge. Psychical, Religious, Scientific and Personal* (London, 1932)

Hilton, Boyd, *The Age of Atonement. The Influence of Evangelicalism on Social and Economic Thought 1795–1865* (Oxford, 1988)

Houlbrooke, Ralph (ed.), *Death, Ritual and Bereavement* (London, 1989)

Hughes, H. Stuart, *Consciousness and Society* (Brighton, 1979. 1st pubd 1958)

Hynes, Samuel, *A War Imagined. The First World War and English Culture* (London, 1990)

Inglis, K. S., *Churches and the working classes in Victorian England* (London, 1963)

Jalland, Pat, *Death in the Victorian Family* (Oxford, 1996)

Jay, Elisabeth, *Faith and Doubt in Victorian Britain* (London, 1986)

Jenkins, Tim, *Religion in everyday life. An ethnographical approach* (New York and Oxford, 1999)

John, Juliet, ' "A body without a head": The Idea of Mass Culture in Dickens's American Notes (1842)', *Journal of Victorian Culture*, 12, 2 (Autumn 2007), 173–202.

Jones, G. S., *Languages of Class. Studies in English Working Class History 1832–1982* (Cambridge, 1983)

Kelly, J. N. D., *Early Christian Doctrines*, 5th edn (London, 1977. 1st pubd 1958)

King, Alex, *Memorials of the Great War in Britain. The Symbolism and Politics of Remembrance* (Oxford, 1998)

Knight, Frances, *The Nineteenth Century Church and English Society* (Cambridge, 1995)

Kollar, Rene, *Searching for Raymond. Anglicanism, Spiritualism and Bereavement between the Two World Wars* (Maryland, 2000)

Lake, P. with Questier, M., *The Antichrist's Lewd Hat. Protestants, Papists and Players in Post-Reformation England* (New Haven and London, 2002)

Lambek, M. (ed.), *A Reader in the Anthropology of Religion* (Malden, MA and Oxford, 2002)

Lamont, Peter, *The First Psychic. The Peculiar Mystery of a Notorious Victorian Wizard* (London, 2005)

——, 'Spiritualism and a mid-Victorian Crisis of Evidence', *Historical Journal*, 47 (December 2004), 897–921.

Lampe, G. W. H., *Doctrine in the Church of England (1938): the report of the Commission on Christian Doctrine. With a new introduction by G. W. H. Lampe* (London, 1982)

Larsen, Timothy, *Crisis of Doubt. Honest Faith in Nineteenth-Century England* (Oxford, 2006)

Lead, Brian; Woods, Roger, *Harry Houdini. Legend and Legacy* (Accrington, 1993)

Leavis, Q. D., *Fiction and the Reading Public* (London, 1932)

Lerner, Laurence, *Angels and Absences. Child Deaths in the Nineteenth Century* (Nashville and London, 1997)

Lockhart, J. G., *Cosmo Gordon Lang* (London, 1949)

——, *Charles Lindley Viscount Halifax*, 2 Vols (London, 1935)

Lohse, Bernhard (transl. Roy Harrisville), *Martin Luther's Theology. Its history and systematic development* (Edinburgh, 1999)

Machin, G. I. T., *Politics and the Churches in Great Britain, 1869–1921* (Oxford, 1987)

Mack, Phyllis, *Visionary Women. Ecstatic prophecy in seventeenth-century England* (Berkeley, CA, 1992)

——, *Secularisation in Western Europe 1848–1914* (London, 2000)

Maiden, John, *National Religion and the Prayer Book Controversy, 1927–28* (Woodbridge, 2009)

Matthew, H. C. G., *Gladstone 1809–1898* (Oxford, 1997)

McCabe, Joseph, *Spiritualism. A popular history from 1847* (London, 1920)

McDannell, Colleen; Lang, Bernhard, *Heaven. A History* (New Haven, 1988)

McFague, Sallie, *Metaphorical Theology. Models of God in Religious Language* (London, 1983)

McGrath, Alister, *Luther's theology of the cross. Martin Luther's theological breakthrough* (Oxford, 1985)

——, *A Life of John Calvin. A study in the shaping of Western Culture* (Oxford, 1990)

McLeod, Hugh, *Religion and the Working Classes in Nineteenth Century Britain* (London, 1984)

——, *Religion and Society in England 1850–1914* (Basingstoke, 1996)

——, *Secularisation in Western Europe 1848–1914* (Basingstoke, 2000)

McLeod, H.; Ustorf, W., *The decline of Christendom in Western Europe, 1750–2000* (Cambridge, 2003)

Morris, J. N., *Religion and urban change: Croydon 1840–1914* (Woodbridge, 1992)

——, *F. D. Maurice and the crisis of Christian authority* (Oxford, 2005)

————, 'The strange death of Christian Britain: another look at the secularization debate', *Historical Journal*, 46, 4 (2003), 963–76

Mosse, George L., *The Culture of Western Europe. The Nineteenth and Twentieth Centuries. An Introduction* (London, 1963)

————, *Fallen Soldiers. Reshaping the Memory of the World Wars* (Oxford, 1990)

Nelson, Geoffrey K., *Spiritualism and Society* (London, 1969)

Noppen, J. P. van, *Metaphor and Theology* (Theolinguistics 2) (Brussels, 1983)

O'Keefe, D. L., *Stolen Lightening. The Social Theory of Magic* (Oxford, 1982)

Oppenheim, Janet, *The Other World. Spiritualism and Psychic Research in England, 1850–1914* (Cambridge, 1985)

Owen, Alex, *The Darkened Room. Women, Power and Spiritualism in Late Victorian England* (London, 1989)

————, *The Place of Enchantment. British Occultism and the Culture of the Modern* (Chicago, 2004)

Paget, Stephen, *Henry Scott Holland* (London, 1921)

Parker, T. H., *Calvin. An introduction to his thought* (London, 1995)

Parsons, G. (ed.), *Religion in Victorian Britain. Vol. II, Controversies* (Manchester, 1988)

Podmore, Frank, *Modern Spiritualism. A history and a criticism*, 2 Vols (London, 1902)

Porter, Roy, *Myths of the English* (Cambridge, 1992)

Prickett, S., *Romanticism and Religion. The Tradition of Coleridge and Wordsworth in the Victorian Church* (Cambridge, 1976)

Reardon, B. M. G., *From Coleridge to Gore. A Century of Religious Thought in Britain* (London, 1971)

Rowell, Geoffrey, *Hell and the Victorians. A study of the nineteenth-century theological controversies concerning eternal punishment and the future life* (Oxford, 2000. 1st pubd 1974)

Schor, Esther, *Bearing the Dead. The British Culture of Mourning from the Enlightenment to Victoria* (Princetown, 1994)

Shaw, Jane, *Miracles in Enlightenment England* (New Haven and London, 2006)

Snape, Michael, *God and the British Soldier. Religion and the British Army in the First and Second World Wars* (London, 2005)

Stout, John Joseph, *Sunrise to Eternity. A study in Jacob Boehme's Life and Thought* (Philadelphia, 1957)

Strong, L. A. G., *Flying Angel. The story of the missions to seamen* (London, 1956)

Taylor, Anne, *Annie Besant. A Biography* (Oxford, 1992)

Thomas, Keith, *Religion and the Decline of Magic* (London, 1991. 1st pubd 1971)

Turner, Alice, *The history of Hell* (London, 1996)

Underwood, P., *A short history of the Ghost Club Society* (Haslemere, 2000)

Vickery, Amanda, 'Golden age to separate spheres? A review of the categories and chronology of English women's history', *Historical Journal*, 36, 2 (1993), 383–414

Waite, A. E. (et al.), *Three Famous Mystics* (London, 1939)

Walker, D. P., *The Decline of Hell. Seventeenth Century Discussions of Eternal Torment* (London, 1964)

Walsham, A., *Providence in Early Modern England* (Oxford, 1999)

Watson, J. R., *An annotated anthology of hymns* (Oxford, 2002)

Whalley, Joachim (ed.), *Mirrors of Mortality. Studies in the Social History of Death* (London, 1981)

Wheeler, Michael, *Heaven, Hell and the Victorians* (Cambridge, 1994)

Wickham, E. R., *Church and people in an industrial city* (London, 1957)

Wilkinson, Alan, *The Church of England and the First World War* (London, 1996. 1st pubd 1977)

Williams, S. C., *Religious Belief and Popular Culture in Southwark c.1880–1939* (Oxford, 1999)

———, 'The language of belief: an alternative agenda for the study of Victorian working-class religion', *Journal of Victorian Culture*, 1, 2 (Autumn 1996), 303–17

Wilson, Bryan, *Religion in a Secular Society* (London, 1966)

———, *Religion in Sociological Perspective* (Oxford, 1982)

Windscheffel, Ruth Clayton, 'Politics, Religion and Text: W. E. Gladstone and Spiritualism', *Journal of Victorian Culture*, 11, 1 (Spring 2006), 1–29

Winter, Alison, *Mesmerized. Powers of the Mind in Victorian Britain* (Chicago and London, 1998)

Winter, Jay, *Sites of Memory, Sites of Mourning. The Great War in European Cultural History* (Cambridge, 1995)

———, 'Spiritualism and the First World War', in R. W. Davis and R. J. Helmstadter, *Religion and Irreligion in Victorian Society* (London, 1992), 185–200

Wolfe, Kenneth, *The churches and the British Broadcasting Corporation 1922–1956* (London, 1984)

Wolffe, John, *Great Deaths. Grieving, Religion and Nationhood in Victorian and Edwardian Britain* (Oxford, 2000)

Wolfreys, Julian, *Victorian Hauntings. Spectrality, Gothic, the Uncanny and Literature* (Basingstoke, 2002)

Yates, Nigel, *Anglican Ritualism in Victorian Britain, 1830–1910* (Oxford, 1999)

Unpublished Theses

Byrne, Georgina, 'The Church of England, spiritualism and ideas of the afterlife 1850–1939' (PhD thesis, Kings College London, 2007)

Grimley, Matthew, 'Citizenship, community and the Church of England: Anglican theories of the state c. 1926–1939' (D. Phil thesis, Oxford University, 1998)

Mews, Stuart P., 'Religion and English Society in the First World War' (PhD thesis, Cambridge University, 1874)

Stryker, Laurinda, 'Languages of Sacrifice and Suffering in England in the First World War' (PhD thesis, Cambridge University, 1992)

Tomkins, Sandra, 'Britain and the Influenza Epidemic of 1918–19' (PhD thesis, Cambridge University, 1989)

Index

STUDIES IN MODERN BRITISH RELIGIOUS HISTORY

Previously published volumes in this series